AF816812

The Generative AI Career Masterplan

Navigate the future of AI with practical insights from industry pioneers at AI-first organizations

Dr. Ali Arsanjani

Sadid Hasan

Maxime Labonne

Andreas Horn

Leonid Kuligin

<packt>

The Generative AI Career Masterplan

This book was written by Dr. Ali Arsanjani, Sadid Hasan, Maxime Labonne, Andreas Horn, and Leonid Kuligin. Generative AI tools were used only to assist with ideation, phrasing, and diagram drafts, and all technical content and code were created, verified, and tested by the authors and Packt's editorial team. Packt does not accept AI-generated content that replaces expert authorship.

Portfolio Director: Gebin George
Relationship Lead: Ali Abidi
Project Manager: Prajakta Naik
Content Engineer: Aditi Chatterjee/Afzal Shaikh
Technical Editor: Sumant Jadhav
Indexer: Manju Arasan
Production Designer: Alishon Falcon
Growth Lead: Dipali Malwatkar

First published: July 2026

Production reference: 1310726

Published by Packt Publishing Ltd.

Grosvenor House

11 St Paul's Square

Birmingham

B3 1RB, UK.

ISBN 978-1-80669-145-6
`www.packtpub.com`

I would like to dedicate this book to my family, who inspire me. I would like to extend my deepest gratitude to my grandparents for their nurturing guidance, love, and wisdom; to my father; to my mother for being a role model for so many, and for giving me the motivation to excel; and to my wife and son, my companions on the path to spiritual evolution and tireless self-sacrifice.

– Dr. Ali Arsanjani

I begin by thanking the Almighty, whose blessings have carried me through every stage of my life. I am deeply grateful to my parents for grounding me in learning and purpose, and to my family, friends, and the people who walked beside me, each of whom has shaped my growth in meaningful ways. Finally, I dedicate this book to my wife, Tanzila, and my daughter, Norah—my greatest sources of love and support. Without them, neither this work nor the person I have become would be possible.

– Sadid Hasan

I want to thank my family and partner. Your unwavering support and patience made this book possible.

– Maxime Labonne

To my wife, Ksenia, whose unwavering love and optimism have been my constant support over all these years; to my mother-in-law, Tatyana, whose belief in me, even in my craziest endeavors, has been an incredible source of strength; and to my kids, Matvey and Milena: I hope you'll read it one day.

– Leonid Kuligin

Contributors

About the authors

Dr. Ali Arsanjani is a pre-eminent technical executive who bridges architectural rigor and large-scale organizational strategy with industrial-scale execution. Widely recognized as the "father of SOA", he has led transformational initiatives across multiple organizations. He currently serves as Director of Applied AI Engineering at Google Cloud, where he leads the GenAI Blackbelts, a center of excellence that bridges research, forward-deployed engineering, and enterprise implementation. In this role, he drives strategic co-engineering programs with Google's most critical customers and partners, accelerating enterprise adoption of generative AI and agentic AI. With executive roots as Head of Machine Learning at AWS and CTO for Analytics at IBM, Dr. Arsanjani has managed global teams of more than 6,000 practitioners. An IBM Master Inventor, his patent portfolio includes foundational contributions to service decomposition and context-aware routing. With executive roots as Head of ML at AWS and CTO for Analytics at IBM, Dr. Arsanjani has managed global teams of over 6,000 practitioners. An IBM Master Inventor, his patent portfolio includes foundational contributions to service decomposition and context-aware routing. Today, he pioneers generative AI and agentic AI, introducing best practices and protocols (e.g., A2A) to ensure autonomous systems remain transparent, auditable, and grounded in ethical governance. A dedicated educator, he has impacted thousands of students as an Adjunct Professor at Maharishi International University, the University of California, San Diego, and San José State University. His scholarly work, cited more than 4,800 times, spans enterprise architecture, distributed systems, and neuro-machine interaction. Dr. Arsanjani remains a leading force in synthesizing deep technical mastery with the strategic vision required to navigate the Agentic Age.

Sadid Hasan, Ph.D., is a Principal AI leader in the Microsoft AI Development Acceleration Program within the Office of the CTO, where he drives enterprise-scale research and development of advanced Generative and Agentic AI capabilities, products, and solutions for Office Copilots and Azure AIOps initiatives. With more than 20 years of experience in AI research and innovation, he has led and contributed to groundbreaking work across generative AI, natural language processing, and machine learning, authoring hundreds of peer-reviewed publications and patents. Before joining Microsoft, Sadid served as Executive Director of AI at CVS Health and as Senior Scientist and Technical Lead of the AI Group at Philips Research. Widely recognized as a thought leader, he frequently delivers keynote speeches, serves on program committees for top AI conferences, and contributes actively to the global AI research and practitioner community. He is dedicated to advancing the state of the art in AI, accelerating adoption across industries such as healthcare, education, legal, finance, and marketing, and developing the next generation of AI leaders to make transformational impact worldwide. He was recently named one of the 100 most influential AI leaders in the United States.

Maxime Labonne is Head of Post-Training at Liquid AI. He holds a Ph.D. in Machine Learning from the Polytechnic Institute of Paris and is a Google Developer Expert in AI/ML. He has made significant contributions to the open-source community, including the LLM Course, tutorials on fine-tuning, tools such as LLM AutoEval, and best-in-class models such as NeuralDaredevil. He is the author of the best-selling books *LLM Engineer's Handbook* and *Hands-On Graph Neural Networks Using Python*.

Andreas Horn is an enterprise AI and automation leader with over a decade of experience helping organizations turn emerging technology into practical, scalable operating capability. He has worked with some of the world's leading technology companies, including IBM and Microsoft, and has advised large enterprises on redesigning operations around AI, automation, and resilience. His experience spans complex transformation programs in regulated and high-stakes environments, where technical depth must be matched by governance, operational discipline, and business value. Andreas's work focuses on moving AI beyond experimentation into measurable, reliable, and production-ready use. He advises senior leaders on enterprise AI adoption, speaks frequently on AI-powered operations and organizational change, and works at the intersection of technology, execution, and long-term capability building. He also teaches AI and innovation at universities, helping professionals and students understand how emerging technologies translate into real-world business impact.

Leonid Kuligin is a staff AI engineer at Google Cloud, working on generative AI and classical machine learning solutions, such as demand forecasting or optimization problems. Leonid is one of the key maintainers of Google Cloud integrations on LangChain, and a visiting lecturer at CDTM (TUM and LMU). Prior to Google, Leonid gained more than 20 years of experience in building B2C and B2B applications based on complex machine learning and data processing solutions such as search, maps, and investment management in German, Russian, and US technological, financial, and retail companies.

About the reviewers

Tre Rodriguez is an AI and Data Systems Consultant and the founder of Magic Data Engineering. She helps businesses replace manual, fragmented workflows with intelligent operational infrastructure that improves execution, decision-making, and day-to-day efficiency.

With a background in problem-solving, leadership training, and consulting for small and medium-sized businesses, Tre has worked across industries including technology, financial services, medical devices, healthcare, and nonprofits. Her work focuses on reducing operational complexity and helping founders and executives manage growing businesses more effectively.

Shruti Dhumak is a senior technology executive and the Head of Customer Engineering at Google, where she leads large-scale enterprise transformation through data, cloud, and AI. She is recognized for building and scaling high-performing teams and aligning complex technology strategies with executive priorities. Shruti partners closely with C-suite leaders to enable sustainable growth and measurable business outcomes, bringing a strong focus on operational excellence and customer impact. As a technical expert in advanced cloud architectures and autonomous agentic systems, she serves as a trusted advisor and mentor, passionate about results-driven leadership and advancing the next generation of technology leaders.

Raj Ganesh Jayaraman is a Senior GenAI/ML Solutions Architect at AWS, bringing over 11 years of experience designing large-scale AI and machine learning systems. He leads digital transformation initiatives, helping organizations move from proofs of concept to reliable, production-grade AI. His expertise spans agentic AI, RAG, multi-agent systems, and cloud computing. He holds an MS from the University of Illinois Chicago and six AWS certifications.

An active community contributor, Raj publishes research in leading journals, serves on Technical Program Committees, and reviews technical books. He also presents at global events, including AWS re:Invent and Databricks Summit.

Table of Contents

Chapter 12: Conquering the AI Job Market – Strategic Search Techniques and Interview Excellence 239

Preface

Generative AI (Gen AI) is redefining the future of work at an unprecedented pace. What began as a breakthrough in content generation has rapidly evolved into a technology that is transforming industries, reshaping business strategies, and creating entirely new career paths. As organizations across every sector adopt **large language models (LLMs)**, AI agents, and intelligent automation, professionals are faced with both an exciting opportunity and an urgent need to develop new skills. Success in this new era requires more than simply learning how to use AI tools; it demands an understanding of the technologies behind them, the skills that complement them, and the strategies needed to build a resilient, future-ready career.

This book is designed to help you navigate that journey. Rather than focusing solely on the technical aspects of generative AI, this book takes a holistic approach, combining foundational AI concepts, practical engineering knowledge, career planning, and professional development into a single, structured roadmap.

You will begin by understanding how generative AI is reshaping the employment landscape, the emerging roles within the AI ecosystem, and the skills employers increasingly value. From there, you will explore the technologies that power modern AI applications, including prompt engineering, **retrieval-augmented generation (RAG)**, vector databases, AI agents, and the essential tools and frameworks used by practitioners. The book then strengthens both your technical foundation and your uniquely human capabilities by covering programming fundamentals, machine learning concepts, prompt engineering, critical thinking, communication, creativity, and ethical AI.

Building on these foundations, you will discover how generative AI is being applied across industries such as software development, finance, healthcare, marketing, education, and supply chain management while learning how modern LLM-powered applications are designed, deployed, and extended using multi-agent systems.

Finally, the book shifts its focus to career success, guiding you through personal branding, AI-assisted job searching, interview preparation, networking, and long-term professional growth. Drawing on industry best practices and expert insights, it also emphasizes the importance of authenticity, responsible AI adoption, lifelong learning, and active participation in the AI community.

Whether your goal is to land your first AI role, pivot into a new career, or grow into a technical or leadership position, this book provides a practical roadmap to help you get there. It combines industry trends, technical knowledge, career guidance, and actionable advice to equip you with the confidence to navigate the rapidly evolving world of generative AI and build a rewarding, future-ready career.

Who this book is for

This book is for graduates, professionals, and leaders seeking to future-proof their careers and capitalize on the rise of Generative AI. Whether you're entering the job market, transitioning from a traditional tech or non-tech role, or aiming to lead AI transformation, this guide provides the clarity, tools, and confidence to take control of your trajectory. It's an indispensable resource for engineers, data scientists, product managers, business analysts, educators, and executives determined to stay relevant in the new world of work.

What this book covers

Chapter 1, Generative AI – Revolutionizing the Future of Work, Strategy, and the Global Economy, explores how generative AI is reshaping industries, careers, and the future of work. You'll understand both the opportunities and risks it presents, learn why AI literacy has become essential across professions, and begin identifying how to position yourself for long-term career success.

Chapter 2, Decoding GenAI – Core Concepts for Every Professional, introduces the foundational concepts behind generative AI and large language models without assuming a deep technical background. You'll learn the terminology, core principles, and AI literacy needed to understand how modern AI systems work and how they create value across industries.

Chapter 3, Mapping Your Path – Roles and Roadmaps in GenAI, helps you identify where you fit in the rapidly evolving AI job market by exploring emerging Gen AI roles, required skills, and career progression paths. You'll learn how to leverage your existing experience, evaluate different career options, and create a roadmap for long-term growth in the AI industry.

Chapter 4, Generative AI Architectures and Advanced Concepts, builds a deeper understanding of the technologies that power modern generative AI systems. You'll explore transformer architectures, prompt engineering, RAG, vector databases, AI agents, function calling, and LLMOps, gaining the technical foundation needed to understand and work with production AI systems.

Chapter 5, Essential Tools and Platforms, introduces the tools, frameworks, and platforms that power today's Gen AI ecosystem. You'll learn when and how to use popular LLMs, developer frameworks, and open-source tools, enabling you to select the right technologies for your learning goals and professional role.

Chapter 6, Mastering Hard Skills – The Technical Edge, puts emphasis on the core technical competencies that form the foundation of AI careers. From Python and machine learning fundamentals to prompt engineering and deep learning frameworks, you'll discover the practical skills that employers value most in technical AI roles.

Chapter 7, Cultivating Technical and Human Skills for the Agentic AI Era, covers the human skills that remain essential in an AI-driven workplace. You'll learn why critical thinking, creativity, communication, adaptability, and ethical judgment are becoming increasingly valuable and how they complement AI rather than compete with it.

Chapter 8, Strategic Career Moves – Entry, Transition, and Upskilling, illustrates practical strategies for entering the AI field, transitioning from another career, or advancing your existing expertise. You'll discover how to build an effective learning path, use AI to accelerate your career preparation, and identify certifications, projects, and experiences that strengthen your professional profile.

Chapter 9, Applied Generative AI – Industry Use Cases and Multi-Agent Systems, demonstrates how generative AI is transforming industries through real-world applications and intelligent automation. You'll explore practical use cases across multiple domains while learning the key stages involved in building, deploying, and scaling modern LLM-powered applications.

Chapter 10, Building and Deploying LLM Applications, explores the journey from a proof of concept to a production-ready generative AI application. It covers application development strategies, evaluation frameworks, production deployment, reliability, observability, and deployment considerations, equipping you with the principles and best practices for building scalable, maintainable, and production-grade LLM applications.

Chapter 11, Crafting Your AI Identity – Personal Branding for Impact, explains how to establish a compelling professional presence in the AI community. You'll discover strategies for building an authentic personal brand, using AI tools responsibly, and creating an online profile that showcases your expertise while remaining uniquely your own.

Chapter 12, Conquering the AI Job Market – Strategic Search Techniques and Interview Tips, equips you with practical techniques for securing AI roles in today's competitive job market. You'll learn how to optimize resumes and online profiles, prepare for technical and behavioral interviews, use AI tools effectively throughout your job search, and confidently showcase your skills to potential employers.

Chapter 13, Expert Insights and Sustaining Growth – Building a Career That Compounds, teaches you how to build a rewarding, long-term career in generative AI through continuous learning, community involvement, and mentorship. You'll gain practical advice from industry perspectives, learn to avoid common pitfalls, and develop the mindset needed to grow alongside this rapidly evolving field.

To get the most out of this book

Readers should have a basic understanding of Python programming, familiarity with machine learning concepts, and a basic understanding of large language models. This book assumes readers have some experience with AI development environments and are comfortable working with APIs.

Software/hardware covered in the book	Operating system requirements
Python 3.x	Windows, macOS, or Linux
OpenAI API key	Windows, macOS, or Linux

Disclaimer on images

Some images in this title are presented for contextual purposes, and the readability of the graphic is not crucial to the discussion. Please refer to our free graphic bundle to download the images.

Download the color images

We also provide a PDF file that has color images of the screenshots/diagrams used in this book. You can download it here: `https://packt.link/gbp/9781806691456`.

Conventions used

There are a number of text conventions used throughout this book.

`CodeInText`: Indicates code words in text, database table names, folder names, filenames, file extensions, pathnames, dummy URLs, user input, and Twitter handles. For example: "Create a comprehensive soak test script `milvus_soak_test.py`:"

A block of code is set as follows:

```
from trl import SFTConfig, SFTTrainer

config = SFTConfig(
    output_dir="./output",
    num_train_epochs=1,
    per_device_train_batch_size=1,
    learning_rate=5e-5,
    lr_scheduler_type="linear",
```

Any command-line input or output is written as follows:

```
pip install vectordb-bench==1.0.11
```

Bold: Indicates a new term, an important word, or words that you see on the screen. For instance, words in menus or dialog boxes appear in the text like this. For example: " For load testing Milvus, we'll use **Locust**, an open-source load testing tool based on Python. "

Warnings or important notes appear like this.

Tips and tricks appear like this.

Get in touch

Feedback from our readers is always welcome.

General feedback: If you have questions about any aspect of this book or have any general feedback, please email us at `customercare@packt.com` and mention the book's title in the subject of your message.

Errata: Although we have taken every care to ensure the accuracy of our content, mistakes do happen. If you have found a mistake in this book, we would be grateful if you reported this to us. Please visit `http://www.packt.com/submit-errata`, click **Submit Errata**, and fill in the form.

Piracy: If you come across any illegal copies of our works in any form on the internet, we would be grateful if you would provide us with the location address or website name. Please contact us at `copyright@packt.com` with a link to the material.

If you are interested in becoming an author: If there is a topic that you have expertise in and you are interested in either writing or contributing to a book, please visit `http://authors.packt.com/`.

Share your thoughts

Once you've read The Generative AI Career Masterplan, we'd love to hear your thoughts! Scan the QR code below to go straight to the Amazon review page for this book and share your feedback.

`https://packt.link/r/1806691450`

Your review is important to us and the tech community and will help us make sure we're delivering excellent quality content.

Free benefits with your book

This book comes with free benefits to support your learning. Activate them now for instant access (see the "*How to Unlock*" section for instructions).

Here's a quick overview of what you can instantly unlock with your purchase:

DRM-Free PDF Version

Download DRM-free PDF and ePub copies of this book.

7-Day Packt Library Access

Get 7-day unlimited access to 8,000+ books and videos. No credit card required.

Available for first-time Packt+ trial users only.

Next-Gen Reader Access

Read this book on Packt Reader with progress sync, dark mode and note-taking.

How to Unlock

Scan the QR code (or go to `packtpub.com/unlock`). Search for this book by name, confirm the edition, and then follow the steps on the page.

UNLOCK NOW

Note: Keep your invoice handy. Purchases made directly from Packt don't require one.

Share your thoughts

Once you have read *The Generative AI Career Masterplan*, we would love to hear your thoughts! Scan the QR code below to go straight to the Amazon review page for this book and share your feedback.

Your review is important to the tech community and us, and it will help us make sure we're delivering excellent quality content.

Join our Discord and Reddit Space

You're not the only one navigating fragmented tools, constant updates, and unclear best practices. Join a growing community of professionals exchanging insights that don't make it into documentation.

Join our Discord at `https://packt.link/z8ivB` or scan the QR code below:	Follow us on Reddit at `https://packt.link/0rExL` or scan the QR code below:

Part 1

The Gen AI Landscape: Understanding the Revolution

Part 1 introduces the rapidly evolving world of generative AI and establishes the knowledge needed to navigate it with confidence. You'll explore why Gen AI is transforming industries and careers, build a solid understanding of its core concepts and capabilities, and examine the growing ecosystem of roles and career pathways emerging around the technology. By the end of this part, you'll have a clear understanding of the Gen AI landscape, the skills and knowledge that matter most, and a roadmap for positioning yourself to succeed in this fast-changing field.

This part contains the following chapters:

1

Generative AI – Revolutionizing the Future of Work, Strategy, and the Global Economy

> *"The impact of GenAI is not happening in a vacuum. It is deeply intertwined with broader macroeconomic trends that are collectively reshaping the global labor market."*
>
> *– Dr. Ali Arsanjani*

The AI revolution has shown how quickly the technology landscape can evolve and influence the way people think, work, respond to change, and collaborate. What was once limited to discussions on blogs, social media, and podcasts has now become an essential skill for individuals across virtually every domain. The advent of **generative artificial intelligence (GenAI)** marks another pivotal milestone in this technological evolution. GenAI is fundamentally reshaping the world of work, resource management, corporate strategy, and the broader macroeconomic environment.

This chapter explores the multifaceted impact of generative AI, examining both its opportunities and the risks it poses to jobs, how it is compelling organizations to rethink corporate strategy and career progression, and its deep-seated connections with major global trends. As AI capabilities continue to evolve, their influence extends well beyond automation, transforming how organizations innovate and compete. We will also explore the agentic enterprise, an emerging specialization of GenAI that represents the next stage in the evolution of intelligent systems within modern organizations.

We will cover the following key topics in the chapter:

- Understanding the advantages and risks of GenAI for jobs
- Re-thinking corporate strategy and career paths
- How AI intersects with macroeconomic trends
- A collective reshaping of the labor market
- The agentic enterprise – a refinement of GenAI

Understanding the advantages and risks of GenAI for jobs

GenAI is like a double-edged sword. It is not only a technological upgrade but also a transformative force with the potential to both create and displace, augment and automate. Recent empirical evidence has moved this discussion from speculation to observable reality, revealing a complex and often polarizing impact on the workforce.

Augmenting work and expanding possibilities with AI

A substantial body of research suggests that GenAI is more likely to **augment human capabilities** and change jobs than to replace them entirely.

- **Productivity boom and skill equalization:** GenAI is a powerful tool for boosting productivity. A study of over 5,000 customer support agents found that access to an AI conversational assistant boosted average worker productivity by **14%**. Crucially, the largest gains (a **35% boost**) went to new and low-skilled workers, suggesting AI can act as a great equalizer within a company by accelerating on-the-job training (`https://www.hrdive.com/news/generative-ai-chatgpt-increased-customer-service-agent-productivity/648925/`).
- **Job augmentation over replacement:** Projections from organizations like the International Labor Organization (ILO) suggest a majority of jobs will be changed or augmented by AI, with a smaller percentage being completely automated. The "EPOCH" framework from MIT Sloan identifies key human-intensive capabilities complementary to AI: **empathy, presence, opinion, creativity,** and **hope**. These will remain highly valued (`https://www.ilo.org/publications/generative-ai-and-jobs-2025-update`).
- **Creation of new roles:** Historically, technological shifts have led to the creation of new types of jobs. GenAI is expected to continue this trend, creating roles like **"AI Orchestrators"** and **"AI Ethicists"** that require new skills in system design and cross-functional collaboration.

- **Addressing labor shortages:** In economies facing aging populations (such as Japan) and declining birth rates, generative AI can be a crucial tool to fill labor gaps and maintain productivity. It is estimated that GenAI could handle up to 30% of currently worked hours by 2030 (`https://www.mckinsey.com/mgi/our-research/generative-ai-and-the-future-of-work-in-america`).

Along with opportunities and expansion there are also viable risks and challenges that are associated and you need to consider them before adoption.

The challenges and risks: Displacement, bias, and new threats

The transformative power of GenAI also brings significant challenges and risks that require careful management. Let's look at these risks and threats:

- **Disproportionate impact on entry-level jobs:** A Stanford University analysis of millions of ADP payroll records, titled "Canaries in the Coal Mine?", found that since late 2022, early-career workers aged 22-25 in "AI-exposed" occupations (like software development, customer service, and accounting) experienced a **13% relative decline in employment**. Researchers attribute this to AI's ability to replicate **"codified knowledge"** (book-learning) more easily than the **"tacit knowledge"** of experienced professionals. This adjustment is occurring primarily through the elimination of positions rather than wage cuts (`https://digitaleconomy.stanford.edu/app/uploads/2025/11/CanariesintheCoalMine_Nov25.pdf`).
- **Accelerating wage polarization:** The economic shift is creating a sharply divided workforce. According to PwC's 2024 Global AI Jobs Barometer (`https://www.pwc.com/gx/en/news-room/press-releases/2024/pwc-2024-global-ai-jobs-barometer.html`), the average **wage premium for workers with specialized AI skills surged to 25%**, with some analyses showing it as high as 56%. In the U.S., this premium can be as high as 53% for roles like database designers. This trend risks widening the gap between high- and low-income earners as industries rapidly automate.
- **Algorithmic bias and discrimination:** AI systems can inherit and amplify human biases present in their training data. A key driver of this is the severe "diversity disaster" in the AI field itself, where women can make up as little as **12%** of AI researchers. This homogeneity leads to the creation of biased algorithms that can have discriminatory outcomes in hiring, lending, and healthcare.

- **Case study – Amazon's AI recruiting tool:** Amazon's experimental AI recruiting tool was scrapped after it was found to be discriminatory against women. The model was trained on a decade of Amazon's own resume data, which was heavily skewed toward male candidates. The AI taught itself that male candidates were preferable, penalizing resumes that contained the word "women's" (e.g., "women's chess club captain") and downgrading graduates from two all-women's colleges. Amazon ultimately disbanded the project, unable to guarantee the system wouldn't devise new discriminatory methods.
- **Uneven impact on demographics:** Automation disproportionately affects women and minority workers, who are more concentrated in roles at high risk of automation, such as office support and clerical services. This is exacerbated by the **"digital divide,"** which limits opportunities for these groups to retrain and transition into new, high-tech jobs.
- **Emerging cybersecurity threats:** The same technology powering this transformation also equips malicious actors with powerful new tools. These threats include AI-powered phishing, polymorphic malware that evades detection, and prompt injection attacks.

These challenges demand fundamental changes in how organizations operate and how individuals build their careers. In the next section, we will focus in that direction.

Rethinking corporate strategy and career paths

GenAI is forcing a fundamental rethink of how businesses operate, compete, and structure their workforce. This is giving rise to new **"AI-first"** business models, operational disciplines, and a radical reshaping of the career ladder.

The agentic enterprise and the AI corporate citizen

A transformative new model, the *agentic enterprise*, is emerging, centered on a symbiotic partnership between humans and AI. In this model, AI agents go a step further from being tools and become autonomous actors who are capable of reasoning, planning, and executing complex, multi-step workflows. This shifts the human role from "human-in-the-loop" supervision to a strategic **"human-above-the-loop"** framework.

- **Case study – Klarna's AI-powered customer service:** Fintech giant Klarna provides a compelling real-world implementation of this model. Its AI assistant is able to handle *two-thirds of all customer service chats*, which is the equivalent work of *700 full-time human agents*. It is also projected to deliver a *$40 million profit improvement*. The average time to resolve an issue plummeted from 11 minutes to *under 2 minutes*.

- **The AI corporate citizen framework:** As AI autonomy grows, a more formal framework is emerging to treat AI agents as *corporate citizens*. This involves integrating them into the corporate structure with unique identities, auditable permissions, and clear accountability.
    - **Accountability and governance:** Accountability is established through *Automated Lineage and Auditability*, an immutable logging system that traces every AI decision. To ensure ethical alignment, the concept of *Constitutional AI* embeds core corporate policies and values directly into the agents' operational logic.
    - **Performance measurement:** Performance is tracked with a new class of KPIs beyond simple efficiency, including strategic metrics, such as **Time-to-Insight** or **Innovation Capacity.**

Another important attribute that would help in organizational success in the AI era is resilience.

Building corporate resilience amid uncertainty

In an era of economic uncertainty and supply chain fragility, corporations are deploying generative AI to build resilience and create more predictive, agile operations. Organizations are applying generative AI across several critical business functions, including:

- **Supply chain optimization:** Unilever is embedding AI across its vast supply chain. For its ice cream division, it uses AI to analyze weather data to refine demand forecasts, improving accuracy by 10% in some markets. Furthermore, Microsoft provides GenAI tools like the Copilot in Dynamics 365 Supply Chain Management, which proactively monitors global events to identify potential supplier risks and drafts communications to mitigate disruptions (`https://www.unilever.com/news/news-search/2025/how-ai-is-transforming-unilever-ice-creams-end-to-end-supply-chain/`).
- **Financial strategy and risk management: Chief Financial Officers** (**CFOs**) are using GenAI to automate financial forecasts and run complex **'what-if' risk scenarios**. By leveraging models like **recurrent neural networks** (**RNNs**) and incorporating real-time sentiment analysis, they can simulate the impact of market shifts on cash flow and profitability, moving from a reactive to a proactive stance.
- **Revolutionizing marketing and customer segmentation:** AI is enabling *hyper-personalization at scale*. A groundbreaking application is the use of AI to create synthetic environments for campaign testing. AI models generate lookalike audiences, which are simulated user profiles that mirror real consumer traits. This allows marketers to test new products and messaging on these synthetic audiences to predict campaign performance before a full-scale launch, reducing risk and cost.

The changing nature of work is also redefining how careers begin and progress. As organizations integrate AI into their workflows, many entry-level responsibilities are being automated, reshaping long-established career paths.

Automating the entry level and reshaping the career ladder

The automation of foundational tasks is profoundly reshaping career paths, particularly in professional services, disrupting the classic apprenticeship model. The impact of AI on the modern workforce can be seen across several important areas, including:

- **Disruption in professional services:** McKinsey & Company's *Lilli* synthesizes information from over 100,000 documents, automating a core part of a junior consultant's role. Similarly, *Harvey AI*, used by top law firms, automates legal research and contract analysis, challenging the traditional training model for junior lawyers.
- **The evolving workforce and new professions:** The value of human workers is shifting from research to the ability to query AI, evaluate its output, and integrate its insights. This is creating and formalizing new roles:
    - Demand is growing for AI Trainers ($63k–$116k+ salary), Generative Design Specialists ($154k–$236k+), and Digital Labor Coordinators.
    - We need to watch out for the rise of the AI supervisor. Human roles are evolving into AI Agent Supervisors or AI Orchestrators, who design, manage, and refine AI workflows. This is supported by new cross-functional *Agent Ops* teams and strategic leadership roles like the **Chief AI Officer (CAIO)**.
- **Formalizing AI in performance reviews**: Meta has announced that starting in **2026**, *AI-driven impact* will be a formal criterion in employee performance appraisals, reflecting an urgent push across the tech sector to integrate AI skills.

The effects of AI are not only evident within organizations and across career paths, but also at the macroeconomic level. Its widespread adoption is influencing economic growth, workforce dynamics, and the competitive landscape across nations.

How AI intersects with macroeconomic trends

The impact of GenAI is not happening in a vacuum. It is deeply intertwined with broader macroeconomic trends that are collectively reshaping the global labor market. Let's explore a few such intersections:

The green transition

GenAI presents a significant paradox for the global push toward sustainability. It's both a force for environmental good and a source of new environmental challenges. This dual impact can be understood through the following key developments:

- **AI as a sustainability tool:** Google DeepMind's GNoME project has used AI to discover 2.2 million new crystal structures, including 380,000 stable candidates for green technologies like better batteries, accelerating research by what would have taken nearly 800 years.
- **The environmental footprint of AI:** Training large models is incredibly energy-intensive. The carbon footprint of AI systems alone could be between 32.6 and 79.7 million tons of CO_2 emissions in 2025, while the water footprint could reach 312.5–764.6 billion L (`https://www.sciencedirect.com/science/article/pii/S2666389925002788`).
- **The "Green AI" movement:** In response, this movement promotes energy-efficient AI through techniques like model pruning and the use of specialized, energy-efficient hardware.

The macroeconomic impact of AI cannot be understood in isolation from the geopolitical and regulatory forces shaping its development. As nations compete for technological leadership, fragmented policies and diverging regulations are creating an increasingly complex global AI landscape.

Geo-economic fragmentation and regulatory balkanization

Increasing geopolitical tensions are leading to a fragmented global economy, impacting AI development by restricting technology and data access. This has given rise to a **"regulatory Balkanization,"** where major powers have adopted starkly different approaches to AI governance, creating significant compliance challenges for multinational corporations.

The following examples highlight the contrasting regulatory approaches adopted in various regions:

- **European Union (EU):** The EU's **AI Act** establishes a comprehensive, risk-based framework, categorizing AI systems and placing stringent requirements on high-risk applications in areas like employment.
- **United States (US):** The U.S. has a more fragmented, voluntary framework, relying on executive orders and the non-binding National Institute of Standards and Technology (NIST) AI Risk Management Framework, prioritizing innovation but lacking a single federal law.
- **China:** China's approach is state-led and control-oriented, aligning AI with national interests and social stability through targeted regulations and data sovereignty mandates.

The consequences of these global shifts extend beyond markets and regulation. Together, they are transforming employment patterns, workforce demands, and the skills needed to thrive in an AI-driven economy.

A collective reshaping of the labor market

As generative AI intersects with broader economic trends, the labor market is undergoing a major transformation, which is pushing governments, companies, and labor groups to respond proactively.

Labor's counteroffensive – unions negotiate for AI protections

Recognizing the threats of displacement and algorithmic bias, labor unions are making technology a central issue in negotiations, securing concrete contractual rights:

- **Writers Guild of America (WGA):** Following a 2023 strike, the WGA secured a landmark agreement that *AI cannot write or rewrite literary material* or be used as source material, and studios must disclose if material is AI-generated.
- **Marriott hotel workers (UNITE HERE):** A 2018 agreement requires Marriott to provide **165 days' advance notice** before introducing new technology, to bargain with the union over its effects, and to provide *retraining* for affected workers.
- **AFL-CIO's "worker-centered AI" principles:** In 2025, the largest U.S. union federation established a "Workers First Initiative on AI," calling for stronger collective bargaining rights and guardrails against surveillance (`https://aflcio.org/press/releases/afl-cio-launches-workers-first-initiative-ai-put-american-workers-future-artificial`).

In the next section, we will see how GenAI is bridging the skill gap.

Bridging the skills gap

To counteract the disproportionate impact of automation and build a more inclusive AI workforce, targeted initiatives are being developed to bridge the skills gap:

- **Microsoft's AI Skills 4 Women:** This program aims to democratize access to AI education for women, offering a free, online, three-hour course with no prior technical background required, providing foundational knowledge in AI fundamentals, prompt engineering, and ethics.
- **Policy innovations and a speculative future:** One promising policy is *wage insurance*, which subsidizes a portion of the wage difference if a displaced worker finds re-employment at a lower salary, encouraging quicker transitions. Looking ahead, a speculative concept is the **"union of agents,"** where AI agents could engage in collective bargaining on behalf of human workers.

Navigating this new era requires a proactive approach to reskilling, lifelong learning, and innovative policies to harness AI's power for a more prosperous and inclusive future.

The trends discussed throughout this chapter point to a broader transformation in the role of AI. Building on the foundations of generative AI, organizations are now embracing agentic systems that can execute tasks, coordinate workflows, and support decision-making with minimal human intervention.

The agentic enterprise – a refinement of GenAI

The emergence of the **agentic enterprise** is driven by the shift from AI as a static tool (like a sophisticated search engine) to AI as an autonomous agent capable of complex reasoning, planning, and execution. This model fundamentally redefines the relationship between human workers and technology.

Defining the agentic enterprise

The *agentic enterprise* is an organizational structure centered on a symbiotic partnership between human employees and sophisticated, goal-oriented AI systems (AI Agents). In this environment, AI agents are delegated authority to initiate, manage, and complete complex, multi-step business processes without constant human intervention.

Let's look at the core mechanics of an AI agent. Unlike conventional software, an AI agent possesses four key attributes (as shown in *Figure 1.1*):

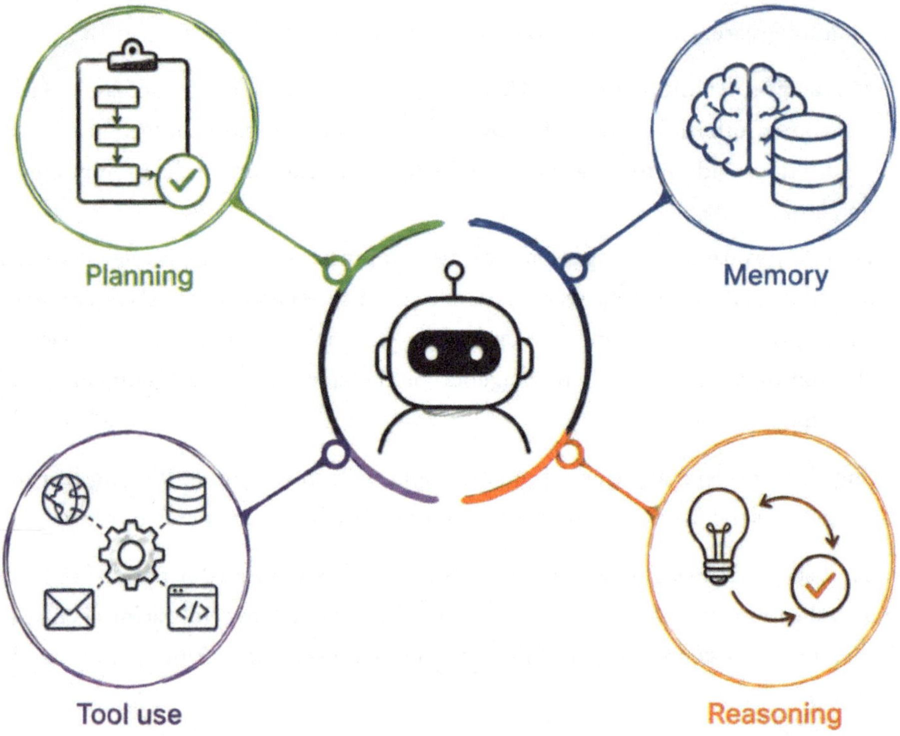

Figure 1.1: Key attributes of AI agents

Here's a closer look at each of these core mechanics:

1. **Planning:** Breaking down a high-level goal (e.g., "Launch a Q4 promotional campaign") into discrete, executable steps.
2. **Memory:** Storing context and previous interactions to inform future decisions and maintain long-term coherence.
3. **Tool use:** Accessing and interacting with external systems (databases, APIs, CRMs, email clients) to execute tasks.
4. **Reasoning:** Self-correcting and iterating on its plan when it encounters an error or ambiguous situation.

So far, our discussion has focused primarily on the technological, organizational, and economic dimensions of AI. We now turn our attention to the human aspect and examine how the evolving role of AI is redefining the relationship between people and intelligent systems.

The shift to human-above-the-loop

The most significant organizational change is the movement away from the traditional *human-in-the-loop* model, where humans validate every small step, to the *human-above-the-loop* strategic framework. The following table shows the differences between the two concepts:

Role	Human-in-the-loop (old model)	Human-above-the-loop (agentic model)
Human role	Task execution, validation, and quality assurance	Strategic oversight, setting high-level goals, auditing outcomes, and ethical governance
AI role	Assisting with single tasks (e.g., writing an email draft)	Autonomous execution of multi-step workflows (e.g., identifying risk, drafting mitigation strategy, scheduling, and approval)

Table 1.1: A comparison of human-in-the-loop and human-above-the-loop approaches

In this new structure, humans leverage their unique capabilities, such as **empathy, presence, opinion, creativity, and hope (EPOCH),** to manage the AI's goals and interpret the broader business context, leaving the execution of codified, repeatable tasks to the agents.

As AI agents become embedded in everyday business operations, organizations need a framework that ensures they act in ways that are aligned with business objectives, governance principles, and ethical standards.

The AI corporate citizen framework

As AI agents gain autonomy, they are increasingly being treated as **corporate citizens.** This framework establishes the necessary governance to ensure the agents operate ethically, lawfully, and with accountability within the enterprise structure.

Here are a few ways to embed accountability and auditing in AI agents:

- **Automated lineage and auditability:** This is a crucial governance requirement. An immutable logging system is implemented to trace every AI decision back to the specific logic, data inputs, and corporate policies used. This creates a transparent, clear audit trail, establishing accountability when an agent makes an error or a biased decision.
- **Constitutional AI:** To align AI behavior with corporate values, **Constitutional AI** embeds core corporate policies, ethical guidelines, and legal requirements directly into the agents' operational logic. The AI uses this "constitution" to govern its own actions and self-evaluate its outputs before execution.

For auditing purposes, you'll also need KPIs that track performance and support decision-making.

New performance metrics (KPIs)

Simple efficiency metrics are insufficient for managing autonomous agents. The agentic enterprise uses new KPIs to measure strategic impact:

- **Strategic KPIs:**
    - **Time-to-insight:** How quickly an agent can move from raw data to a validated, actionable recommendation
    - **Innovation capacity:** The volume and quality of novel solutions or designs that agents propose
- **Business impact metrics:** ROI, Customer Satisfaction (CSAT) scores, and conversion rates directly attributable to agent activities.
- **Technical Metrics:** Accuracy, Latency, and Cost-per-Action

In the final section, we will explore some new roles as well as the organizational implications.

Organizational implications and new roles

The agentic enterprise demands a complete reorganization of job roles and internal departments. Let's explore a few of these new roles:

The rise of the AI orchestrator

The human role evolves into that of an **AI agent supervisor** or **AI orchestrator**. These professionals are cross-functional experts responsible for:

- **Designing workflows:** Translating business objectives into executable AI agent workflows
- **Agent refinement:** Iteratively debugging and refining the agents' goals, tools, and constitutional boundaries
- **Risk management:** Monitoring agent behavior for "hallucinations," bias, or operational drift

This requires the creation of new **Agent Ops** or Agent Operations teams and dedicated strategic leadership, often formalized by the role of the **Chief AI Officer (CAIO)**, to steer the entire strategy.

Efficiency gains (Klarna case study revisited)

The Klarna example powerfully illustrates the potential of the agentic enterprise:

- **Scale and cost savings:** An AI assistant handles two-thirds of all customer service chats, accomplishing the work equivalent of **700 full-time human agents**, projected to yield a **$40 million profit improvement**.

- **Customer experience:** The average time to resolve a customer issue plummeted from 11 minutes to **under 2 minutes**, demonstrating superior efficiency without sacrificing customer satisfaction. This efficiency gain is only possible because the agent can autonomously access all necessary systems (billing, order history, FAQs) to complete the task end-to-end.

The new emerging roles reflect a broader shift toward organizations where humans and AI collaborate to create greater value together.

Summary

In this chapter, you explored how generative AI is reshaping the future of work at multiple levels, from individual careers and organizational strategy to the broader global economy. You examined both the opportunities and challenges of GenAI, including its impact on jobs, workforce transformation, corporate decision-making, and macroeconomic trends. You also learned how the rise of the agentic enterprise is redefining human–AI collaboration, introducing new operating models, governance frameworks, and organizational roles that will shape the next generation of AI-enabled businesses.

Understanding these shifts is essential because the impact of generative AI extends far beyond adopting new tools. It requires rethinking how organizations create value, how professionals develop new skills, and how businesses govern increasingly autonomous AI systems responsibly. By gaining this broader perspective, you are better equipped to understand not only where AI is creating opportunities but also how to navigate the strategic, ethical, and organizational changes that accompany its adoption.

In the next chapter, we will dive into the core concepts of generative AI, helping you build a strong foundation for your AI journey and future career.

2

Decoding GenAI – Core Concepts for Every Professional

"GenAI has moved from a research ambition to an everyday capability, and understanding its core ideas is now part of modern professional literacy."

– Sadid Hasan

In the summer of 1956, a small group of scientists at Dartmouth College in Hanover, New Hampshire, USA, hypothesized that every aspect of learning or intelligence could be so precisely described that a machine could simulate it to demonstrate Artificial Intelligence. They envisioned creating machines that could use language, form abstractions, solve problems requiring human intelligence, and even improve themselves over time. Nearly 70 years later, the recent breakthroughs in Generative AI (GenAI) are finally realizing large pieces of that vision. GenAI systems are typically built on large foundational models that are capable of generating new content (text, images, audio, video, code, etc.) in response to natural language prompts. In AI terminology, natural language refers to the ordinary languages that humans speak and write, such as English, Spanish, Mandarin, and Arabic, rather than programming languages or mathematical notation. When GenAI systems accept natural language prompts, it means you can interact with them using everyday sentences and questions instead of specialized code or syntax. This ability to understand and generate human language is what makes modern AI systems feel more conversational, intuitive, and accessible to people across a wide range of disciplines.

Why does this matter for every professional, not just developers, scientists, or engineers? Because GenAI is rapidly becoming a ubiquitous assistant and collaborator in workplaces across industries, including healthcare, education, science, biotechnology, finance, marketing, legal, and more.. Unlike earlier AI models and systems, which often required specialized training data and were limited to narrow tasks, GenAI represents a paradigm shift. These systems are trained on large-scale, general-domain data, allowing them to perform a wide range of tasks. Users can draft emails, brainstorm marketing copy, analyze spreadsheets, write code, or create training videos, all through simple natural language prompts.

Therefore, mastering the core concepts of GenAI, from how it works to how to use it wisely (often referred to as AI literacy), is now as essential as computer literacy was a generation ago. In fact, a recent industry report found that 62% of employers now expect candidates and employees to have at least some familiarity with AI, driving the rollout of training programs and certifications aimed at non-technical professionals seeking to become AI champions within their organizations (`https://cloud.google.com/blog/topics/training-certifications/new-google-cloud-certification-in-generative-ai`).

This chapter introduces the essential concepts behind GenAI systems, focusing on what every modern professional needs to understand. We begin by clarifying what makes GenAI fundamentally different from traditional AI systems, considering the shift from discriminative models that classify data to generative models that can create new content from natural language prompts. We then explore the core concepts that enable these systems, including deep learning, in-context learning, embeddings, and vector search, and examine how they shape the way users interact with the foundational models, such as **Large Language Models** (**LLMs**). Next, we look at the emerging discipline of AI literacy, highlighting why skills such as prompt design, critical evaluation, and understanding model limitations are becoming indispensable across all professional roles. Finally, we connect these foundations to the broader strategic landscape, showing how GenAI fluency is evolving into a key competency for leaders, managers, and non-technical professionals navigating AI-driven transformation.

By the end of this chapter, you will be able to distinguish between discriminative and generative tasks and understand why GenAI's ability to produce new content represents a major shift in how organizations operate. You will also understand the fundamentals of how LLMs interpret prompts through mechanisms like in-context learning, and how to craft prompts that are structured, testable, and aligned with model behavior. Further, you will learn the importance of AI literacy, from recognizing hallucinations and bias to evaluating outputs responsibly, and understand how GenAI skills translate into strategic value in the workplace.

In this chapter, we will cover the following topics:

- The fundamental shift in AI models
- The deep learning foundations of GenAI
- In-context learning – how GenAI adapts on the fly
- Prompt engineering – the art art of asking AI the right way
- AI literacy – a new skill for the modern professional

> In generative AI, a *hallucination* refers to a response that sounds confident but is factually incorrect, made up, or unsupported by the data the model was trained on. A *bias* refers to systematic patterns in a model's output that unfairly favor or disadvantage certain groups, viewpoints, or outcomes, often reflecting imbalances or stereotypes present in the training data. Recognizing both is an essential part of responsible AI literacy.

From discriminative to generative – a fundamental shift

To appreciate GenAI's impact, let's first clarify how generative tasks differ from traditional discriminative tasks in AI. In simple terms, a discriminative AI model learns to distinguish or decide. It takes some input data and assigns it a label or category or chooses among given options. A classic example is a spam filter: the AI model looks at an email and classifies it as one of the two possible labels/categories: *spam* or *not spam*. Another example is a medical AI model that analyzes an X-ray image and outputs a probable differential diagnosis. Such models draw a boundary between possible outcomes/categories in the data, e.g., what email features separate a spam from a legitimate email, and use that to make decisions. What they don't do is generate new material. They can tell you which existing category something falls into but not imagine something outside of what they've seen.

By contrast, a GenAI model learns the underlying patterns and distribution of the training data to be able to create new examples that look like they could belong in that dataset. In this context, the distribution refers to the overall pattern or *shape of the data* to denote aspects like how often certain features appear, how they relate to one another, and what typical versus unusual examples look like. For instance, if a model is trained on thousands of emails, it doesn't memorize each message; instead, it learns common structures like greetings, transitions, tone, and closing phrases. When it generates a new email, it draws from this learned pattern space to produce something that fits the style of the original dataset. This is why a generative model doesn't just classify spam vs. not spam; it can generate an email similar to a person's writing style. In essence, generative models aim to capture the full richness of the training data, so they can sample from it to produce novel outputs.

In more technical terms, discriminative models learn decision boundaries, while generative models learn data distributions. The following table highlights the difference:

AI model type	Primary goal	Typical output	Example use case
Discriminative	Distinguish between classes or outcomes given input data.	A label, category, or prediction about the input.	Classify an email as spam vs. not spam; recognize a handwritten digit as 0–9.
Generative	Generate new data samples resembling the training data.	A novel data instance (text, image, etc.) created by the model.	Write a paragraph in the style of a poet; generate a photorealistic image of an animal.

Table 2.1: Discriminative vs. generative models

A key insight is that generative models, in principle, subsume discriminative abilities. The idea is that if a model can learn the data well enough to generate new examples, it effectively captures key patterns in that data, which allows it to answer questions or perform classifications. For instance, GPT-4 can write an essay (generative task) and also answer a multiple-choice question (discriminative task by choosing an answer) using the same model. However, the reverse is not true: a narrowly trained discriminative model, such as logistic regression for spam detection, has no capacity to generate a plausible email from scratch.

GenAI's ability to produce content opens up fundamentally new applications. We can now have AI draft text, design art, or formulate ideas, not just evaluate them. This transforms AI from a back-office analytics tool to a front-line creative and thought partner. A GenAI system can serve as a tireless junior copywriter, a prototype graphic designer, or a data analyst that can not only chart trends but also write a plain-English report about them.

It's important to reemphasize that GenAI generates outputs by extrapolating from patterns learned from training data. For example, if a model is trained only on English text, it won't be able to generate in fluent French. Moreover, if there are gaps or biases in the training data, those may be reflected in the outputs as well. In practice, GenAI often feels very creative, and it can surprise and inspire; however, it can also make errors or produce nonsensical results when prompted beyond its knowledge. We will discuss these limitations later, but first, let us explore what enabled the rise of GenAI.

> The Dartmouth proposal in 1956 planted the seed for AI, but progress in the creative, generative aspects of AI was slow for a long time. Early AI and expert systems in the 60s–80s were mostly rule-based and discriminative. The ability for a machine to produce fluent language or realistic images had to wait for both theoretical and architectural breakthroughs, and the accumulation of massive datasets and computing power. For decades, AI could play chess and classify images, but it couldn't write a novel or draw a unique picture. That began to change in the 2010s, as new techniques (which we'll cover next) unlocked the generative potential of machines. It has been a long journey, but understanding where we came from helps highlight why GenAI is considered a turning point in the evolution of AI.

The deep learning foundations of GenAI

What has changed in the last decade to make GenAI possible? Short answer is *data* (and the algorithms and necessary computing power to make use of it). The advent of deep learning in the 2010s is one of the most important factors. Deep learning refers to neural networks with many layers ("deep" networks) that can automatically learn complex representations of data. Traditional machine learning hit a point of diminishing returns as data scaled up. Models would plateau in performance even with more training examples. Deep learning researchers found that with the right architecture and sufficient computational power, model performance could continue to improve with more data, as richer patterns, nuances, and structures in data could be captured by bigger models on bigger datasets. Importantly, this leap in computational power was enabled by GPUs, whose massive parallel processing capabilities made it feasible to train large neural networks at scale, turning what once took months into days or even hours, thereby unlocking the modern era of GenAI.

The scaling ability was critical for generative tasks: to convincingly produce content, a model must learn from vast amounts of knowledge, for example, the subtleties of natural language or the textures of images. Achieving this required training on large datasets, including billions of words or millions of images, that deep learning models could fully exploit. By the late 2010s, this led to the rise of foundation models, where large neural networks were trained on broad, diverse data (for example, text from across the Internet) without a specific task in mind, and later adapted to many downstream applications. Among these foundation models, some were explicitly designed for generative tasks. At the same time, new architectures such as transformers provided far more effective ways to capture long-range dependencies in text and images, meaning they can understand relationships between elements that are far apart from each other. For example, in a long sentence, the meaning of a word at the end may depend on something that was introduced many words earlier; traditional models struggled to connect those distant pieces, but transformers can track and relate them with much greater accuracy. This ability to maintain context over long spans is one of the key reasons modern models perform so well on complex language and vision tasks. Cloud computing expanded access to large-scale training by offering flexible, on-demand compute resources, while open-source frameworks like TensorFlow and PyTorch standardized development workflows that helped accelerate experimentation across the research community. Together, these advances created the foundation for today's GenAI systems.

Let's dive into some deep learning architecture breakthroughs that enabled today's GenAI:

- **Transformer-based Large Language Models (LLMs):** The transformer architecture revolutionized natural language processing (Vaswani et al., 2017) by introducing an attention mechanism that allows models to consider contextual information from all parts of a sequence simultaneously, rather than processing text strictly from left to right. This made it possible to train extremely large language models, often with hundreds of billions of parameters (which are the adjustable numerical values a model learns during training) on vast text corpora (i.e., large collections of written material such as books, articles, websites, and transcripts). Such models are typically trained in a generative fashion as they learn to predict the next token (the model's basic unit of text, which may be a whole word or part of one, and can differ based on the underlying tokenization algorithm) in a sequence given all preceding tokens. Although this objective appears simple, scaling it up produces models capable of generating coherent paragraphs, translating between languages, answering questions, and performing a wide range of language-based tasks. Many modern GenAI models and systems like GPT, BERT, PaLM, LLaMA, etc. rely on the transformer architecture to power chatbots, writing assistants, and a growing ecosystem of text generation tools.

  However, raw pre-training of large language models alone is not the only reason for the recent leap in GenAI capability. The modern recipe combines large-scale pre-training with a multi-stage post-training process starting with supervised fine-tuning (SFT)—a step where the model learns from curated input–output examples to follow instructions more reliably, followed by reinforcement learning from human feedback (RLHF), which uses human preference ratings to align model behavior with what people consider helpful or appropriate. More recently, reinforcement learning with verifiable rewards (RLVR) has emerged as a powerful extension, enabling models to optimize against objective, automatically checkable signals (such as correctness or constraint satisfaction) rather than relying solely on subjective human judgments. This shift has fueled the rise of reasoning-oriented models such as o1, o3, and DeepSeek-R1, which demonstrated that longer RL runs and extended "thinking time" can systematically improve performance by encouraging the model to generate richer intermediate reasoning traces before producing a final answer. These developments suggest that test-time compute (that is, how long a model is allowed to think) can become a controllable axis of GenAI capability.

At the same time, researchers demonstrated with a new generation of small language models (SLMs) that high-quality data and targeted training can enable models with orders of magnitude fewer parameters to achieve performance competitive with much larger LLMs. These compact models are far more efficient to train and run, enabling inference and on-device fine-tuning on consumer hardware or edge devices, meaning small, everyday computing devices like smartphones, tablets, laptops, or wearables that operate outside the cloud and perform AI tasks locally. This paradigm shift helped improve accessibility, allowing organizations and individuals to deploy capable smaller language models without the massive computational footprint traditionally associated with LLMs. Together, these advances illustrated that the progress of GenAI is no longer driven solely by data or model size, but by smarter and more efficient training pipelines, better data, and new ways of enabling models to reason.

- **Generative adversarial networks (GANs):** Proposed by Ian Goodfellow et al. in 2014, GANs introduced a game-theoretic approach for generation in which two neural networks are trained in opposition, where a generator tries to create realistic data, such as images, and a discriminator tries to detect if an image is real or generated (`https://proceedings.neurips.cc/paper_files/paper/2014/hash/f033ed80deb0234979a61f95710dbe25-Abstract.html`). Through this adversarial process, the generator becomes progressively better at producing outputs that can fool the discriminator. GANs have proven highly effective for tasks such as image synthesis, image enhancement, and artistic style generation. However, they can be difficult to train due to issues such as mode collapse (where the model keeps generating the same limited set of outputs instead of producing diverse examples) and instability (meaning the training process can oscillate, diverge, or fail to converge to a reliable solution). As a result, their applicability tends to be concentrated in domains with well-structured data, particularly images.
- **Variational autoencoders (VAEs):** Around the mid-2010s, VAEs offered another approach to generation, where an autoencoder is a neural net that compresses data into a latent representation—a compact, numerical encoding that captures the essential features or structure of the input, such as the overall shape of an image or the style of a handwriting

sample—and then reconstructs it. A VAE extends this idea by making the latent representation probabilistic, modeling it as a distribution of possible encodings and then sampling from that distribution to generate new data. This formulation helped formalize the notion of a latent space: a continuous, structured space in which one can interpolate smoothly between points and produce outputs that blend characteristics in meaningful ways. Although individual VAEs may not achieve the same level of photorealism as GANs, they offer strong advantages for controlled and interpretable generation. As a result, VAEs have been applied in domains such as face synthesis, handwriting generation, and chemical molecular structure design.

- **Diffusion models:** Emerging as a major breakthrough in the early 2020s, diffusion models quickly became one of the most powerful approaches to generative image modeling. These models begin with pure random noise and learn to denoise it step by step, gradually transforming it into a sample from a target distribution, for example, images of cats. Conceptually, one can imagine progressively blurring an image until it becomes static; a diffusion model learns the reverse trajectory, reconstructing a coherent image through a sequence of small, learned noise-removal operations. Foundational work by Ho et al. (2020) demonstrated the effectiveness of this denoising diffusion framework, and subsequent systems such as DALL·E 2 and Stable Diffusion models showcased their ability to produce high-resolution, detailed images from text prompts (`https://proceedings.neurips.cc/paper/2020/hash/4c5bcfec8584af0d967f1ab10179ca4b-Abstract.html`). Diffusion models have rapidly become state-of-the-art for text-to-image generation, as they tend to capture fine-grained detail more effectively than GANs and offer greater stability during training.

Despite their differences, all of the above approaches share a common foundation: they rely on training deep neural networks on large datasets. The specifics range from modeling the distribution of pixels to the distribution of words, but all rely on immense computing power and data. For example, GPT-3 was trained on massive internet-scale data and has 175 billion parameters. This exhaustive learning is what empowers generative models to be so flexible. An LLM isn't explicitly taught grammar, facts, or common sense; it absorbs them implicitly from the data. Likewise, an image model might learn the concept of "zebra" with all the stripes and shapes not through explicit human instruction, but by identifying patterns across thousands of animal images; over time, it forms internal representations (often described as clusters in latent space) that correspond to such concepts.

For a non-technical professional, it's not necessary to grasp the math of these models, but a high-level understanding is important to be familiar with the model capabilities and their limitations. Being aware of the fact that an LLM has learned from essentially all public text up to a certain date explains why it might know a lot of general knowledge but will lack awareness of events after its training data cutoff date. Knowing that these models generate content by leveraging learned patterns from data helps one to be alert to issues like bias (if the training data had biases, outputs can), or factual errors (the model doesn't truly know facts, it only strings together likely words, so it can make up plausible-sounding falsehoods, known as *hallucinations* or *fabrications*). In short, deep learning made GenAI possible, but it also introduced a new kind of opacity: these models contain millions or billions of learned parameters whose internal dynamics may not be fully interpretable. This lack of transparency is one reason why developing a critical eye toward AI-generated output is essential, and why AI literacy has become so important. Before turning to AI literacy, however, there is one more deep learning-enabled capability to address, because it has fundamentally changed how we interact with modern GenAI models: in-context learning.

In-context learning – how GenAI adapts on the fly

One of the most remarkable aspects of modern generative models, especially LLMs, is their ability to learn new tasks from just a few examples or instructions at runtime, without any retraining. This phenomenon is known as **in-context learning (ICL)**. The capability emerges from the scale and structure of deep neural networks, which learn internal representations that allow them to generalize from the patterns present in a prompt without updating their weights. In effect, the model uses the prompt itself as a temporary training signal, inferring the desired behavior and carrying it out on the fly.

Consider this scenario: You have an AI language model that was never explicitly programmed to do translation. However, you can use the prompt as follows:

```
Translate the following English sentences to Bangla.

English: Where is the library?
Bangla: লাইব্রেরিটা কোথায়?

English: How are you today?
Bangla: আজ আপনি কেমন আছেন?

English: Nice to meet you.
Bangla:
```

If you give the preceding as input, chances are the model will output "আপনার সঙ্গে পরিচিত হয়ে ভালো লাগলো।" – a correct Bangla translation of "Nice to meet you." What happened here? In the prompt, the model identified a pattern of "English: [sentence] -> Bangla: [sentence]" for two examples, and then a third English sentence. Even though it wasn't explicitly trained to be a translator, it has enough general language understanding from pre-training to infer, in context, that it should produce the Bangla version of the third sentence. It learned the task from the prompt.

In-context learning is possible because during training, the model saw many instances of text where a task is demonstrated (for example, Q&A pairs, or lists of translations, or chronology of events, etc.). The GPT-3 research (Brown et al., 2020) was the first to highlight this capability in large language models, framing it as **few-shot learning**. In this setting, the model treats the examples provided in the prompt as a temporary training signal, inferring the intended task and generalizing from those examples within a single interaction, without updating its parameters (`https://papers.nips.cc/paper/2020/hash/1457c0d6bfcb4967418bfb8ac142f64a-Abstract.html`).

From a user perspective, this is greatly empowering, as it means you can get the model to do things it was never explicitly built to do, by simply demonstrating or describing the task in the prompt. Need it to format data in a table? Show it an example. Want it to behave like a customer and give objections in a role-play? Just prompt: "You are a customer who is hesitant..." and so on. Essentially, natural language prompts are not just questions but can include instructions, examples, role definitions, a few data points etc. and the model can interpret all that to infer user intent.

A few important aspects of in-context learning to note:

- **Zero-shot vs. few-shot:** Zero-shot prompting is when you ask the model to do a task with no examples, just an instruction (e.g., `Translate to French: Good morning.`). Few-shot prompting is when you include a couple of examples in the prompt (as in the English-->Bangla translation example) to guide the model. Few-shot prompts often improve accuracy because they remove ambiguity about what you want. If the task can be interpreted in different ways, an example makes it clear for the model to understand the user intent better.
- **Chain-of-thought prompting:** Sometimes, you want the model to not just give an answer but to reason through a problem. You can prompt it to "think step by step." For example: "Q: What's 100 divided by 2, plus 3? Let's solve it step by step." If the model follows properly, it might output: "First divide 100 by 2 to get 50. Then add 3 to get 53. So, the answer is 53." This technique forces the model to break down the task, which can lead to more correct

results on complex problems (especially math or logic). It's like asking the model to show its work. Interestingly, research has found many models do better when you explicitly request this kind of chain-of-thought reasoning approach because it helps avoid lapses in complex tasks.

- **Context window limitations:** Early language models were constrained by a strict context window, which is the fixed amount of text (prompt + response) they could process at once. Older systems such as GPT-3 operated within only a few thousand tokens, which meant the model could not "remember" anything beyond that limit. Long conversations would gradually push earlier messages out of scope, and large documents had to be fed in pieces. GPT-4 expanded this window to tens of thousands of tokens, but the fundamental limitation remained: once the window was full, additional text simply could not be incorporated. External tools could chunk or retrieve information, but these were workarounds rather than inherent model capabilities. In effect, the context window functioned as the model's working memory and that memory was finite. However, recent research has begun to challenge this architectural ceiling. For example, state-space models, such as Samba, demonstrated how hybrid designs can achieve effectively unbounded context by avoiding the quadratic bottleneck of self-attention (you can learn more about Samba models at `https://arxiv.org/abs/2406.07522`). Instead of forcing all text into a single window, these models maintain and update a latent state that can, in principle, extend indefinitely. Complementary approaches such as recursive language models and retrieval-augmented systems further expanded usable context by storing and re-injecting relevant information rather than requiring the entire history to fit inside the model at once. These innovations enabled a shift from fixed-window constraints toward architectures where context length becomes a practical rather than structural limitation.
- **Learning across sessions:** It's important to emphasize that in-context learning does not produce permanent learning inside the model itself, as the underlying weights don't change. If you show the model five examples of how to format a report and it performs well, you'll need to provide those examples again the next time you invoke it. Each session effectively starts fresh unless some external "memory" mechanism is used to re-inject prior information. This stands in contrast to training or fine-tuning, where the model's parameters are updated and the new behavior becomes part of its long-term capabilities. As newer GenAI/agentic systems introduce persistent memory layers outside the core model with regard to storing and leveraging preferences, instructions, or past interactions, they help bridge this gap by automatically supplying the context that in-context learning alone cannot retain.

From a professional standpoint, understanding in-context learning means recognizing that you can actively shape an AI system's behavior through your prompt. The model will attempt to follow whatever task structure, examples, or instructions you provide. When it produces an incorrect or incomplete result, you usually don't need to start over; simply rephrasing the request or adding an example of the desired output is often enough for the model to adjust and respond more accurately.

Although recent systems are improving with advanced memory features and larger context windows, how the model or system can effectively leverage all information in a long conversation is still an open problem. Therefore, if key instructions are provided many paragraphs earlier, it's often necessary to restate them or anchor them in the prompt in a more persistent way. Some interfaces support system or context messages/instructions that remain fixed at the top, ensuring that essential guidance stays within the model's active working context.

In summary, in-context learning gives GenAI a powerful form of instant flexibility. Rather than requiring a custom model for every task, a single large model can handle a wide range of workflows simply through appropriate prompting. This has major practical implications: the same system can support legal, marketing, finance, HR, and engineering teams in different ways without being explicitly trained for each domain (although specialized models fine-tuned on domain-specific datasets such as code-focused models like Codex naturally offer deeper capability in their respective areas). In effect, the *training* happens in the prompt, where the user provides the structure, examples, or constraints that guide the model's behavior. This places substantial control in the hands of the user, which naturally leads to the importance of prompt engineering.

Prompt engineering – the art of asking AI the right way

By now, it should be clear that the way you prompt a GenAI model is crucial. Prompt engineering is often described as both an art and a science of guiding the model toward the output you want. Unlike traditional software, where debugging code is the natural response when something goes wrong, working with GenAI often means rephrasing your request, adding context, or clarifying your intent. This calls for a different mindset: you're communicating with a system that is highly literal and relies entirely on patterns in data rather than shared human intuition, so the clarity and structure of your prompt directly shape the quality of the result. Recent research has also shown that even seemingly small factors, such as how a prompt is formatted or simply repeating the same instruction, can meaningfully influence performance (you can check the following resources for further information: `https://arxiv.org/abs/2411.10541` and `https://arxiv.org/abs/2512.14982`). This precision matters even more as we move into an era of coding and collaborative agents (for example, GitHub Copilot CLI) that can take autonomous actions, call APIs, use tools, and ground themselves into relevant context as needed to accomplish given tasks. The paradigm is shifting from conversational queries to assistive workflows, from responses to resolutions, from automation to execution, and ultimately from conversations to meaningful, accelerated outcomes.

Modern systems also tend to mirror the user, which is why two people using the same model can get very different outcomes depending on how clearly they articulate goals and constraints. In that sense, AI doesn't replace foundational skills like reading comprehension and structured writing; rather, it makes them more important, because prompting is essentially structured writing that rewards clarity, logic, and precision.

Here are some key principles and tips for effective prompting, which any professional can apply:

- **Be clear and specific:** Being vague in your prompt may lead to generic output. If you ask, `Tell me about bank accounts`, you might get a generic essay about bank accounts. But if you actually wanted to know how to open a certain type of account, you should ask that specifically. Include details in your prompt about what exactly you want and in what format. For example: `List the three main requirements to open a personal checking account at a U.S. bank, in bullet points.`" Now the model knows it should output a bullet list, probably short, and focused on requirements.
- **Set the role or tone (if needed):** You can ask the model to speak as if it were someone or something. This often helps get a relevant style. For example, with the prompt: `Act as an elementary school science teacher and explain climate change`, the output will likely be simpler and more informative, suitable for kids. Or if you say: `Respond in a friendly, empathetic tone`, the model will adjust wording accordingly. The model has seen numerous texts of different styles during training, so prompting it with a role can steer the output toward the right direction.
- **Provide examples in the prompt:** As discussed in in-context learning, showing an example of the desired output can considerably improve quality. If you want a certain format, illustrate it. For example, `Translate the following phrases to French. Example: Good night -> Bonne nuit. Now translate: See you tomorrow ->`. By giving that example, you leave no doubt how the output should look (the model will likely continue with the output: "À demain"). Even without a full example, sometimes mentioning the style helps: `Summarize the article in one paragraph of no more than 5 sentences.` This is explicit instruction on format and length to help the model provide the desired output.

- **Iterate and refine:** A complicated prompt is often imperfect on the first attempt. Professionals who get the most out of GenAI rely on an iterative approach: they pose a question, examine the output, and then refine the prompt to address any issues. If the response is too shallow, you might add a line like `Give more detailed explanations for each point.` If it's too verbose, you could specify `Keep the answer under 200 words.` Prompt engineering is best understood as a guided conversation in which you can progressively steer the model toward what you need. In practice, it's generally an interactive process rather than a one-shot directive.
- **Ask for steps or reasoning for complex tasks:** If you want the AI system to solve a complex problem, it often helps to prompt it to show its reasoning, explanations, or intermediate steps. This makes it easier to understand how the model arrived at its final output and to debug when something doesn't look right. Although large language models can handle many reasoning tasks, they are still language systems at their core, so they often struggle with multi-step calculations required for complex mathematical and logical reasoning unless guided carefully. Asking for explicit reasoning helps the model break the problem into smaller parts, verify its own steps, and produce more reliable results. For example: "You are an expert accountant. Calculate the break-even point for the following scenario and explain each step clearly." This prompt signals that you expect a step-by-step solution, not just a final number. And if the model makes a mistake, you can easily see where its reasoning went off track.
- **Be mindful of bias and framing:** The model will often mirror the way you ask something. For example, the prompt "Why is Product X better than Product Y?" already assumes X is superior, and the model will likely comply (a behavior known as sycophancy) by generating reasons that support that assumption. If you want an objective comparison, a better prompt would be: "Compare Product X and Product Y, discussing their respective advantages and disadvantages." In the same way, any question framed from a particular angle will tend to produce an answer aligned with that angle. This happens partly because supervised fine-tuning teaches the model to imitate human-written answers, and reinforcement learning from human feedback rewards responses that appear helpful, agreeable, and aligned with user preferences. Together, these model post-training stages (after pre-training LLMs) nudge the model toward agreeing with the user rather than challenging them. Newer AI systems try to reduce this by optimizing internal reasoning trajectories to help models evaluate their own confidence, explore alternative interpretations, and avoid blindly endorsing the user's viewpoint. Still, as a professional, especially in fields where objectivity matters, phrasing prompts neutrally remains one of

the most reliable ways to get balanced output. This is why domain expertise is essential so that humans can remain in the loop to interpret, validate, and correct AI-generated answers, ensuring that decisions are grounded in real knowledge rather than the model's tendency to sound confident even when it is wrong.

- **Use constraints or context:** You can embed pieces of context or specific requirements directly into your prompt for the model to use. For example: `Using the information below, draft an email to the team about our Q3 sales figures: [insert a short table or summary of figures]`. Modern models can read and incorporate structured or unstructured data you provide, weaving it naturally into the output. **Retrieval-augmented generation (RAG)** extends this idea by automatically pulling in relevant information from your documents or external knowledge sources at query time, grounding the model's answer in real, up-to-date data rather than relying solely on what it learned during training. Whether you supply the context manually or the system retrieves it through RAG, it's still important to verify that the model hasn't misread or distorted any aspects. Manual context injection is best when the information is small, specific, and already in front of you, giving you precision and full control, while RAG is better when the relevant information is spread across many documents, too large to paste into a prompt, or frequently changing. The key is choosing the method that matches the scope of the task and the amount of information involved. Providing appropriate context is part of a broader practice, often called context engineering, which focuses on shaping what information the model receives, how it is formatted, and how it is framed so the model can reason effectively and produce an output that best satisfies the user's intent. You can learn more about context engineering using the following resource: `https://www.langchain.com/blog/the-rise-of-context-engineering`.
- **Handle sensitive or confidential info carefully:** While this is less about prompt wording and more about good judgment, responsible AI practice requires avoiding the entry of confidential or sensitive information into public, non-secure GenAI tools, as this may introduce unnecessary risks to data privacy and security. GenAI systems are best approached with the same caution applied to any online service or digital workflow, where sensitive information is handled with care and established data usage policies and guidelines are consistently observed.

Prompt engineering is ultimately about clear communication and intentional guidance: the model is flexible, literal, and eager to comply, so the quality of the output often improves when the request is reframed, given more detail, or clarified. What proves most effective is a straightforward yet imaginative way of asking for what you need via framing the request in the right terms, experimenting with roles or domain-specific language, and treating the exchange as a collaborative, iterative process. Although models continue to improve in following plain instructions, the core principle remains unchanged: people who know what they want and express it clearly achieve far better results. In this sense, prompt engineering is becoming a foundational digital literacy skill grounded in natural language, like crafting effective search queries or using basic spreadsheet formulas. As these systems become more capable and more deeply embedded in everyday work, a broader set of competencies becomes essential for not just knowing how to prompt a model but understanding how to use AI responsibly and interpret its outputs with confidence.

AI-literacy – a new skill for the modern professional

Back in the 1990s, not everyone assumed that "computer literacy" would become universally essential. Yet today it is difficult to imagine any professional role that does not rely on computers in some form. AI literacy is reaching a similar inflection point: the basic understanding of AI concepts and the ability to use AI tools is becoming a part of everyday professional competence. The rapid rise of GenAI has transformed this from a niche technical topic into a broad workforce imperative, with many employers now expecting AI familiarity even in general roles. With that shift underway, it is worth examining what AI literacy means in the context of GenAI and why it is becoming so important for long-term career development.

What AI literacy means for professionals

AI literacy goes beyond knowing how to use AI tools; it involves understanding their capabilities, limitations, and appropriate applications in professional settings. As AI becomes increasingly embedded in everyday workflows, this foundational knowledge is emerging as a critical skill for professionals across industries.

AI literacy for a professional can be understood across several layers:

- **Conceptual understanding:** AI literacy doesn't require a PhD in machine learning, but it does call for familiarity with a few core ideas, for example, what it means for a model to be "trained," what a parameter represents, how a rule-based system differs from one that learns from data etc. By this point in this chapter, you should understand the difference between generative and discriminative models and why GenAI represents such a significant shift. You also know that an AI system can produce confident but inaccurate outputs (hallucinations), because it relies on learned patterns from training data. This kind of conceptual grounding helps you set realistic expectations for what the state-of-the-art AI systems can and cannot do. For example, knowing that an image generator is trained on existing images reminds you that it may reproduce certain styles or biases and that it doesn't "imagine" visuals in the human sense but recombines patterns from its training data. With this understanding, you're far better equipped to use AI effectively and avoid common pitfalls.

- **Practical skills (Tool use):** This involves being able to work effectively with AI-powered applications that support everyday professional tasks. It might mean using a conversational AI system to research information or draft content, relying on image-generation tools to create concept art, or using voice-based assistants to automate routine actions. Many modern productivity apps or platforms now include built-in GenAI features that can summarize information, draft text, or help structure documents and data. AI literacy includes knowing how to make practical use of these capabilities. For example, an AI-literate analyst might use a GenAI tool to produce several ways of visualizing a dataset, and then evaluate which option best fits the narrative they need to communicate, thus saving time while still reviewing each suggestion for accuracy, clarity, and relevance.
- **Critical evaluation:** This is a foundational element of AI literacy. It involves approaching AI-generated outputs with informed judgment rather than automatic acceptance, recognizing that these systems may have inherent limitations and that their results require human interpretation. For example, when AI produces text, images, or recommendations, you should assess the output for accuracy, appropriateness, and potential bias. You should understand where human judgment must intervene to validate, refine, or contextualize what the AI system provides, and you should remain attentive to moments when the AI's reasoning may be incomplete or misleading. In practice, AI literacy means knowing when and how human expertise should complement the model to ensure that the final outcome is reliable, responsible, and genuinely impactful.
- **Awareness of latest AI developments:** You don't need to follow every research paper, but AI is advancing quickly enough that capabilities can shift dramatically within a short period of time. AI literacy includes maintaining a general sense of this trajectory, recognizing that new AI techniques, tools, and norms are evolving constantly, and that what seemed out of reach last year may now be straightforward to accomplish. Staying curious and periodically updated through tech news, professional networks, or training courses should help you recognize new opportunities and avoid emerging risks. When you're aware of what current AI systems can and cannot do, you're better positioned to anticipate vulnerabilities, adapt your workflows, and spot practical ways to continually expand your skillset.

The impact of AI literacy on careers

AI literacy increasingly shapes how individuals grow in their roles in the AI era and how they adapt, compete, and advance in their careers. Those who understand how to use AI effectively can improve productivity, make better decisions, and stay competitive as workplace expectations evolve.

A few reasons why AI literacy is so important for careers:

- **Enhanced productivity:** Individuals who know how to leverage AI tools can often accomplish more in less time. For example, a data analyst might use AI to generate routine code or documentation, and a journalist might rely on AI to transcribe and summarize interviews instead of doing it manually. Research consistently points to substantial productivity gains from GenAI across a wide range of occupations (`https://www.microsoft.com/en-us/research/project/the-new-future-of-work/`). However, these gains can only emerge when people understand how to use the tools effectively. Without those skills, the tools are likely to be underused (potentially leading to *capability overhang*, a situation where an AI system is capable of far more than users realize or know how to leverage) or applied in ways that limit their potential impact.
- **Better decision-making:** AI can surface patterns and insights, but they are only valuable when the human interpreting them understands their context and limitations. An AI-literate professional does not accept a prediction at face value; rather, they examine the underlying assumptions, weigh the output against their own expertise, and consider factors the AI system may not capture. At the same time, they remain open to the signals the AI reveals, for example, patterns or trends that might be difficult to manually detect in large, complex datasets. For instance, a project manager might use an AI tool to forecast delivery risks, then integrate those insights with their understanding of team dynamics and upcoming organizational changes to make a more grounded decision. In practice, the strongest decisions emerge when human judgment and AI-generated insights work together, with the human providing the critical understanding needed to guide and refine the model's output.
- **Career opportunities and security:** As AI becomes more embedded in everyday work, having foundational AI skills is increasingly an advantage. Just as proficiency with tools like Word or Excel eventually became standard expectations, many roles will soon assume a basic level of comfort with AI-assisted writing, analysis, and problem-solving. Those who build these skills are better positioned to stay competitive and adapt as their fields evolve, while those who ignore them may find it harder to keep pace. Importantly, adapting

does not require becoming an AI specialist; it simply means learning how to incorporate AI into your work in a thoughtful and effective way. Developing this fluency helps ensure that your capabilities continue to grow with technological advances, rather than falling behind them.

- **Strategic leadership:** For managers and leaders, AI literacy is essential for making informed strategic decisions about adopting AI within their teams, products, or organizations. When senior leaders lack an understanding of GenAI, they may overlook transformative opportunities or implement solutions in ways that create operational or ethical problems. Leaders who are AI-literate can more readily identify where AI might streamline processes, enhance customer experiences, or enable new business models. Increasingly, this is why many organizations are directing AI education toward non-technical leaders. These leaders do not need to know how to build the AI systems themselves, but they do need to know how to ask the right questions: What data is the model trained on? How do we mitigate bias? What is the expected return on investment? How do we prepare our teams to use it effectively? What risks arise if we rely on it for this process? These are now leadership questions as much as technical ones.

On the societal side, broad AI literacy helps communities engage in thoughtful conversations about how AI should be used and governed. When many people have a basic understanding of these technologies, public discussions about ethics, privacy, and policy become more balanced and constructive. Instead of debates being driven by either hype or fear, a wider shared understanding supports more grounded, inclusive decision-making. But that's zooming out; let's return to the workplace.

What can you do to build AI literacy? Beyond reading a book like this, one of the most effective approaches is hands-on experimentation. If you have access to a GenAI tool, try applying it to different tasks. Curiosity is your ally. Challenge the system with something from your own work: Can it draft this email? Did it miss something important? Does it understand our internal terminology, or do I need to supply that context? Over time, you will develop an intuitive sense of what the AI handles well and where it tends to stumble. That mental model of the system's strengths and limitations is invaluable; it helps you quickly determine which tool, if any, is appropriate for a given task. For example, an AI-literate lawyer might recognize that AI is excellent for suggesting a contract outline or summarizing lengthy depositions, but not reliable enough to cite case law without verification. Based on this understanding, they would use it for what it accelerates (creating early drafts and synthesis), while reserving the critical, accuracy-dependent work for human expertise.

Many organizations are investing in training their employees on GenAI tools, recognizing that technology alone doesn't create value as people need to learn new workflows to unlock its benefits. If your workplace offers opportunities to learn or experiment with AI, it's worth taking advantage of them, and if not, there are plenty of accessible online resources designed for non-technical learners. These can reinforce and expand the concepts introduced in this book and help you build confidence through guided practice. Building AI literacy also means developing an awareness of the ethical considerations surrounding AI use, for example, understanding the concepts of fairness, transparency, and intellectual property to ensure your skills grow responsibly alongside the technology.

Summary

GenAI has moved from a research ambition to an everyday capability, and understanding its core ideas is now part of modern professional literacy. In this chapter, we explored foundational concepts such as generative versus discriminative tasks, in-context learning, and the basics of prompt design, building the groundwork for using AI thoughtfully and effectively in your work. As you apply these ideas, you'll likely find new ways to streamline tasks, make more informed decisions, and approach problems with greater creativity, all while relying on your own judgment and ethical awareness to guide AI toward meaningful outcomes. The next chapters will build on this foundation by showing how these concepts translate into specific roles and practical strategies for integrating GenAI into your career. The future will favor those who can work confidently alongside these systems, and with the understanding you've gained here, you're well positioned to grow meaningfully in your career with the evolving technological landscape.

In the next chapter, we will discuss the five families of GenAI careers and dive into specific roles along with their skill sets and responsibilities.

3

Mapping Your Path – Roles and Roadmaps in GenAI

> *"A clearer way to understand the GenAI career landscape is to look beyond shifting job titles and focus instead on the stable patterns of work that appear across organizations."*
>
> *– Sadid Hasan*

In the last chapter, you built a foundation for understanding how generative AI works and how to use it effectively. Now we turn to what that knowledge means for your career and the roles emerging in this new landscape.

We are in a period where progress in **GenAI** is accelerating at an extraordinary pace, opening doors that most professionals have never seen before. This rapid expansion is generating a wide range of new opportunities across industries. People can feel this momentum all around them, and many are now focused on understanding where their own strengths fit within this evolving landscape and how to move forward with clarity and purpose. In this context, the question is no longer "What job title should I pursue?". That framing is too narrow. The more relevant question is: "Which role aligns with how I think and work, and how do I move from where I am today to where the field is heading?". Recent workforce insights such as, *LinkedIn Jobs on the Rise 2026* report highlights strong growth in AI-related roles, while also noting that many professionals are eager to build the skills needed to thrive in this changing environment. (`https://www.linkedin.com/pulse/linkedin-jobs-rise-2026-25-fastest-growing-roles-us-linkedin-news-dlb1c/`)

A more durable way to navigate this landscape is to rely on signals that extend beyond any single product or technology innovation cycle. Labor market trends, technical best practices, and governance frameworks, such as LinkedIn's *AI Labor Market Update*, the NIST AI policy frameworks, and ISO/IEC 42001 AI management system standards offer a stable vocabulary for describing roles, skills, and responsible deployment.

This chapter builds on that foundation in three ways: First, it explains how GenAI roles are shifting from model-centric work, where teams focus on training or fine-tuning a single model in isolation, to system-centric work, where the model becomes just one component in a larger AI system that includes retrieval pipelines, business logic, evaluation frameworks, monitoring signals, and human-in-the-loop workflows, as organizations move from experimentation to real-world deployment. A concrete example of this shift is an enterprise customer-support agent: a production system where a RAG pipeline retrieves the latest policies and product documentation; application engineers integrate the model into the support platform with proper authentication and permissions; evaluation teams run automated and human-rated tests to measure accuracy, hallucination rates, and policy compliance; monitoring teams track drift, latency, and safety violations in real time; governance teams define guardrails, escalation paths, and audit requirements; and product designers shape how the agent fits into a customer support specialist's workflow. In such systems, no single role *owns the model*; instead, multiple roles collaborate around a complex, end-to-end pipeline where reliability, grounding, safety, and workflow integration matter as much as the model itself, illustrating the system-centric work in production.

Second, it introduces five broad role **families**: builders, shapers, guardians, enablers, and adopters to help you understand the field in terms of strengths and responsibilities rather than job titles that vary across companies, and to show how these families map onto the operating models most enterprises actually use. In practice, large organizations rarely rely on a single structure; instead, they blend centralized AI platform teams, domain-aligned product groups, and embedded specialists working in what many companies describe simply as central teams plus satellite teams or shared platforms plus local ownership. Builders often sit in the central platform group, creating shared components such as RAG pipelines, evaluation tools, and model-serving infrastructure; shapers typically live in product teams where they translate business needs into AI-enabled workflows; guardians span both central governance groups and embedded risk partners who ensure responsible use across domains; enablers are frequently embedded in business units, helping real teams adopt and operationalize AI systems; and adopters represent the domain experts who integrate these systems into real work, providing the usage patterns and feedback that ultimately shape system evolution.

This chapter then expands these families with descriptions of both established roles and the newer ones emerging from agentic systems, evaluation practices, and AI operations. Finally, it offers practical pathways for readers at different stages of their careers, **from students and early career professionals to mid-career switchers and organizational leaders navigating AI driven transformation**.

This chapter will cover the following topics:

- The shift from "models" to "systems"
- Why agentic AI changes the career map
- A practical map – five families of GenAI careers
- Core roles in GenAI – purpose, practice, and evidence
- Roadmaps and leveling matrices
- Career pivot playbooks

The shift from "models" to "systems"

In the earliest stage of the GenAI wave, the model was the center of attention: scale, emergent capability, and benchmark performance. The focus has since shifted toward deployment. Once GenAI enters real workflows, it is evaluated less by its best demonstration and more by its reliability under every day, diverse, and sometimes adversarial conditions. Labor-market signals reflect this transition indirectly through the skills employers emphasize. For example, *LinkedIn Jobs on the Rise 2026* report ranks AI engineering among the fastest-growing roles and explicitly lists concepts and tools like **Retrieval-Augmented Generation (RAG)**, various deep learning libraries, and agentic engineering platforms among common skills, pointing toward system building rather than model training alone. This is because a model (such as LLM) does not guarantee the right information at the right time, nor does it guarantee stable behavior under evolving context due to its underlying non-deterministic approach and training objectives (as discussed in the previous chapters).

To make GenAI reliable in practice, a deployable system must surround the model with mechanisms and responsible AI guardrails that bound its behavior. These include retrieval to ground outputs in relevant data, tool calling to transform language into actions, evaluation to quantify success and detect regressions, and monitoring to identify drift, abuse, and failure patterns, all of which contribute to building a more generalizable and eventually a self-improving system. Because generative models can produce varied outputs, traditional deterministic testing is often insufficient. As a result, structured evaluation approaches are needed to reflect real-world conditions. Even if a system performs well at launch, prompt updates, model updates, and data changes may cause regressions. Therefore, **LLMOps** practices treat the LLM system lifecycle as a continuous loop involving data curation, experimentation, evaluation, validation, deployment, monitoring, and feedback such that quality does not depend on a single moment in time.

> While building systems, teams should be clear about what's essential versus what can wait. At the minimum viable architecture level, this means grounding or retrieval to keep answers accurate, a few targeted evaluation checks to catch obvious failures, and basic monitoring for errors and missue—just enough to keep early prototypes safe without overengineering. Advanced capabilities such as automated regression suites, drift detection, human-review workflows, and policy-driven governance may come later, once the system proves useful and starts to scale. The key principle is simple: build the smallest reliable system first, then layer in sophistication only as real-world usage demands it.

The following subsections build on this idea by showing how teams encounter recurring gaps when moving from prototypes to production and why the resulting demand for GenAI skills is spreading far beyond traditional technical roles.

From prototype momentum to product reality – understanding the gap

A familiar pattern repeats across organizations adopting GenAI: a team prototypes a conversational assistant (question answering system). In controlled tests and demonstrations, it appears trustworthy, but in early user trials, it begins to produce confident errors, incomplete answers, or inconsistent behavior. This gap is not an accident; rather, it is a predictable outcome of deploying non-deterministic systems at scale. Evaluation best practices therefore recommend eval-driven development, logging real interactions, and building test suites that reflect production distributions (i.e., real-world inputs and phrasing patterns that users naturally produce) rather than curated examples. This shift helps clarify where value is created in GenAI systems. The roles that are growing are those that systematically close the prototype-to-product gap: engineering focuses on grounding and orchestration, operations on measurement and monitoring, product on defining success criteria and driving adoption, and governance on ensuring accountability, safety, and risk control.

Why the demand is broad (and why this matters for career transitions)

Public workforce reporting suggests that GenAI-driven demand is not confined to a narrow sector. LinkedIn's *AI Labor Market Update* reports the diffusion of AI engineering talent across industries and rapid growth of AI literacy beyond technical roles (`https://business.linkedin.com/content/dam/me/economicgraph/en-us/PDF/ai-labor-market-update-january-2026.pdf`).

Complementing this, the World Economic Forum has cited LinkedIn data indicating that AI has created new roles at scale and that upskilling is a central workforce strategy. This reinforces the view that AI adoption expands the role ecosystem rather than merely shifting existing titles. For readers considering a career transition, this broad demand matters because it creates multiple entry points; one can enter the ecosystem through engineering, product, operations, security, governance, or domain-applied roles, all of which increasingly interact with GenAI systems. This means that career pathways are no longer limited to technical specialists, but are accessible to professionals across a wide range of backgrounds.

Why agentic AI changes the career map

Within the GenAI paradigm, Agentic AI refers to systems that can pursue goals through multi-step processes, often using tools, accessing resources, and reacting to intermediate outcomes. The unit of work shifts from **generating responses** to **completing tasks**, which changes both capability and obligation.

This shift has two major implications:

1. From a capability perspective, tool calling turns a language model into a controller for external functions. For example, OpenAI's tool-calling documentation describes the canonical pattern: define tools as schemas, allow the model to call them, execute the calls in application code, and feed results back to the model to produce grounded output.
2. From a risk perspective, tool access expands the attack surface and the consequence surface. For example, *OWASP's Top 10 for LLM Applications (2025)* highlights key risks such as prompt injection, sensitive information disclosure, supply chain risk, improper output handling, and excessive agency, where an agent is permitted to act on behalf of a user (`https://genai.owasp.org/resource/owasp-top-10-for-llm-applications-2025/`).

Market signals also align with this shift. Gartner's 2025 press release on AI innovations identifies AI agents as a fast-advancing technology and emphasizes the need for foundational enablers such as AI-ready data and trust/risk/security management for sustainable scaling (`https://www.gartner.com/en/newsroom/press-releases/2025-08-05-gartner-hype-cycle-identifies-top-ai-innovations-in-2025`). Agentic AI also makes governance practical rather than aspirational, but only to the extent that organizations can close gaps in tooling, ownership, and policy adoption—areas where governance maturity still lags the pace of agentic capabilities. Responsible AI guidance for agent-based workloads emphasizes human oversight, safety boundaries, and ongoing monitoring. As agents become common in productivity environments, governance becomes a core competence across product and engineering roles.

As organizations adopt tool-enabled systems, a scaling problem emerges: each tool integration has historically required custom development, increasing cost and security exposure. Public initiatives such as the **Model Context Protocol (MCP),** a lightweight standard that lets AI systems safely request data or trigger actions from external tools, aim to make these connections consistent across applications, for example, by allowing an agent to retrieve a customer's order status or open a support ticket through a permissioned interface. You can learn more about MCP and get started with this resource: `https://modelcontextprotocol.io/docs/getting-started/intro`

For careers, this signals a growing specialization layer: integration, platform engineering, and AI harness engineering, which together form the backbone of how enterprises turn raw model capabilities into safe, reliable, and scalable systems. Most organizations are now investing heavily in an internal platform layer that provides shared APIs, evaluation tooling, guardrails, orchestration services, and reusable modelinteraction patterns for product teams. Within this layer, engineers define the governance primitives that make tool-calling and agent workflows safe and observable; these include consent models (rules that specify what an AI agent is allowed to request), permission scopes (boundaries that limit what a tool or data source can access), tool schemas (structured definitions of a tool's required inputs and expected outputs), and audit trails (records that capture what the system did and why). AI harness engineering extends this by building the scaffolding around models: test harnesses, evaluation runners, safety checks, simulation environments, and controlled execution layers that validate behavior before and after deployment. Together, these capabilities sit between traditional software integration and AI-specific safety requirements, forming a distinct and increasingly critical career path as enterprises mature their AI platforms.

You can learn more about harness engineering at: `https://openai.com/index/harness-engineering/`

A practical map – five families of GenAI careers

A clearer way to understand the GenAI career landscape is to look beyond shifting job titles and focus instead on the stable patterns of work that appear across organizations. To provide that clarity, we can group the emerging roles into five broad families: **Builders** (Technical creation), **Shapers** (Product and strategy translation), **Guardians** (Risk, safety, and accountability), **Enablers** (Operational integration and workflow embedding), and **Adopters** (Domain-driven application and amplification). Together, these families offer a practical map of how teams create and leverage value as GenAI systems move from early prototypes to dependable, widely adopted products.

The following figure illustrates these five families:

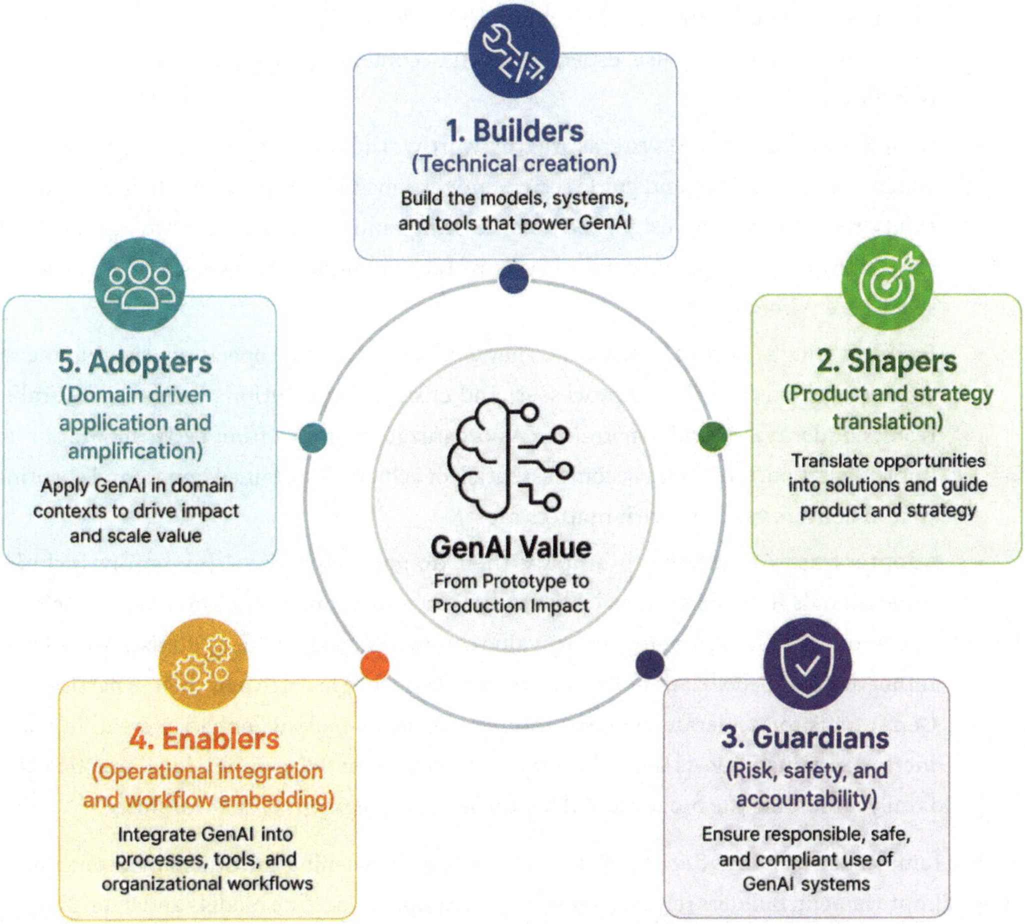

Figure 3.1: Five families of GenAI careers

Let's look at each of these families in more detail:

- **Builders** are responsible for creating the technical foundation that makes GenAI systems work in practice. Their work spans the full lifecycle of system development: curating and preparing data, devising algorithms, training or fine-tuning models, designing retrieval pipelines, building orchestration layers, developing evaluation workflows, and improving performance as systems scale. This family includes engineering, research, and scientific roles involving people who advance model capabilities, refine data quality, and ensure that systems behave reliably under real-world conditions.
- **Shapers** focus on turning technical capability into meaningful product outcomes. They define user problems, shape adoption strategies, and establish success metrics that can be measured and improved. Their strength lies in translating potential into solutions that people can actually use, especially as AI becomes embedded across industries and workflows.
- **Guardians** ensure that AI systems are trustworthy. They convert principles into practical controls, manage risks, and guide secure and responsible deployment. Their work spans safety reviews, policy design, red-team testing, and risk management, where these functions grow in importance as AI systems take on higher-stakes tasks and operate in sensitive environments.
- **Enablers** bring AI into real workflows. They work directly within operational environments, connect systems to existing processes, and ensure that solutions deliver measurable results under real-world constraints. As organizations move from experimentation to implementation, these roles become essential for achieving sustained impact and ensuring that AI delivers value where it matters most.
- **Adopters** use AI systems to amplify their domain expertise. This family includes professionals in fields such as healthcare, law, education, finance, marketing, science, operations, and so on, where primary value comes from people's deep domain knowledge rather than AI specialization. Their work evolves as they learn to pair their expertise with GenAI tools to accelerate analysis, improve decision-making, enhance creativity, and increase productivity. As GenAI becomes woven into everyday professional practice, this family represents the broadest and fastest-growing segment of the workforce.

All five families form an interdependent system, each strengthening the others in a continuous loop of improvement. Builders rely on feedback from Adopters to refine models and data; Shapers depend on Enablers to understand what adoption looks like in practice; Guardians draw on insights from every family to strengthen safety and accountability; and Adopters benefit from the steady improvements that emerge from this shared loop. This interconnected structure is what allows GenAI to move from isolated prototypes to systems that genuinely improve work, decision-making, and human capability. It is also what ensures that the impact of AI is not only technically impressive but socially meaningful. For anyone considering a career in this space, it is worth recognizing that each family is essential to the whole: no single group can create lasting value on its own, and the strongest contributions come from understanding how your work fits into this broader cycle of societal benefit.

How to use the map – a stable decision method

A practical way to navigate the GenAI career landscape is by choosing the family first and treating job titles as variations in naming rather than fixed definitions. For example, roles such as AI Engineer, LLM Engineer, and GenAI Engineer frequently overlap in their system-building responsibilities. Similarly, areas like Responsible AI, AI Governance, and AI Risk often converge on similar work in risk and control implementation.

A simple three-step approach can help guide career decisions:

1. Choose a family: Starting with the family provides a clearer anchor point in a field where terminology shifts faster than the underlying patterns of work.
2. Choose a role: Within that family, select a role that aligns with your current strengths and the capabilities you want to grow.
3. Define evidence: Focus on demonstrating your capability through tangible outputs, such as a portfolio project, an evaluation framework, or a learning plan that shows measurable progress.

This approach keeps career decisions grounded even as job titles evolve. By focusing on stable patterns of work rather than shifting terminology, you can build a trajectory that remains relevant as the field continues to change.

Core roles in GenAI – purpose, practice, and evidence

This section focuses on a set of core roles that define today's evolving GenAI career landscape. Titles may shift as the field matures, but the underlying patterns of work remain stable. Each role is described through a consistent structure that stays useful even as organizations reorganize or technologies change. For every role, the section outlines its formal purpose, how it shows up in modern workplaces, the responsibilities that shape day-to-day execution, the layered skill stack that supports effective practice, and the kinds of portfolio evidence that demonstrate competence. Where relevant, it also clarifies common misconceptions that can obscure what the role actually requires or how professionals can transition into it.

GenAI Engineer/AI Engineer

The GenAI engineer exists to build **LLM-powered** capabilities that operate reliably in products and workflows. In practice, this role has shifted decisively toward system building: retrieval-grounded generation, orchestration, integration, evaluation, and continuous optimization. Modern deployments expect engineers to design retrieval pipelines that tie outputs to authoritative sources, integrate structured tool calling for safe and auditable actions, maintain evaluation suites that detect regressions across prompt, model, and data changes, and instrument observability through traces, logs, and dashboards to diagnose failures and drift. Increasingly, this also means working through significant enterprise integration complexity, for example, by connecting to CRM systems (customer relationship management platforms for sales and support), ERP systems (enterprise resource planning tools for finance, supply chain, and operations), navigating legacy APIs (older or inconsistent integration interfaces), reconciling inconsistent schemas (mismatched data structures across systems), and handling unstructured data (text, documents, logs, and other free-form content) that rarely resembles curated examples. They are also responsible for balancing quality, latency, and cost through iterative measurement and optimization, and for supporting safe rollout strategies across the full LLMOps lifecycle.

The skill stack for this role spans several layers. At the foundation are Python, software engineering principles, and data handling. On top of that sit LLM-specific capabilities such as prompt design, chunking and embedding strategies, retrieval methods, and structured tool calls. A strong quality discipline is essential, including evaluation design, test case curation, automated scoring, and systematic error analysis. **Operational competence**, including monitoring, incident response, cost and latency management, deployment patterns, and feedback loops, is increasingly becoming central. Finally, engineers need basic security and governance literacy, including threat-modeling awareness and guardrail patterns for safe interaction.

Portfolio evidence for this role can be built publicly and often speaks louder than titles. For example, a retrieval-augmented assistant over a public corpus, with clear documentation of chunking and grounding decisions, demonstrates system-level thinking. A simple tool-calling agent that performs one safe action with explicit user confirmation shows an understanding of structured actions. An evaluation harness with a dataset, rubric, and small dashboard illustrates a commitment to measurement. A short writeup (such as technical blogs, publications) explaining observed failure modes and how they were mitigated signals maturity and practical insight to broaden impact. For practitioners already working inside enterprises, where data sensitivity limits what can be shared externally, equivalent internal artifacts carry equal or greater weight: design documents that explain retrieval and orchestration choices, evaluation reports that track regressions across model or data changes, architecture diagrams that show how agents integrate with CRM or ERP systems, and post-incident analyses that document how failures were diagnosed and resolved. Together, these public and internal artifacts provide credible evidence of system-building capability in environments where most meaningful work cannot be open-sourced.

Several misconceptions commonly slow down transitions into this role. One is the belief that a polished demo implies production readiness; in reality, demos hide variability, and reliability comes from evaluation and monitoring. Another is the assumption that retrieval is optional, when grounding has become central to enterprise usefulness. In simple terms, this means that many people still imagine an LLM can operate effectively on its own, but in real organizations the model must pull in actual company data, such as policies, product details, customer records, procedures, documents etc. during answering. Without retrieval, the model is essentially predicting from its learned patterns; with retrieval, it is anchored in the company's real facts, which makes answers accurate, current, and defensible. This grounding step is what turns a general-purpose model into something enterprises can trust in production, which is why retrieval is no longer a nice-to-have but a core requirement for almost every meaningful use case. A third is the idea that monitoring can wait until later, even though modern LLM systems require observability and feedback loops right from the start.

ML Scientist/Applied Scientist

The Machine Learning Scientist, often titled Applied Scientist in industry settings, exists to improve model and system performance through rigorous experimentation, algorithmic innovation, and careful validation of reliability. This role sits at the intersection of research and production, translating scientific insight into measurable system gains. In practice, the work reflects the accelerating pace of capability development across the field and the growing need for scientific rigor that can be applied directly to real-world systems. As organizations deploy increasingly complex models, the scientist's responsibility is to ensure that these systems behave predictably, robustly, and in alignment with intended use. Yet a persistent challenge in enterprises is thelast-mile problem: the handoff from research to engineering to production, where promising experiments often stall due to integration constraints, legacy systems, evaluation gaps, or unclear ownership. Addressing this friction has become a core part of the role: partnering closely with engineering to operationalize findings, shaping production-ready evaluation methods, and ensuring that scientific improvements survive contact with real workloads, data, and infrastructure. This ability to carry ideas across the boundary from insight to impact is increasingly what distinguishes strong scientists in enterprise environments.

Day-to-day work centers on designing experiments that measure quality under realistic scenarios, analyzing failure modes such as hallucination patterns, retrieval mismatches, and robustness gaps, and developing or adapting modeling techniques that address these weaknesses. Scientists frequently work on fine-tuning strategies, re-ranking methods, calibration approaches, and other algorithmic interventions that improve reliability. Collaboration with engineering teams is essential, particularly when translating research signals into deployment-ready improvements or when designing measurement pipelines that capture system behavior at scale. Increasingly, this work intersects with trustworthiness and risk mitigation, as scientific analysis often reveals issues related to information integrity, confabulation (the model producing confident but incorrect statements that sound plausible but are not grounded in real data), or brittleness (the system performing well under ideal conditions but failing abruptly when inputs shift slightly, formats change, or edge cases appear) that must be addressed before systems can be safely adopted.

The **skill stack** for this role spans statistical reasoning, experimental design, and deep familiarity with modern modeling techniques. Strong candidates combine theoretical grounding with practical instincts for how models behave under distribution shift (when real-world data differs from the data used to train or test a model, causing its performance to decline), how to interpret evaluation signals, and how to design experiments that reveal actionable insights. They are comfortable navigating both research code and production constraints, and they understand how to balance innovation with reliability.

Portfolio evidence for this role is best demonstrated through reproducible studies and clear analytical reasoning. For example, a comparative evaluation of retrieval strategies on a public dataset, a calibrated human-evaluation rubric with analysis of disagreement or uncertainty, or technical reports/publications at relevant conference venues or journals explaining proposed scientific contributions and impact, experimental design, results, and limitations can serve as strong indicators of scientific maturity. What matters most is the ability to show how careful experimentation leads to concrete system improvements and how scientific insight translates into measurable, real-world impact.

AI/ML Researcher

The AI/ML Researcher advances the frontier of the field by developing new methods, proposing stronger benchmarks, and deepening our understanding of model behavior. This role is oriented toward discovery: identifying limitations in current approaches, formulating hypotheses, and producing insights that expand what is possible. As AI systems become more capable and more embedded in real-world applications, research increasingly requires attention to measurement, robustness, and transparency. The modern researcher is expected not only to push performance but also to illuminate how and why models behave as they do, and to articulate the implications of those behaviors for safety, governance, and deployment.

In practice, the work blends theoretical exploration with **empirical rigor**. Researchers design experiments that reveal the strengths and weaknesses of emerging architectures, investigate failure modes such as hallucination, brittleness, or distribution shift, and develop new modeling techniques that address these gaps. They often create or refine benchmarks to evaluate progress, propose algorithms that improve generalization or efficiency, and analyze model internals (e.g., the hidden layers, attention patterns, and intermediate signals that reveal how the model processes information and arrives at its outputs) to understand representation, reasoning, or emergent behavior. Collaboration with engineering teams is common, especially when research insights need to be validated at scale or translated into production-ready improvements. Because research now sits close to deployment, there is a growing expectation that researchers understand the societal and operational context in which their innovations will be used.

The skill stack for this role spans mathematical foundations, statistical reasoning, and deep familiarity with modern machine learning methods. Strong researchers combine theoretical intuition with disciplined experimentation, using ablations (i.e., systematically removing or altering one component at a time to see how much it contributes to the overall performance of the system), controlled comparisons, and careful measurement to isolate causal factors. They are comfortable working with large-scale training pipelines, open-source frameworks, and evaluation tools, and they understand how to balance novelty with reproducibility. Increasingly, they also engage with questions of safety, alignment, and governance, recognizing that research choices shape downstream risks and capabilities.

Portfolio evidence for this role typically takes the form of peer-reviewed papers in relevant conferences or journals, or well-documented preprints (i.e., publicly shared research manuscripts posted online before formal peer review, often used to rapidly disseminate new findings) that include reproducible code, clear experimental methodology, and ablation studies where feasible. Participation in **benchmark** development or leaderboard contributions demonstrates engagement with community standards. A research agenda statement that connects methodological innovation to real-world constraints, such as safety, cost, data availability, or deployment considerations, signals maturity and an understanding of how frontier work influences practical systems.

AI Product Manager

The AI Product Manager converts AI capability into durable product value by shaping vision, defining strategy, and ensuring that systems are deployed responsibly and measurably. This role sits at the center of interdisciplinary work, balancing user needs, technical constraints, organizational priorities, and the realities of a rapidly evolving competitive landscape. Because AI systems may introduce uncertainty, nondeterminism (i.e., the fact that the same input can yield different outputs across runs due to sampling, model updates, or context changes), and continuous change, the AI PM must constantly prioritize work items, manage stakeholder expectations, and guide teams through pivots driven by new findings, shifting requirements, or emerging risks. In enterprise settings, a substantial part of this work involves closing AI literacy gaps by educating stakeholders, aligning leadership on what AI can realistically deliver versus hype, and ensuring that decisions are grounded in evidence rather than assumptions. The work requires fluency in both technical and non-technical language, enabling the PM to translate between engineering, design, legal, security, and business stakeholders and to keep the entire team aligned through ambiguity.

In practice, the AI Product Manager begins by defining the user problem with precision and establishing the acceptable boundaries within which an AI system must operate. They set measurable success metrics and specify evaluation requirements that reflect how modern models behave under real-world conditions. Their responsibilities include coordinating engineering, design, security, and governance partners to ensure that the system is effective, trustworthy, and aligned with organizational risk posture. They plan rollout strategies that move from pilot to measurement to refinement to scale, ensuring that each stage produces evidence rather than assumptions. Trust mechanisms, such as citations, explanations, uncertainty cues, and human-override pathways are treated as core product features because user confidence is inseparable from adoption. Throughout this process, the AI PM must assess ROI, understand how AI differentiates the product in the market, and make tradeoffs among quality, latency, cost, and safety while keeping stakeholders aligned on what is feasible and valuable.

The skill stack for this role blends product strategy, user research, and technical literacy. Strong AI PMs understand how retrieval, prompting, evaluation, and model behavior shape user experience, and they can articulate the business impact of different approaches. They are adept at managing expectations by communicating what AI can and cannot do, reframing scope when needed, and ensuring that teams remain coordinated even as the system evolves. Their ability to speak both technical and non-technical language allows them to bridge disciplines, resolve misunderstandings, and maintain momentum through uncertainty at an accelerated speed.

Portfolio evidence for this role is best demonstrated through clear, structured artifacts. For example, a public product brief for an AI feature including key metrics, evaluation plans, and risk considerations shows the ability to translate capability into strategy. A pilot design template that outlines sampling strategy and success thresholds demonstrates rigor in experimentation. A decision log documenting tradeoffs among quality, latency, cost, and safety illustrates the judgment required to guide complex systems toward responsible deployment. These examples demonstrate how an AI Product Manager thinks, how they make decisions, and how they connect user needs to system behavior.

AI UX/Conversation Designer

The AI UX or Conversation Designer shapes the way people interact with AI systems, ensuring that users can understand, trust, and control what the system is doing. This role focuses on the human layer of GenAI: how intent is captured, how ambiguity is resolved, and how the system communicates its reasoning, limitations, and actions. As AI becomes more agentic and more deeply embedded in workflows, the user experience becomes a primary mechanism for expressing fairness, safety, transparency, and accountability. The designer's work determines what the system shows, when it asks for clarification, how it requests consent, and how it signals uncertainty or risk.

In practice, the role centers on crafting interaction patterns that guide users through complex, nondeterministic behaviors in ways that feel intuitive and trustworthy. Designers create conversation flows that reduce ambiguity and elicit the context the system needs to behave safely. They define clear and understandable error states, such as refusals, escalations, and clarifications that prevent misinterpretation and help users recover gracefully. They design transparency mechanisms such as citations, provenance indicators, and user-visible logs of actions so people can see why the system responded the way it did. Collaboration with engineering, product, and research teams is essential, especially when shaping evaluation metrics for helpfulness, trust, and satisfaction. Accessibility and inclusivity remain core expectations, ensuring that AI-assisted experiences work for diverse users and contexts.

The skill stack for this role blends interaction design, linguistic intuition, and an understanding of how LLMs behave under uncertainty. Strong designers can translate model behavior into human-centered patterns, anticipate where confusion or risk may arise, and craft experiences that keep users in control even when the system is unpredictable. They must be comfortable speaking both technical and non-technical language, bridging the gap between model constraints and user expectations.

Portfolio evidence typically includes well-documented conversation flows, prototypes that demonstrate safe and transparent interactions, and short analyses explaining how design decisions address ambiguity, trust, or accessibility. These artifacts show how the designer thinks about user intent, system behavior, and the human factors that make AI experiences reliable and empowering.

Data Scientist (AI focus)

The Data Scientist with an AI focus uses GenAI and agentic workflows to accelerate analytical work while maintaining verification, rigor, and interpretability. This role extends traditional analytics by pairing statistical reasoning with model-assisted summarization, exploration, and pattern detection. As AI literacy grows across organizations, analytics teams increasingly rely on GenAI to speed up data preparation, insight generation, and communication, while the **Data Scientist** remains responsible for ensuring that every AI-assisted output is checked, validated, and grounded in evidence.

In practice, this role blends classical data science with a new layer of AI-augmented workflows. Data Scientists design analysis pipelines where GenAI assists with summarization, hypothesis generation, or code scaffolding, but they maintain control through verification checklists, gold-answer datasets (small, trusted sets of human-verified "correct" outputs used to measure whether the model is behaving as intended), and structured evaluation rubrics. They monitor error rates, track user corrections, and refine prompts or retrieval strategies to improve reliability over time. Their work requires an understanding of when AI can accelerate insight and when human judgment must override or correct model behavior. Because these workflows increasingly involve agents that automate parts of the analytical process, the Data Scientist must also consider transparency, reproducibility, and the auditability of AI-generated steps.

The skill stack for this role spans statistical modeling, data manipulation, and experiment design, combined with a working understanding of LLM behavior, prompt patterns, and retrieval-augmented summarization. Strong practitioners know how to integrate GenAI into notebooks or dashboards without compromising the integrity of the analysis. They can explain model-assisted insights to both technical and non-technical audiences, ensuring that stakeholders understand what is AI-generated, what is verified, and where uncertainty remains.

Portfolio evidence is best demonstrated through transparent, reproducible workflows. A public analysis that uses GenAI for summarization paired with a verification checklist shows the ability to balance speed with rigor. A small dataset of gold answers with an accompanying evaluation rubric demonstrates discipline in measurement. Monitoring signals that track error rates or user corrections over time illustrate maturity in maintaining reliability as AI-assisted workflows evolve.

Prompt Engineer/AI Developer

The prompt engineer or AI Developer designs the instructions, structures, and interaction patterns that make LLM systems controllable, predictable, and aligned with user intent. The role has expanded from crafting clever prompts to shaping full instruction architectures, such as defining templates, tool schemas, retrieval strategies, and multi-step flows that behave like a lightweight programming layer. Because prompts now govern how models reason, call tools, and interact with data, this work increasingly resembles system design. Domain knowledge plays a central role: either the Prompt Engineer brings it directly or collaborates closely with domain experts to ensure that instructions reflect real-world constraints, terminology, and edge cases.

In practice, the role involves creating structured prompt templates that encode roles, constraints, and reasoning steps; defining tool-calling schemas that allow models to perform safe, auditable actions; and designing multi-stage flows that break complex tasks into controlled, verifiable steps. These instructions must be versioned, tested, and evaluated like code, since small changes can produce large behavioral shifts. Collaboration with engineering, product, and domain specialists is essential, where engineers ensure technical feasibility, product teams define boundaries and success criteria, and domain experts provide the contextual knowledge that makes prompts accurate and trustworthy. Because prompts influence safety and compliance, the role also intersects with governance, requiring documentation, rollback plans, and auditability.

The skill stack blends linguistic intuition, system thinking, and an understanding of how LLMs interpret structure, context, and constraints. Strong practitioners can translate ambiguous requirements into precise instructions, anticipate failure modes, and design patterns that remain stable across model versions. They know when domain expertise is required and how to extract it from subject-matter experts, turning tacit knowledge into explicit instructions the model can follow. Their work depends on disciplined iteration including testing variants, measuring regressions, and refining prompts until behavior is reliable.

Portfolio evidence for this role is best shown through reproducible artifacts. A set of prompt templates with clear version history and test coverage demonstrates engineering rigor. Evaluation results comparing prompt variants show the ability to measure and control regressions. A governance checklist for prompt changes covering approvals, rollback plans, and audit trails signals maturity in managing risk. Together, these artifacts reveal how the Prompt Engineer designs, tests, and governs the instruction layer that makes AI systems usable and trustworthy.

Ethical AI Advocate/Responsible AI Specialist

The **Ethical AI Advocate** or **Responsible AI Specialist** ensures that responsible AI principles translate into practical safeguards throughout development and deployment. The role focuses on making AI systems safe, accountable, and aligned with organizational values by turning high-level principles into concrete processes that teams can consistently follow. As AI becomes more embedded in products and workflows, this work becomes operational rather than theoretical, requiring the ability to collaborate across engineering, product, legal, and governance teams.

In practice, the specialist identifies where risks such as bias, confabulation, privacy leakage, or misuse may emerge and works with teams to design controls that prevent or detect them. They help define acceptable system boundaries, document decisions, and ensure that safeguards are built into both the model's behavior and the surrounding product experience. Because AI systems evolve after deployment, they also establish monitoring signals, escalation paths, and incident-response processes that maintain accountability over time. Clear communication across technical and non-technical audiences is essential, since the role often involves explaining risks and tradeoffs in ways that support informed decision-making.

The skill stack combines an understanding of model behavior, governance frameworks, and organizational dynamics. Strong practitioners can translate responsible AI principles into actionable requirements, anticipate where risks may emerge, and design governance workflows that scale across teams. They maintain documentation, approvals, and audit trails that allow organizations to demonstrate compliance and trace decisions throughout the system's lifecycle. Their effectiveness depends on the ability to bridge disciplines such as engineering, product, legal, security, and keep them aligned even when the system or its risk posture changes.

Portfolio evidence typically includes a risk-assessment template that maps system behaviors to risk categories and mitigations, a control framework for GenAI systems that reflects known areas of concern such as safety and robustness, and a monitoring and incident-response plan that describes how quality, safety, and misuse signals are detected and resolved. These artifacts demonstrate the ability to operationalize responsible AI principles in real-world systems.

AI Governance/Risk Manager

The **AI Governance** or **Risk Manager** creates organizational structures that keep AI development accountable, consistent, and auditable. The role turns broad governance principles into policies, controls, and review processes that guide how teams build, document, and deploy AI systems. As AI becomes more pervasive across products and operations, governance shifts from advisory work to an operational discipline focused on clarity, traceability, and organizational readiness.

In practice, the role maintains an inventory of AI systems and classifies them by risk and impact so that oversight scales with potential harm. They define documentation requirements, review gates, and accountability structures to ensure that every system has clear owners and decision records. They coordinate assessments across privacy, security, fairness, and safety, ensuring that evidence is retained and accessible. They also set expectations for monitoring and incident response across deployed systems, establishing how issues are detected, escalated, and resolved in a defensible way.

The skill stack blends governance expertise, risk-management discipline, and enough technical literacy to understand how AI systems behave and where risks may emerge. Strong practitioners can translate principles into actionable controls, design workflows that scale across teams, and communicate clearly with both technical and non-technical audiences to align decisions, documentation, and risk posture.

Portfolio evidence often includes a system inventory with risk classifications, a governance playbook outlining documentation and review requirements, and an assurance plan describing monitoring expectations and incident-response procedures. These artifacts demonstrate the ability to operationalize governance in real systems.

AI Consultant/AI Strategist

The **AI Consultant** or **AI Strategist** helps organizations translate business goals into practical AI adoption plans and guides teams through implementation. The role focuses on identifying where AI can create measurable value by shaping realistic roadmaps and ensuring that technical choices align with business constraints, operational realities, and organizational readiness. As demand for AI transformation grows, this work centers on translation by turning ambition into scoped use cases, clear success criteria, and credible execution paths.

In practice, the strategist works with leaders to identify high-value opportunities, define measurable outcomes, and select system approaches that fit constraints such as data availability, latency requirements, compliance obligations, and integration complexity. They design pilots that generate evidence rather than assumptions, iterate with stakeholders to refine scope, and prepare scale-out plans that account for change management, workflow impact, and long-term sustainability. Because adoption depends on people as much as technology, they also create playbooks and training plans that build AI literacy across teams and help organizations adapt to new ways of working.

The skill stack blends business strategy, technical fluency, and the ability to communicate clearly across executives, engineers, and domain experts. Strong practitioners can frame opportunities in terms of ROI and risk, translate requirements into system choices, and guide organizations through uncertainty with structured experimentation and evidence-based decision-making. Their effectiveness depends on understanding both the capabilities of modern AI systems and the organizational dynamics that determine whether those systems succeed in practice.

Portfolio evidence often includes a set of scoped use cases with success metrics, a pilot plan that demonstrates how evidence was gathered and decisions were made, and an adoption or training playbook that shows how teams were prepared for scale. These artifacts demonstrate the ability to turn strategy into implementation and help organizations adopt AI responsibly and effectively.

Data Annotator/Human-in-the-loop (HITL) Specialist

The data annotator or human-in-the-loop specialist strengthens AI systems by providing the human judgment that models cannot supply on their own. The role focuses on creating high-quality labeled data, reviewing model outputs, and shaping the human feedback loops that improve prompts, retrieval, and model behavior. As organizations adopt more GenAI and agentic workflows, the need for reliable human evaluation grows, making this work central to system quality and trustworthiness.

In practice, the specialist develops clear annotation guidelines, labels, and reviews datasets for training or evaluation, and calibrates human judgment across teams to ensure consistency. They measure inter-annotator agreement, refine instructions when ambiguity appears, and identify edge cases that models struggle with. Their feedback informs prompt design, retrieval strategies, and model tuning, creating a continuous loop between human insight and system improvement. Because their work often defines the *ground truth*, precision, consistency, and domain awareness are essential.

The skill stack combines deep domain knowledge, attention to detail, linguistic and conceptual clarity, and an understanding of how model outputs are used in downstream systems. Strong practitioners can translate vague requirements into precise labeling rules, detect patterns in model errors, and communicate effectively with both technical and non-technical teams. They help ensure that human judgment is applied consistently and that evaluation processes remain reliable as systems evolve.

Portfolio evidence typically includes a set of annotation guidelines with examples and edge-case handling, a labeled dataset or evaluation sample with demonstrated quality controls, and a summary of feedback loops that improved prompts or model behavior. These artifacts show the ability to produce high-quality human signals that meaningfully shape generic or domain-specific AI performance.

Before we end this section, let's summarize and map each of the preceding roles to their skill stack and responsibilities:

Role	Skill stack	Responsibilities
GenAI Engineer / AI Engineer	Programming (mostly Python), software engineering principles, and data handling	System building, designing retrieval pipelines, enterprise integration
ML Scientist / Applied Scientist	Statistical reasoning, experimental design, and modern modeling techniques	Rigorous experimentation, algorithmic innovation, handoff from research to engineering to production
AI/ML Researcher	Mathematical foundations, statistical reasoning, and modern machine learning methods	Identifying limitations in current approaches, formulating hypotheses, and producing insights
AI Product Manager	Product strategy, user research, and technical literacy	Defining the user problem, setting measurable success metrics, specifying evaluation requirements, coordinating with teams, assessing ROI
AI UX/Conversation Designer	Interaction design, linguistic intuition, LLM workflow, design principles	Creating design patterns for systems, defining error states, checking accessibility
Data Scientist	Statistical modeling, data manipulation, experiment design, LLM behavior, prompt patterns, and retrieval-augmented summarization	Design analysis pipelines, code scaffolding, monitor error rates, track user corrections, and refine prompts or retrieval strategies

Prompt Engineer / AI Developer	Linguistic intuition, systems thinking, understanding LLM interpretations	Creating structured prompt templates, defining tool calling, designing multi-stage flows
Ethical AI Advocate / Responsible AI Specialist	Understanding of model behavior, governance frameworks, and organizational dynamics	Defining acceptable system boundaries, document decisions, building guardrails for models and behavior, establishing monitoring signals, escalation paths, and incident response processes
AI Governance/Risk Manager	Governance expertise, risk management discipline, and technical literacy of AI systems' behavior	Maintaining inventory of AI systems, defining documentation requirements, reviewing gates, and accountability structures
AI Consultant/AI Strategist	Business strategy, technical fluency, and strong communication	Identifying high-value opportunities, defining measurable outcomes, selecting system approaches, designing pilots, and creating playbooks and training plans
Data Annotator/Human-in-the-Loop (HITL) Specialist	Deep domain knowledge, attention to detail, linguistic and conceptual clarity, and an understanding of how model outputs are used in downstream systems	Developing clear annotation guidelines, labeling and reviewing datasets, calibrating human judgment, measuring inter-annotator agreement, refining instructions, and identifying edge cases

Table 3.1: Summary of roles, the required skill sets, and their responsibilities

Roles accelerated by agentic systems and production deployment

The roles in the previous section represent the foundational career paths that have emerged as GenAI matured into a broad professional ecosystem. As organizations began deploying AI into real, customer-facing products and workflows at scale, a second set of roles has emerged, driven by the demands of production: reliability, observability, security, and scalable integration. These roles build on core skill sets but operate closer to the critical path of deployment, where systems must behave predictably, withstand adversarial pressure, and integrate cleanly with existing infrastructure. Together, they represent the shift from building AI capabilities to operating AI as durable, accountable infrastructure. These roles include:

- **Agentic AI Engineer:** The Agentic AI Engineer builds tool-using agents that can act with controlled autonomy, making decisions about which tools to invoke, in what order, and under what constraints. The work centers on designing safe orchestration patterns, permission models, and explicit approval checkpoints so that agents remain traceable and predictable. In practice, this means implementing structured tool interfaces, enforcing least-privilege access, hardening systems against prompt injections, and producing auditable traces of every action the agent takes. The role blends engineering, security, and product awareness to ensure that autonomous behavior remains safe, bounded, and reviewable.
- **LLMOps/GenAIOps Engineer:** LLMOps engineers operate AI systems across the full lifecycle from data and experimentation to deployment, monitoring, and feedback. Their work ensures that systems remain healthy after the prototype phase, with continuous evaluation pipelines, regression detection, and rollback mechanisms that keep quality stable as prompts, models, or data change. In practice, they maintain dashboards for quality, latency, cost, and safety signals; coordinate incident response for accuracy or safety issues; and manage the operational rhythms that allow AI systems to evolve without breaking. The role is defined by discipline in measurement, observability, and controlled iteration.
- **AI Evaluation Engineer/LLM Quality Engineer:** The AI Evaluation Engineer designs structured tests and measurement systems that quantify model and system performance. Because generative outputs may vary, evaluation requires defining clear dimensions such as correctness, faithfulness, safety, helpfulness, and building gold sets, rubrics, and automated scoring pipelines that reflect real user needs. In practice, they run regression tests across prompt and model changes, calibrate human evaluators, and work with product and engineering teams to turn metrics into release gates. Their work provides the empirical backbone that makes AI development reliable and repeatable.

- **RAG/Retrieval Engineer:** The Retrieval Engineer grounds generation in authoritative sources by designing and tuning retrieval pipelines. Their work spans ingestion, chunking, embedding selection, retrieval strategy, reranking, and context engineering and assembly, with a strong emphasis on observability because failures often originate in retrieval rather than generation. In practice, they evaluate retrieval quality, diagnose failure modes, optimize chunking and latency trade-offs, and ensure that generated outputs remain tied to verifiable sources. This role requires both system-level thinking and a deep understanding of how retrieval components interact.
- **AI Security Engineer:** The AI Security Engineer protects LLM applications from risks unique to generative systems, including prompt injection, sensitive information leakage, excessive agency, and unsafe output handling. Their work involves threat modeling, red-team testing, permission scoping, and designing mitigations that harden prompts, tools, and data flows. In practice, they analyze how attackers might manipulate model behavior, build safeguards into orchestration layers, and ensure that systems degrade safely under adversarial pressure. The role sits at the intersection of security engineering, AI behavior, and risk management.
- **Forward Deployed Engineer (FDE):** The Forward Deployed Engineer, a new emerging hybrid role delivers working AI systems in real environments by integrating models with actual workflows, data realities, and stakeholder constraints. Their work begins where prototypes end: adapting architectures to messy operational contexts, resolving integration blockers, and ensuring that systems deliver measurable value. In practice, they run pilots, gather evidence, refine designs with stakeholders, and build adoption and training plans that support scale-out. The role requires technical breadth, product intuition, and the ability to navigate organizational dynamics to turn AI concepts into deployed, functioning systems.

Together, these roles reflect the increasing importance of operating, securing, and scaling AI systems in real-world environments, complementing the foundational roles introduced earlier.

Choosing a career field in GenAI

A decision framework for choosing a GenAI career path works best when it is simple, durable, and grounded in your strengths rather than short-term trends.

A practical way to approach this is through a few clear steps:

1. **Take stock of your strengths:** Start by identifying the capabilities you already bring. These may include engineering strengths related to reliability and integration, analytical strengths tied to measurement and experimentation, product strengths for problem

framing and adoption, domain strengths tied to context and operational nuance, or governance strengths related to risk management and compliance.

2. **Choose one primary role family:** Select one role family (as discussed in *A practical map – five families of GenAI careers*) to anchor your development for the next year. Use adjacent families primarily to build collaboration awareness, rather than trying to develop deeply across multiple areas at once. This helps maintain focus and avoids spreading your effort too thin.
3. **Define the evidence you will create:** Focus on producing clear, demonstrable outputs that show your capabilities. This goes beyond building a working demo to include evaluation, monitoring, and evidence that a system behaves as intended over time. A public portfolio built on well-scoped, reproducible projects using open data can make this work visible and credible.
4. **Revisit and refine your direction:** Because the field evolves quickly, revisiting your direction every quarter provides enough stability to build depth while still allowing you to adjust course as your interests or the market shift.

Now that we have explored the core roles in GenAI, the next step is understanding how to grow within them. The next section outlines how professionals typically progress across different role families over time.

Roadmaps and leveling matrices

A leveling matrix clarifies what progress means in GenAI careers. Progress is not only about deeper technical skill but also about broader accountability for outcomes, stronger measurement practices, and clearer governance. Career maturity mirrors AI system maturity: as scope increases, individuals take on more responsibility for defining context, measuring performance and risks, and managing those risks through thoughtful mitigations. The following roadmaps outline how each role family typically develops over the first year, with a focus on practical experience, evidence of competence, and the ability to operate within real constraints:

- **Builders:** The builder track suits software engineers, ML engineers, and applied scientists who want to ship working systems. Early progress comes from building a small end-to-end system, for example, a simple RAG pipeline with clear documentation of failures and weekly iteration. As skills deepen, builders expand into safe tool use, observability, and automated regression testing so that systems behave predictably as they evolve. Over a year, most builders begin to specialize in one layer of the stack, for example, retrieval, evaluation, operations, or security, and produce a public technical report or reproducible project that demonstrates both engineering judgment and measurement discipline.

- **Shapers:** The shaper track fits product managers, designers, and strategy leaders who translate user needs into AI-enabled solutions. Early development focuses on building AI literacy and drafting product briefs that include evaluation criteria and risk boundaries. As experience grows, shapers run pilots with measurable outcomes, refine them through stakeholder feedback, and publish case studies that show how decisions were made. Over a year, they typically develop a repeatable adoption framework that incorporates governance, monitoring expectations, and the organizational patterns needed to scale AI responsibly.
- **Guardians:** The guardian track is ideal for professionals in security, compliance, policy, and responsible AI. Early work involves learning the core risk categories and mapping a sample use case to potential harms and mitigations. As they progress, guardians create governance templates, incident-response playbooks, and review processes that can be applied across teams. Over a year, they demonstrate end-to-end governance by auditing public projects, producing clear documentation, and assembling a toolkit that shows how risks are identified, measured, and managed throughout a system's lifecycle.
- **Enablers:** The enabler track suits consultants, forward-deployed engineers, and human-in-the-loop specialists who focus on real-world integration. Early progress comes from building a use-case inventory and designing a pilot plan with measurable evaluation metrics. As they gain experience, enablers deliver workflow-integration demos, adoption playbooks, and training materials that help teams understand how AI fits into their daily work. Over a year, they standardize implementation patterns across multiple pilots, creating monitoring and governance checklists that make AI deployment repeatable and scalable.
- **Adopters:** The adopter track is designed for domain experts such as marketers, analysts, operators, researchers, educators, and so on, who use AI to amplify their existing expertise rather than build AI systems themselves. Early development focuses on mastering the tools relevant to their domain and understanding how to evaluate outputs for accuracy, safety, and usefulness. As they progress, adopters design repeatable workflows that combine human judgment with AI assistance, document how these workflows improve quality or efficiency, and share examples that demonstrate measurable impact. Over a year, they often become internal champions who help colleagues adopt AI responsibly, contributing to organizational literacy and shaping practical norms for everyday use.

Now that we've explored the different roles and career paths in GenAI, the next step is understanding how individuals can transition into these roles based on where they are starting.

Career pivot playbooks (by reader profile)

The following playbooks are designed for readers starting from different points but share the same underlying principles: build something real, evaluate it rigorously, monitor how it behaves over time, and understand the governance expectations that shape responsible deployment. Each path emphasizes producing credible evidence of competence rather than accumulating disconnected tutorials or theoretical knowledge.

- **Students and new graduates:** Students benefit most from producing a complete, working system that demonstrates both technical capability and disciplined evaluation. For example, early progress can come from building a small RAG assistant with citations and a realistic evaluation set that shows how the system performs under real questions. As skills develop, students add safe tool use, user-approval flows, and basic observability so they can debug failures and understand system behavior. Over a year, the most persuasive outcome is a short technical report that explains the system's performance, highlights failure modes, and documents the mitigations attempted, showing not just what was built, but how it was measured and improved.
- **Early-career professionals:** Early-career professionals should choose a specialization that compounds over time and produces measurable outputs. The first phase often involves prototyping an AI-assisted workflow they understand well and defining a clear rubric for what success looks like. As they gain confidence, they operationalize the workflow with monitoring, cost controls, and automated regression tests so that changes can be made safely. Over a year, the goal is to lead a small cross-functional initiative, documenting standards, patterns, and best practices that others can adopt, demonstrating both technical depth and the ability to drive organizational impact.
- **Mid-career switchers:** Mid-career switchers succeed by combining their domain expertise with enough system literacy to translate real-world problems into AI-enabled solutions. Early progress may come from building a domain-grounded demonstrator using public sources and clearly defined boundaries, showing how AI can augment existing workflows. As they advance, they align their demonstrator with governance expectations, documenting risks, mitigations, and decision rationales in a way that reflects professional practice. Over a year, they often position themselves into boundary roles, such as AI product management, governance, evaluation, or forward-deployed engineering, where their domain knowledge becomes a differentiator and accelerates their career trajectory.

- **Leaders and managers:** Leaders shape organizational adoption by establishing clarity, accountability, and measurement. Early progress involves creating an inventory of AI initiatives, classifying their risks, and defining baseline evaluation requirements so teams know what *good* looks like. As they mature in the role, leaders establish governance structures, security review expectations, and cross-functional processes that ensure AI systems are deployed responsibly. Over a year, they focus on standardizing evaluation pipelines, strengthening monitoring practices, and investing in organization-wide AI literacy so that teams can innovate safely and sustainably with accelerated speed.

Summary

A GenAI career is built the same way robust AI systems are built, for example, through clear objectives, disciplined iteration, and evidence that the system (or the professional) behaves reliably under real conditions. The key theme of this chapter is to denote that modern AI work is defined less by specific tools and more by the ability to design, evaluate, monitor, and govern systems that operate in dynamic environments. Labor-market signals consistently show that roles requiring system thinking, such as retrieval grounding, orchestration, evaluation, operations, security, and governance are expanding because organizations now depend on AI as infrastructure rather than novelty. Broader workforce reporting reinforces that AI is reshaping roles across industries and that upskilling is now central to staying relevant as AI becomes embedded in everyday work. Technical guidance across the field emphasizes that nondeterminism demands evaluation discipline, lifecycle awareness, and a mindset oriented toward continuous measurement rather than one-off demos. Therefore, the most durable career strategy is not to chase emerging titles but to build a trajectory anchored in systems and evidence as we discussed so far: choose a role family, build a minimal system, evaluate it rigorously, monitor how it behaves over time, and align it with responsible governance. This discipline remains stable even as models, frameworks, and organizational structures evolve.

Foundational skills compound across model generations and remain valuable regardless of how quickly tools change. Mathematics provides intuition for optimization, generalization, and uncertainty, where these concepts underpin how models behave and why they fail. Software engineering remains essential, not because professionals need to implement new optimizers from scratch, but because modern AI systems still depend on human judgment to integrate models into reliable architectures. Even as code-generation models become more capable, engineers must review, and refine the code they produce, decide when, and how to grant agency, design safe tool-calling patterns, and ensure that systems handle failures predictably. The work is less about writing every line by hand and more about shaping the scaffolding around the model, such as through retrieval pipelines, orchestration layers, permission boundaries, and monitoring hooks that keep the system trustworthy in production. Evaluation has become equally foundational because generative systems produce variable outputs; knowing how to design metrics, build datasets, and measure regressions is now as fundamental as writing clean, reviewable code. Governance literacy compounds as adoption scales, enabling professionals to reason about risk, accountability, and organizational readiness. These foundations endure because they reflect the stable principles beneath rapidly changing interfaces.

A strong GenAI portfolio demonstrates end-to-end system thinking rather than isolated experiments. For example, credible portfolios may show retrieval grounding, evaluation discipline, monitoring signals, and clear safety boundaries toward downstream impact to benefit the end-users. A simple progression might begin with a grounded assistant over a public corpus, evolve into a tool-using workflow with explicit user confirmation, and culminate in an evaluation harness and monitoring dashboard that track regressions across iterations. Each artifact benefits from a short engineering memo describing the goal, constraints, evaluation plan, results, and observed failure modes, mirroring the documentation expected in real deployments. Non-engineering roles can produce equally rigorous evidence: product managers can publish evaluation plans and success metrics; governance professionals can publish risk assessments and control checklists; human-in-the-loop specialists can publish annotation guidelines and rubric designs. These artifacts are persuasive because they address the real bottlenecks of AI deployment—measurement, reliability, and accountability.

Interview processes increasingly reflect the complexity of deployed AI systems. Engineering and applied science roles often test whether candidates can explain underlying foundational concepts and end-to-end architectures, for example, retrieval grounding, tool orchestration, and failure handling. Evaluation and operations roles emphasize metric design, dataset construction, regression testing, and incident response, reflecting skills that ensure systems behave predictably over time. Security roles probe understanding of risks such as prompt injection, data leakage, and excessive agency, along with mitigations grounded in least privilege, isolation, and auditability. Product and design roles assess whether candidates can define success metrics, plan safe rollouts, and design human oversight points that are meaningful rather than ceremonial. Across all roles, the unifying theme is the ability to reason about reliability, measurement, and safety in systems that do not behave deterministically, and to use that discipline not only to advance individual careers but to ensure that the AI systems we build ultimately strengthen institutions, empower people, and contribute to outcomes that benefit society as a whole.

In the next chapter we will explore the building blocks of modern GenAI systems and different model architectures.

Part 2

The Gen AI Tech Stack: Architectures, Tools, and Advanced Concepts

Part 2 explores the technologies, architectures, and engineering concepts that power modern generative AI applications. You'll develop a practical understanding of the core building blocks behind LLM-based systems, including prompt engineering, **retrieval-augmented generation** (**RAG**), vector databases, function calling, AI agents, and LLMOps. The part also introduces the essential tools, frameworks, and platforms used across the Gen AI ecosystem, helping you understand when and how to apply them to build, deploy, and manage production-ready AI solutions.

This part contains the following chapters:

- *Chapter 4, Generative AI Architectures and Advanced Concepts*
- *Chapter 5, Essential Tools and Platforms*

4

Generative AI Architectures and Advanced Concepts

Model-specific optimization has become essential as different AI models demonstrate distinct response patterns and capabilities... Always favor the model provider's documentation to learn how to interact with a specific model.

– Maxime Labonne

In this chapter, we explore the core building blocks behind modern **generative AI (GenAI)** systems. We start with architectures to see how models have evolved beyond the original Transformer to improve efficiency and reduce costs. We then cover how to effectively communicate with these models through prompt engineering, before diving into **retrieval-augmented generation (RAG)** systems that ground AI responses in your data. Finally, we see how to combine these components into AI agents that can plan and execute multi-step tasks.

By the end of this chapter, you'll be able to compare Transformer variants, such as **multi-head attention (MHA)**, **multi-query attention (MQA)**, and **grouped-query attention (GQA)** and know when to use each. You'll understand **Mixture of Experts (MoE)** trade-offs between capacity and compute, hybrid architectures that mix attention with other operators, and how diffusion models generate media. You'll also know how to craft structured, testable prompts with proper evaluation frameworks, build robust RAG pipelines from ingestion to generation, select appropriate vector stores, and architect reliable AI agents with clear tool schemas, memory strategies, and guardrails.

In this chapter, we're going to cover the following main topics:

- Generative architectures
- Prompt engineering
- RAG system design
- AI agents

Generative architectures

Architectures represent the blueprint of how models process inputs to generate outputs. Since the introduction of the Transformer, researchers have experimented with new ways of structuring neural networks to improve efficiency, extend context length, and reduce compute and memory costs.

In this section, we discuss four major architectural families that define modern generative AI. It begins with Transformers, tracing their refinements, then moves to MoEs for efficient scaling, followed by hybrid models that combine attention with other operators. Finally, it introduces diffusion models, which power image and video generation by denoising noise into coherent outputs.

Transformer architectures

Introduced in 2017, the Transformer architecture was the first one to entirely rely on the attention mechanism. Attention lets the model dynamically weigh how much each token should influence every other token when processing a sequence, so meaning is built from context rather than from fixed position or proximity. This is what makes it possible to capture long-range dependencies, since any token can directly attend to any other regardless of distance. This architecture was successfully applied to different modalities like language, vision, audio, and beyond. But attention also introduced heavy memory and compute costs, prompting a series of refinements over the years.

The original design, **Multi-Head Attention (MHA)**, used many parallel attention heads. Each head captured different relational patterns between tokens, making the model expressive and powerful. Yet this richness came at a cost: memory usage and processing time grow sharply with the length of the input (roughly four times more cost when you double the input length). In practice, the VRAM (the GPU's dedicated memory) usage explodes with long inputs, limiting its actual usability.

To address this, researchers introduced **Multi-Query Attention (MQA)**. Instead of maintaining separate keys and values for every head, MQA shared them across queries. This simple change cut memory usage and accelerated inference, though it sacrificed some of the nuanced modeling of MHA.

A compromise soon followed: **Grouped-Query Attention (GQA)**. Here, queries are divided into groups, each with its own set of shared keys and values. This struck a balance between MHA's expressiveness and MQA's efficiency. GQA has since become the workhorse of modern production models such as Llama, Mistral, and Qwen.

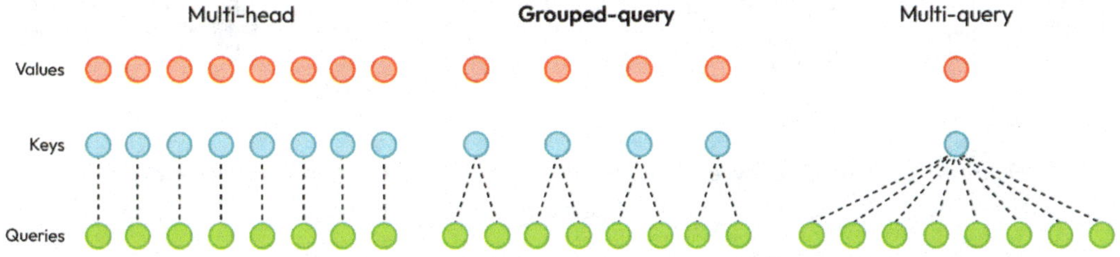

Figure 4.1: Comparison between MHA, MQA, and GQA

Note that MHA, MQA, and GQA are rarely used with their original, unoptimized implementations. Modern frameworks and kernels (low-level software routines optimized for efficient GPU execution, such as `PagedAttention` and `FlashAttention`) provide memory-efficient implementations of all three attention variants. These optimized kernels allow today's large-scale transformers to deploy MQA and GQA in practice, combining the theoretical efficiency of these designs with real-world speedups.

In addition to these innovations, another architectural pattern emerged over the years: the mixture of experts.

Mixtures of Experts

Mixture of Experts (**MoE**) is a way to scale model capacity without paying the full compute cost on every token. For each token, a router picks a small subset of "experts" (**Feed-Forward Networks** or **FFNs**) to run, so only a fraction of the parameters is active at a time. Although the idea traces back to the 1990s, modern, sparsely activated MoEs have gained a lot of traction lately. This is especially true since the release of DeepSeek-R1, which demonstrated that MoE architectures could achieve competitive performance with frontier models (like GPT-5 and Claude Opus) while being significantly more cost-efficient to train and run.

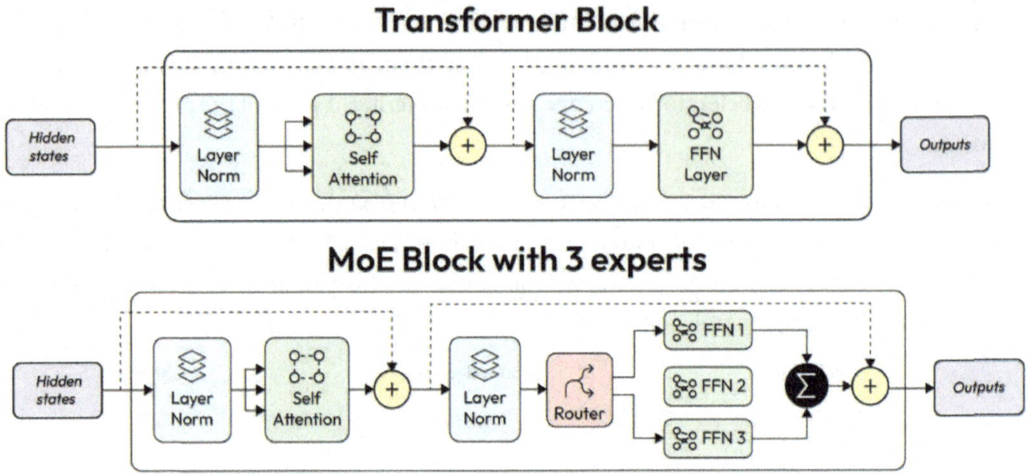

Figure 4.2: Comparison between a traditional Transformer block and a MoE block with three experts

The modern MoE took shape in 2021 with Google's Switch Transformer and GLaM, which together established the core trade-off space that still guides today's systems: how many experts to activate per token and how to keep the workload balanced across them.

While the architecture of closed-source models like GPT, Claude, and Gemini is not publicly disclosed, they're very likely to be MoEs. Open-weight MoEs reached mainstream developers in late 2023 with Mixtral 8×7B. Mixtral routes each token to two out of eight experts inside the feed-forward block, so it carries 46.7B total parameters but 12.9B active per token. This was an early, widely adopted proof that sparse activation could be product-ready.

By 2024-2025, frontier models pushed sparsity even further. DeepSeek-V3 and R1 scale to 671B total parameters with about 37B active per token, pairing massive capacity with tight routing and training optimizations to keep compute and bandwidth in check. It demonstrated that very large MoE models can be trained and served economically.

OpenAI's GPT-OSS-120B brought another open-weight entrant to this class: an MoE transformer with 120B total parameters but only 5.1B active per token, designed to run on a single 80 GB GPU thanks to aggressive quantization of the expert weights. Despite the modest active compute, it reports near-parity with o4-mini on core reasoning benchmarks.

Alibaba's Qwen line standardized MoE across sizes, from the flagship Qwen3-235B-A22B (235B total, 22B active per token) to the very-sparse Qwen3-Next-80B-A3B (80B total, 3B active). The Qwen 3.6 release extends the same approach, with Qwen3.6-35B-A3B activating only 3B of its 35B parameters per token while reaching frontier-level coding quality at a fraction of the cost.

This leads us to one other major innovation: what if instead of improving attention mechanisms, we just replaced these layers entirely?

Hybrid architectures

Pure attention models, such as in the original Transformer, are no longer the only option available to design **large language models (LLMs)**. Hybrid architectures mix attention with cheaper alternatives that summarize past information rather than attending to every token in detail. Attention is precise but expensive: it lets the model pull exact information from any earlier point in the input. Lighter building blocks, such as state space models (SSMs), gated convolutions, and small recurrent layers, give up some of that precision in exchange for far lower compute and memory cost. Recent systems combine the two, interleaving or fusing layers so the model keeps most of attention's recall ability at a fraction of the price.

The most common example is interleaving Transformer with Mamba (an SSM) layers. It can also be used in dense models (like NVIDIA's Nemotron-Nano-9B-v2) or in an MoE architecture (like AI21's Jamba). The result is a hybrid that improves throughput and memory footprint while remaining competitive on standard language tasks and long contexts.

It's also possible to interleave attention layers with a lighter version of it, like **Sliding Window Attention (SWA)**. By restricting attention to a fixed window around each token, SWA dramatically reduced memory scaling, especially for long sequences. Models like NVIDIA's Hymba and Gemma 3 have shown that this strategy can cut KV cache (the memory that stores past tokens during generation) requirements in half while keeping performance nearly intact.

Liquid AI's LFM2 series (and its successor LFM2.5) applies this approach to edge deployment. LFM2 combines GQA (6 layers) with short-range, multiplicatively gated convolution blocks (10 layers). This provides two times faster prefill/decode compared with similar-sized models on CPU without impacting performance.

To finish our overview of generative AI model architectures, we need to mention one additional family: diffusion models.

Diffusion models

Diffusion models generate images by learning to reverse a simple process: start from pure noise and repeatedly clean it up until a coherent picture appears (see *Figure 4.3*). During training, the model sees real images with varying amounts of noise sprinkled on top and learns the "cleaning move" for each noise level. At generation time, a text prompt is added to steer the denoising process toward a specific image, like a Ghibli character.

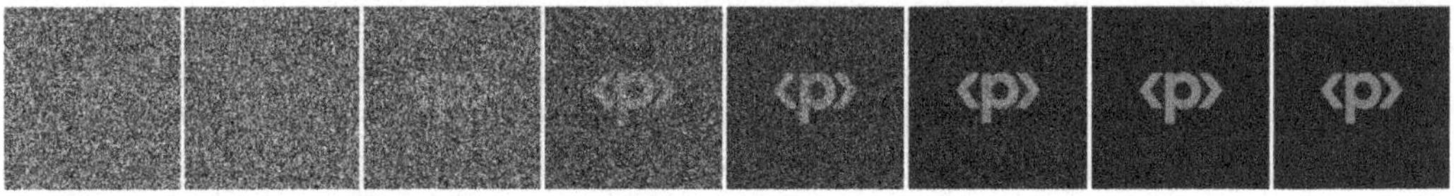

Figure 4.3: Step-by-step illustration of the denoising process used by diffusion models to generate an image from noise

Like with MoEs, the architectures used by closed-source model providers like OpenAI and Google are not publicly disclosed. Open-weight models, by contrast, are released with their parameters publicly downloadable so anyone can run, study, or fine-tune them locally. Stable Diffusion (Stability AI) and FLUX.1 (Black Forest Labs) are well-known examples, and both have moved toward more capable transformer-based architectures over time. They can be deployed on consumer-grade GPUs and fine-tuned to learn a specific style, topic, or other desired features.

Production use cases now extend well beyond standalone image generation, with diffusion models embedded inside creative tools (such as Adobe Firefly) and design workflows where they generate concept variations from text descriptions and rough sketches.

The same shift has happened for video generation. Modern video generators such as Google's Veo 3 and Runway's Gen-4 rely on large diffusion transformers. The shared idea is to denoise "spacetime patches" of latent video, so each step of the process refines both the spatial detail of each frame and the temporal continuity between frames. These models scale to longer durations and higher resolutions while keeping controls for editing, conditioning, and synchronized audio. OpenAI's Sora 2 (discontinued in April 2026) was an influential early example of this design.

Researchers have also applied the diffusion idea to text generation. The main advantage is speed: instead of producing tokens one after another like an attention-based model, a diffusion text model can refine many tokens in parallel. Google's Gemini Diffusion and Inception Labs' Mercury are early examples of this approach for large language models, and they hint at a path where text generation could become an order of magnitude faster without sacrificing quality.

Despite the role of architectural breakthroughs, the field of GenAI has not been shaped by architectures alone. In the next section, we will explore how to design robust applications with AI to leverage the full potential of these models.

Prompt engineering

A prompt is defined as a natural language text provided as input to a model to perform a specific task. Prompt engineering remains an experimental discipline at its core, but the difference between casual experimentation and production-grade systems lies in how that experimentation is organized.

Evaluating prompts

Instead of relying on intuition alone, adopting a reliable evaluation framework can provide actionable feedback and save a lot of engineering time. Typically, this involves generating variations of prompts, running them against standardized test sets, and comparing outputs against predefined quality metrics (such as accuracy, factuality, latency, or alignment with business requirements). This way of measuring prompt performance in a systematic manner is how successful teams operate.

> Prompts generated by language models tend to be verbose and ill-defined. While this can provide a helpful first draft, it is always recommended to read them carefully and add the kind of accurate and actionable instructions that are often lacking. Note that models tend to benefit from XML and Markdown formatting to structure prompts with headers, lists, and XML tags to isolate blocks, such as input documents.

A common pattern is to separate prompts into modular components, as shown in the example below. System prompts (also called "developer prompts" by OpenAI) establish behavioral context and guardrails. Instructions provide clear task definitions in unambiguous language. Contextual information injects relevant knowledge (often retrieved dynamically) so the model operates with awareness of the domain. By structuring prompts this way, engineers can adjust individual parts independently and test their effects in controlled experiments.

In practice, these evaluations can be implemented in a custom way or rely on frameworks like promptfoo, DeepEval, RAGAS, or cloud-specific APIs like OpenAI Evals:

```
System
You are a data extraction assistant. I will provide a JSON schema and an
input text. Your task is to fill out the JSON schema based on the input
```

```
text.

Instruction

Only output the following JSON with the correct values extracted from the
input text and nothing else:
{
  "project_name": "Name of the project",
  "client_name": "Name of the client",
  "cost": "Cost in dollars"
}

Context
Input text:{}
```

The preceding prompt can be further improved with structured outputs. Each cloud model has a specific API to guarantee correct JSON formatting. This is significantly more reliable than asking "output JSON" and trying to parse the answer afterward. We can rewrite the prompt with structured outputs as follows with the OpenAI API:

```
from openai import OpenAI
from pydantic import BaseModel

client = OpenAI()

class DataExtraction(BaseModel):
    project_name: str
    client_name: str
    cost: int

response = client.responses.parse(
    model="gpt-5-2025-08-07",
    input=[
        {
            "role": "developer",
            "content": (
```

```
            "You are a data extraction assistant. "
            "I will provide a JSON schema and an input text. "
            "Your task is to fill out the JSON schema based on the 
input text."
        ),
    },
    {
        "role": "user",
        "content": "...",
    },
  ],
  text_format=DataExtraction,
)

data_extracted = response.output_parsed
```

Here, if successfully processed, the variable in `data_extracted` is guaranteed to be an object with the fields defined in `DataExtraction`. This guarantee is extremely important in many applications where post-hoc parsing can lead to increased cost and latency.

Prompting techniques

The field of prompt engineering is often introduced via important prompting techniques. So far, we've only considered the scenario where we directly ask for the final answer. In this case, because no example is provided, it is often referred to as **zero-shot prompting**.

The following example shows zero-shot prompting used for a classification task, with three possible options. The assistant's answer is included to show the expected answer:

```
Instruction
Classify the sentiment of the following text as positive, negative, or 
neutral:

"I absolutely loved the new restaurant downtown. The food was incredible, 
and the service was outstanding!"

Assistant
Positive
```

On the other hand, providing examples helps you steer the model toward a specific task or format. This is called **few-shot prompting** (or few-shot learning). While recent advances in AI slightly decreased the popularity of few-shot prompting, it is still an efficient tool when a model struggles to follow a specific task or format. The challenge lies in curating these examples: they must cover both the common cases and the tricky edge cases discovered in production. Having a reliable evaluation framework can also help here to maintain a library of few-shot examples and test them in real-world scenarios. It is also advised to only use it when needed, as it severely increases the number of tokens processed, and hence the cost of each request.

We can revise our zero-shot prompting example to add additional data points to provide more context as follows:

```
Instruction
Classify the sentiment as positive, negative, or neutral:

Text: "The movie was boring and too long."
Sentiment: Negative

Text: "It was okay, nothing special."
Sentiment: Neutral

Text: "I absolutely loved the new restaurant downtown. The food was
incredible and the service was outstanding!"

Sentiment:

Assistant
Positive
```

Chain-of-Thought prompting consists of prompting the model in a way that encourages step-by-step reasoning, which generally increases accuracy but consumes more tokens. A simple instruction like "think step by step" can sometimes help, but systematic experimentation reveals that domain-specific reasoning scaffolds yield stronger results. For instance, in financial applications, prompts can be structured to force explicit evaluation of market factors, risk metrics, and historical trends. In legal analysis, they might guide the model to first identify precedents, then interpret statutory language, and finally weigh risks. Each version can be compared against benchmarks to determine whether the added structure improves consistency and reduces errors.

In the following example, the assistant's answer displays step-by-step reasoning to provide a deeper analysis:

```
Instruction
Classify the sentiment of the following text as positive, negative,
or neutral. Think step by step about the language used, the emotions
expressed, and the overall tone before making your final classification.

"I absolutely loved the new restaurant downtown. The food was incredible
and the service was outstanding!"

Assistant
Let me analyze this step by step:

Step 1: Identify key emotional words
- "loved" - strong positive emotion
- "incredible" - very positive descriptor
- "outstanding" - highly positive evaluation

Step 2: Examine the overall tone
- Enthusiastic language throughout
- No negative qualifiers or criticisms
- Exclamation mark suggests excitement

Step 3: Consider context
- Restaurant review expressing satisfaction
- Multiple aspects praised (food AND service)
- No mixed signals or contradictions

Final Classification:
Positive

The text demonstrates clear positive sentiment through consistently
enthusiastic language and praise.
```

> When using reasoning models (often referred to as "thinking mode"), the model implicitly creates its own internal chain-of-thought. In this case, it is advised to only provide high-level instructions and let the model process them on their own. The real chain-of-thought used by the model is hidden by most cloud providers, which only display a high-level summary of it. These summaries can be unfaithful and deceptive, so it is not recommended to rely on them for an audit.

Role-based prompting provides another intuitive dimension of experimentation. Assigning the model a persona (for example, as a customer support agent or a technical analyst) can significantly influence tone, depth, and reliability. This is often used in conjunction with other techniques to steer the model toward a certain tone.

In our example, we can define a persona with a broader framework that details the type of reasoning that is expected in this role.

```
Instruction
You are analyzing customer feedback for a restaurant. Classify the
sentiment using this framework:
1. First, identify specific aspects mentioned (food, service, ambiance,
price, etc.)
2. For each aspect, determine if the language is positive, negative, or
neutral
3. Weigh the intensity of emotional language used
4. Consider if there are any qualifiers that modify the overall sentiment
5. Make your final classification
Text: "I absolutely loved the new restaurant downtown. The food was
incredible and the service was outstanding!"

Assistant
Step 1 - Aspects mentioned:
- Location: "downtown" (neutral descriptor)
- Food quality: mentioned
- Service quality: mentioned

Step 2 - Sentiment per aspect:
- Food: "incredible" → strongly positive
- Service: "outstanding" → strongly positive
```

```
Step 3 - Emotional intensity:
"absolutely loved" → very high positive intensity
- Superlative language throughout

Step 4 - Qualifiers present:
No "but," "however," or negative qualifiers
No hedging language
- Consistent praise

Step 5 - Final classification: Positive

The feedback shows strong positive sentiment across multiple dimensions,
with high emotional intensity and no negative qualifiers.
```

Model-specific optimization has become essential as different AI models demonstrate distinct response patterns and capabilities. For example, the Claude 4 family excels when provided with explicit structure using XML-like tags that help organize its reasoning process. Gemini requires particularly clear formatting and separation cues, but demonstrates exceptional capability with long context exceeding one million tokens. Always favor the model provider's documentation to learn how to interact with a specific model.

However, despite recent advances in long context processing, models still struggle to reliably understand extremely long inputs like an entire book. This is why **retrieval-augmented generation (RAG)** is still relevant nowadays.

RAG system design

RAG is a technique that retrieves relevant documents and includes them as context in the input prompt to improve the model's response accuracy. The documents are kept in a vector store, a specialized database that holds each document as a numerical vector and supports fast similarity search over very large collections. A successful approach to handle this complexity is to adopt a modular architecture with different stages: document ingestion, query understanding, retrieval, reranking, and generation.

Designing a RAG pipeline

Let's detail each stage of the RAG pipeline to provide a more granular understanding of the techniques involved.

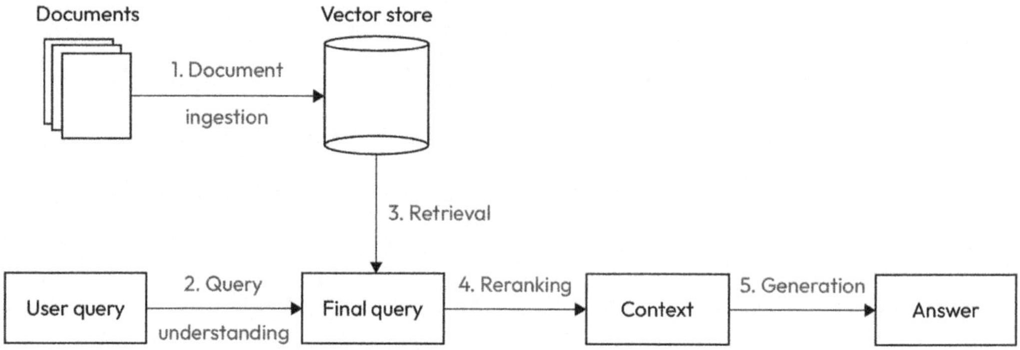

Figure 4.4: High-level components of a typical RAG architecture

The first step consists of adding documents to a vector store, also called **document ingestion**. During this process, documents are normalized, deduplicated, segmented, and enriched with metadata you can later filter or rank on. Documents are typically split into chunks with a segment size and an overlap that ideally vary by document type. It is also important to preserve some structures like headings, tables, and code blocks to keep recall high.

Once the documents are stored, users can interact with the RAG system. **Query understanding** turns a user request into one or more retrieval intents, that is, the specific things the system needs to search for in order to answer. In practice, useful tactics include rephrasing the user query in several different ways to catch synonyms, generating a draft answer first and using its embedding to find similar real documents (**hypothetical document embeddings**, or **HyDE**), and breaking complex questions into smaller sub-questions that can be answered one at a time. A small planning layer should also decide when not to retrieve at all (for example, routing to a tool or database when the user needs live data rather than documents). These strategies raise recall without overwhelming downstream reranking or generation.

Retrieval corresponds to the strategy used to retrieve stored documents based on the user query. There are two main families of retrieval algorithms. Dense retrieval encodes queries and passages as vectors and finds neighbors via approximate nearest-neighbor search, a fast way to find the closest vectors in a large collection without comparing every single one. It excels at semantic similarity and paraphrases, as shown in open-domain question answering. Sparse lexical retrieval with BM25 (a classic algorithm that ranks documents by word frequency) matches on exact terms and is particularly strong for rare entities, IDs, numbers, and code tokens. Because each method fails where the other succeeds, a robust pattern is to retrieve modest candidate sets from both, then merge them with Reciprocal Rank Fusion (a simple formula that combines two ranked lists into one by rewarding documents that appear near the top of either list). For more advanced systems, learned sparse retrievers (like SPLADE) and late-interaction retrievers (like ColBERT) blend the strengths of both approaches.

Reranking is a thin but high-leverage layer. Instead of sending all the documents we retrieved to the generator, we can use a small cross-encoder reranker (a model that reads the query and a candidate passage together and scores how well they match) to reorder our shortlist, so the generator sees the best documents first. It is also possible to tune how many candidates to rerank to balance latency and precision, as well as keep the context window small. A final deduplication step with **Maximal Marginal Relevance (MMR)**, which picks documents that are both relevant and different from what has already been selected, helps avoid feeding the generator three near-identical passages. Technical reports consistently show rerankers as a high-leverage improvement for enterprise RAG.

Finally, **generation** combines the retrieved documents and the user query to perform a given task. Through clever prompt engineering, it can also encourage grounded answers, cite sources inline, and degrade gracefully when evidence is thin (for example, ask a clarifying question or return partial answers with links). An additional orchestrator can be used to route away from RAG when a tool call is more appropriate, then integrate tool outputs into the final response. This keeps answers faithful and avoids forcing retrieval into tasks it doesn't fit.

In addition to these essential components, enterprise RAG can benefit from two more advanced architectures: multimodal RAG and GraphRAG.

Multimodal RAG extends the basic pattern to evidence beyond text to images, charts, and even sometimes audio and video. It typically uses **vision-language models (VLMs)** to interpret and embed that content for retrieval. The pipeline is the same, but the ingestion step also extracts text from diagrams and tables, stores image features alongside captions and Optical Character Recognition (OCR), and normalizes metadata so filters work across modalities. In practice, it is recommended to start with text-first retrieval plus a VLM reranker for image-heavy domains, then escalate to full multimodal fusion as needed.

For graph-shaped retrieval, **GraphRAG** combines extracted entities, relations, and textual evidence to support questions that depend on connections between pieces of information: who-did-what-to-whom, questions that require chaining several facts together (for instance, "who is the CEO of the company that acquired X?"), and summaries that cover everything related to a given entity. It can outperform standard vector search when the relationships between items carry meaningful information, but it requires upfront work to extract those relationships and maintain a clean graph. For many use cases, traditional approaches with hybrid retrieval and rerankers achieve similar performance with far less complexity.

Vector stores

When it comes to choosing a vector store, it is advised to start simple and move to more complex solutions when the number of documents or missing features becomes an issue. We distinguish three main families of databases for this purpose:

- **Managed vector databases**: Pick this when you want guaranteed service levels and prefer paying for the index instead of operating it. Best for small teams or spiky workloads that value time-to-market over infrastructure control. Examples: Pinecone and managed open-source offerings.
- **Open-source vector databases**: pick this when you want guaranteed service levels and prefer paying for the index instead of operating it. Best for small teams or spiky workloads that value time-to-market over infrastructure control. Examples: Milvus, Qdrant, Weaviate, or Vespa.
- **SQL-integrated extensions**: Pick this when you want guaranteed service levels and prefer paying for the index instead of operating it. Best for small teams or spiky workloads that value time-to-market over infrastructure control. Example: PostgreSQL with the pgvector extension.

  Vector stores add another layer of complexity, which is why they're not recommended when a simple index like a NumPy array is sufficient.

Evaluating RAG

Evaluation and observability are two essential components of a successful RAG pipeline. This is often implemented with a framework like Ragas or LangSmith. Evaluation should mirror the RAG architecture, measuring retrieval and generation separately and together. For retrieval, standard metrics include recall@k, precision, nDCG@k (see the info box) after reranking on both single-turn and multi-turn user queries. For generation, answer correctness on labeled sets and faithfulness (also called "groundedness") are typically used to ensure that the model's answers are not hallucinated. More advanced evaluation strategies can also introduce noise and subtle errors to test the robustness of the pipeline. When real-world data is limited, it is also possible to use these techniques to synthetically upsample queries and craft adversarial prompts.

Retrieval metrics are easier to understand with a concrete example. For instance, you search for "best pizza restaurants" and the system returns 5 results. In reality, there are 8 great pizza restaurants total in the database, and your top 5 results include 3 of them.

The recall@5 is the proportion of relevant items that are successfully retrieved in the top 5 results. In other words, it answers the question "Out of ALL the good results that exist, how many did I find in my top 5?" In our example, 3 good restaurants found ÷ 8 good restaurants total = 37.5% recall. This tells us that we're missing important items.

The precision@5 measures how many of the retrieved items are actually relevant or "out of the 5 results I showed, how many were actually good?" In our example, 3 good restaurants ÷ 5 total shown = 60% precision. This precision tells us that we're presenting irrelevant results to the user.

Finally, the nDCG@5 evaluates both the relevance of the items and their positions in the ranked list. Imagine that our 5 results are: bad, good, bad, excellent, good (in this order). The nDCG penalizes the system for putting highly relevant items lower in the ranking. If we define bad = 0, good = 1, and excellent = 2, we get an nDCG@5 = 60%, while the ideal ranking (excellent, good, good, bad, bad) would get 100%. This informs us that the best results are not displayed first.

Observability for RAG must be engineered to make failure modes measurable across ingestion, retrieval, reranking, and generation. This should allow us to answer simple questions quickly, like "what did we retrieve, why did the reranker change the order, and which passages were actually used to write the answer?" More traditional metrics like P95 retrieval latency (the speed below which 95% of requests are answered, which captures slow outliers better than an average) should trigger an alert when they drift beyond the threshold. Additional security signals can also be helpful, for example, to detect adversarial prompts based on heuristics (like keywords) or a safety classifier (like ShieldGemma).

In the next section, we will cover the natural extension of RAG systems with the introduction of agentic AI.

AI agents

An AI agent is a model paired with a runtime that wraps around it. That runtime, commonly called a harness, owns everything outside the model itself: which tools the model is allowed to call, how state carries from one turn to the next, which actions require a human's confirmation, how logs and traces are written, and how a user actually interacts with the system. What separates an agent from a plain chatbot or a fixed pipeline is the control loop. The harness lets the model pick what to do, executes that action, captures the result, and asks the model again, repeating until the task is finished or some stopping condition fires. The choices belong to the model, not to the code around it.

Workflows vs. agents

The word "agent" gets thrown around loosely, so it helps to pin down what does and doesn't qualify. The best test is to ask one question: at runtime, who decides what step comes next?

If the answer is the developer, because the steps and their order were committed to code ahead of time, you have a workflow. Workflows can be sophisticated and useful. Picture an invoice processing system that scans a vendor PDF, extracts line items with a model, validates totals against a database, then routes the document for approval. Or a weekly digest generator that pulls articles from an RSS feed, scores each for relevance, summarizes the top ten with a model, and emails the result. Or a customer support triage system that classifies each incoming ticket, attaches a priority tag, and assigns it to a team. In all three, the model is doing meaningful language work at specific points, but the surrounding orchestration is written in code.

If the answer is the model, because nothing in the code is dictating which step comes next (only the model's judgment in the moment), you have an agent. A coding assistant that explores an unfamiliar repository to track down a regression is doing this. A research assistant who reads one paper and then decides which reference to follow up on is doing this. The runtime hands the model context, the model chooses an action, the result feeds back in, and the cycle continues.

The reason to be strict about the line is that every interesting failure mode in agentic systems lives in that one decision step. The model can pick the wrong tool, stop one step too early, or fabricate an argument. Workflows simply do not have this category of failure, because the model is never the one steering. When the sequence of steps is knowable in advance, that predictability is almost always worth more than the flexibility of letting the model choose. Many production systems sold as "agents" turn out, on closer inspection, to be workflows in disguise.

Two patterns are worth highlighting because they are often mistaken for agents:

- A multi-call pipeline that always runs "***extract -> analyze -> recommend***" in the same order, with three separate model calls, is still a workflow. The number of model calls doesn't change the picture because the developer's code is doing the orchestration.
- A function calling endpoint that returns the structured arguments of a single tool call for the caller to execute is constrained decoding. The model is filling in a form, not driving a loop.

In other words, agents are powerful because the model gets to pick, and they're hard for exactly the same reason. If your task does not actually need that runtime decision, a well-tested workflow with good logging will outperform any agent on every axis that matters.

Designing an agentic application

A simple example is a chatbot that calls a single tool, like a web search, to answer a user's question. More advanced agents tackle complex, multi-step goals: coding agents can read a codebase, plan changes, edit files, and run tests across many iterations to complete a software engineering task on their own.

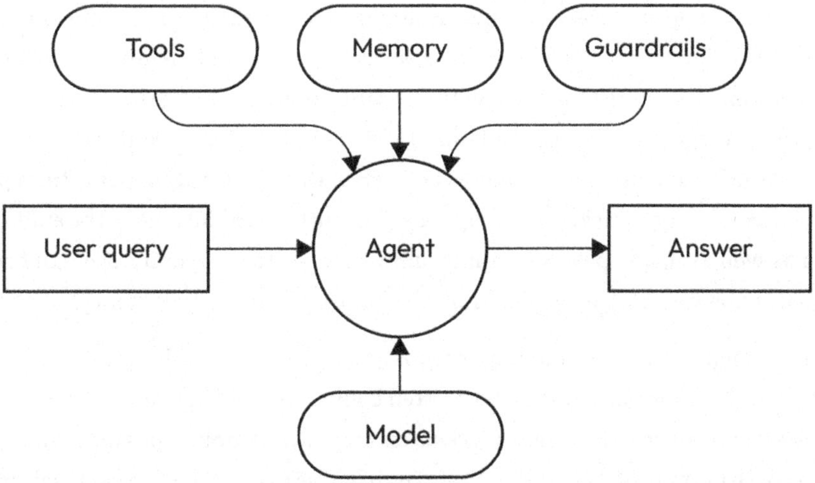

Figure 4.5: Common breakdown of an agent into model, tools, memory, and guardrails.

The harness side of the equation can be broken down many ways. A common shorthand, useful as a starting point, is to think of an agent as having four ingredients:

- **Model**: the underlying model (typically an LLM) that plans and picks the next action.
- **Tools**: functions the model can call, like web search, databases, or code execution.

- **Memory**: short-term scratchpads for the current task and longer-term stores (often a vector database) that persist across sessions.
- **Guardrails**: permissions, rate limits, safety policies, and observability.

This breakdown is convenient but not exhaustive. A real harness also owns the control loop itself (when to keep going, when to stop, how to recover from a failed tool call), the system prompt and scaffolding that shape the model's behavior, and the interface through which the user interacts with the agent. Different harnesses make different trade-offs in each of these, which is part of why the same task can look very different in Claude Code, Cursor, or a custom build.

The simplest reliable pattern is a single agent with tool use and short-term memory. Multi-agent systems (where specialized agents collaborate) can be useful, but they increase latency, complexity, and failure modes, so they should be introduced only when a single agent cannot perform the given task.

Agent design benefits from the same discipline as prompt and RAG work: decomposing the workflow, evaluating each stage, and failing fast with clear fallbacks. When processing the user query, a robust agent should be able to determine that the best action is sometimes "don't retrieve but call a tool," or "don't act but ask a clarifying question." When retrieval is needed, the best practice consists of reusing a RAG pipeline rather than creating a new one inside the agent. Tools should be well-defined with explicit schemas, strict timeouts, and idempotent behavior where possible (so calling the same tool twice with the same input produces the same result, which is essential when an agent retries after a failure). For memory, prefer temporary scratchpads for intra-task reasoning and use durable stores only when the agent truly benefits from persistence (for example, recalling prior tickets for a support assistant). Guardrails should be enforced outside the model as well as inside prompts: apply allow-lists for tools, require user confirmation for high-impact actions, and log every decision with inputs, outputs, and latency.

Evaluation for agents mirrors evaluation for prompts and RAG but adds new layers. At the model level, it is possible to measure task success, step count, and tool call accuracy. For end-to-end quality, it is recommended to run realistic scenarios that include ambiguous inputs and adversarial prompts. As with prompt evaluation, an evaluation harness (LangSmith, DeepEval, or similar) is helpful to replay traces (logs of the sequence of steps the agent took), track behavior after changes, and prevent regressions. Agents should degrade gracefully: if a tool fails, the agent returns a partial, grounded answer with citations or asks for permission to retry, rather than hallucinating.

AI frameworks

Frameworks are libraries you use to build your own agents and workflows. The landscape has shifted significantly in the past two years: as models have grown more capable and tool calling has become a native feature of cloud APIs, much of the orchestration scaffolding that early frameworks provided is no longer essential. The practical question is now less "which framework?" and more "do I need one at all, or can I call the model directly and add a small loop on top?"

When a framework does help, the main options break down by use case. LangGraph (the graph-based agent layer that has become LangChain's main differentiator) is a popular choice for production workflows that need explicit state and control flow. LlamaIndex remains strong for retrieval-heavy applications, with its Workflows API extending it from a pure RAG toolkit into a broader orchestration layer. For multi-agent collaboration, CrewAI offers a simple way to assemble role-based teams; Microsoft's Agent Framework targets the enterprise tier with built-in observability and policy controls.

Cloud providers also ship their own SDKs. OpenAI's Agents SDK and AgentKit are tightly coupled with the Responses API but provide a smooth path from prototype to production. Google's **Agent Development Kit** (**ADK**) plays the same role for Gemini and Vertex AI, while remaining model- and deployment-agnostic.

Agentic harnesses

For most developers, the default way of consuming an agent is no longer a framework but an agentic harness. A harness is a complete agent runtime that already wires together the four ingredients we described earlier: a model, a set of tools, memory management, and guardrails. Where a framework gives you building blocks to assemble your own agent, a harness gives you a working agent that you configure and extend. The shift matters because the engineering work that used to fill weeks (designing a tool schema, managing context windows, handling permissions, logging traces) is now solved once by the harness and reused across projects.

The most mature harnesses live in the software engineering space. Anthropic's Claude Code runs in the terminal and inside IDEs to read codebases, edit files, run commands, and orchestrate subagents on the developer's behalf. OpenAI's Codex CLI does similar work but executes inside sandboxed virtual machines and can deliver results asynchronously as pull requests. Cursor takes an IDE-first approach with rich UI integrations and background cloud agents. Open-source alternatives like Aider, Cline, and OpenCode target the same workflows with different priorities (model-agnostic git workflows, stepwise planning, terminal-native operation). Most production teams in 2026 use two or three of these together, picking each for a specific role: an IDE assistant for daily work, a background harness for long-running tasks, and a deep-context harness for complex refactors.

The pattern extends beyond coding. OpenClaw, an open-source harness that gained traction in early 2026, applies the same idea to personal and productivity tasks, with integrations spanning chat apps, smart home devices, and automation tools. Harnesses tend to be opinionated about workflow but expose hooks, skills, slash commands, and configuration files (like Claude Code's CLAUDE.md, which persists project-specific instructions across sessions) so teams can adapt the tools and behaviors to their domain without rebuilding the foundations. They also typically ship with built-in observability, trace replay, and safety controls, removing a large chunk of the engineering effort that frameworks leave to the developer.

Let's see some practical examples. Notice how each one mixes workflow and agentic steps in different proportions:

- A research assistant who must read many sources and cite evidence. The retrieval and citation steps are workflow-shaped, but routing between sources and asking the user clarifying questions are the agentic parts. LangGraph or LlamaIndex Workflows can host this kind of hybrid and provide trace replay and groundedness checks out of the box.
- Task automation that touches business systems (tickets, spreadsheets, CRM). These are usually mostly workflow, with a small agentic step that decides which tool to invoke. A cloud SDK like OpenAI's Agents SDK, AgentKit, or Google's ADK fits well, with tools modeled as typed functions and user confirmation gates for high-impact operations.
- Software engineering tasks (code review, refactoring, debugging, writing new features). These are genuinely agentic: the model needs to decide what to read, what to change, what to run, and what to do next based on results. An agentic harness like Claude Code, Codex CLI, or OpenClaw is often the fastest path, since they ship with file-editing, command execution, and version-control tools already wired in.

An important best practice when working with agents is to separate "thinking" from "doing." The model should plan and draft actions, but gate irreversible effects (like sending emails or making purchases) behind deterministic checks and human approval. With these practices in place, you can pick the framework or harness that matches your environment and introduce agentic capabilities confidently.

Summary

This chapter covered four fundamental building blocks of modern GenAI systems. We learned about different model architectures, from Transformer variants like Grouped-Query Attention to Mixture of Experts models that scale efficiently, hybrid architectures combining attention with other operators, and diffusion models for image and video generation. Then, we reviewed systematic approaches to communicate with language models through structured prompts, evaluation frameworks, and techniques like few-shot prompting and chain-of-thought reasoning. For retrieval, we covered how to build systems that ground AI responses in your data, including the complete pipeline from document ingestion to generation, advanced patterns like multimodal RAG, and practical guidance on vector databases and evaluation. Finally, we introduced agentic systems that plan and take multi-step actions using four core components: model, tools, memory, and guardrails. We drew a sharp line between workflows (where code orchestrates the steps) and agents (where the model decides what to do next at runtime), and saw how agentic harnesses such as Claude Code have become the default way to consume these systems.

These skills represent the core technical competencies needed to build production-ready AI applications that perform consistently at scale. Whether extracting insights from documents, automating workflows, or creating intelligent assistants, these patterns provide the reliable foundation for real-world AI systems. The systematic approaches to prompt optimization, RAG pipeline design, and agent architecture ensure your applications can handle the complexity and reliability requirements of production environments.

In the next chapter, we'll explore essential tools and platforms in AI.

5

Essential Tools and Platforms

> *"It's easy to convince yourself that your system works well on simple examples and vibe-checks. Make sure that your evaluation set reflects the actual diversity and complexity of real-world queries, including edge cases and failure modes."*
>
> *– Maxime Labonne*

In this chapter, we will explore the practical tools and frameworks essential for building modern AI applications. We'll detail the two main pathways: developing with cloud models from providers like OpenAI, Anthropic, and Google, and building with local, open-weight models. We will cover key agentic frameworks such as LangGraph and LlamaIndex, as well as the complete open-source ecosystem, including the Hugging Face Hub, various inference engines, fine-tuning libraries, and essential evaluation tools.

By the end of this chapter, you'll be able to compare the trade-offs between major cloud API providers and select the right one for your budget and feature requirements. You'll learn to choose the appropriate agentic framework, like LangGraph or LlamaIndex, based on your application's complexity. You'll also gain the skills to navigate the open-weight ecosystem, selecting the best inference tools for local development or production, choosing a fine-tuning framework that matches your hardware constraints, and implementing robust strategies for experiment tracking and model evaluation.

In this chapter, we're going to cover the following main topics:

- Building cloud applications
- Building local applications

Building cloud applications

In this section, we provide an overview of modern AI engineering. We start by detailing the offerings of the three main cloud model providers, as well as a popular aggregator. Then, we focus on two well-known frameworks for building RAG and agentic applications.

Cloud model providers

We will now survey the main cloud model providers. While the specifics of this dynamic market change quickly, the fundamental guidelines and comparisons presented here are designed to remain relevant.

OpenAI

Cloud models are priced per token, typically grouped in batches of one million. To give a sense of scale, one million tokens corresponds to roughly 750,000 English words. That is enough to cover around ten short novels, summarize a hundred research papers, draft a few thousand emails, or sustain a long agent run involving many tool calls. With this in mind, OpenAI's GPT-5 model family is available through the API in different sizes: GPT-5 at $1.25 per million input tokens and $10 per million output tokens, GPT-5 mini at $0.25/$2, and GPT-5 nano at $0.05/$0.40. These models support text and image inputs with text output, with an input limit of 272,000 tokens and an output limit of 128,000 tokens. The output limit also includes "reasoning tokens," which are tokens the model uses to think through a problem internally without showing them to the user.

The GPT-5 family offers different reasoning effort levels that can be adjusted based on task complexity. GPT-5 is priced at half the input cost of GPT-4o while maintaining the same output price, though reasoning tokens count as output tokens, which can increase total token usage. OpenAI's platform includes built-in tools such as web search, file search, and image generation, with tokens used for these tools billed at the model's standard per-token rates.

For workloads that do not require an immediate answer, the Batch API processes non-urgent requests at 50% off standard pricing, with results returned within 24 hours. A semantic caching system recognizes when a new request closely resembles a previous one and reuses the cached input tokens, reducing their cost by 90%. Enterprise features include System and Organization Controls (SOC) 2 Type II certification, **Single Sign-On (SSO)**, role-based access controls, and Business Associate Agreements for **Health Insurance Portability and Accountability Act (HIPAA)** compliance.

Anthropic

Anthropic's Claude model family spans multiple capability tiers. Claude Sonnet 4.5, released in September 2025, maintains the same pricing as Sonnet 4 at $3 per million input tokens and $15 per million output tokens. Claude Opus 4 and 4.1 are priced at $15 per million input tokens and $75 per million output tokens, while Claude Haiku 3.5 costs $0.25/$1.25. Claude 4 models introduce "thinking tokens," charged when models use tools or perform complex reasoning, with these tokens billed separately at $10 per million for Sonnet 4 and $40 per million for Opus 4.1.

Anthropic's prompt caching system lets you store parts of a prompt that you expect to reuse (such as a long document or a system instruction) and pay only a tenth of the usual input price each time the cache is read, for a saving of up to 90% on repeated content. Writing to the cache costs slightly more than a normal input (1.25x for the default 5-minute cache, or 2x for a longer 1-hour cache).

The API includes capabilities such as code execution tools, a connector for the **Model Context Protocol** (**MCP**) for external system integration, a Files API for document management, and extended prompt caching up to one hour. Recent API additions include context editing features that automatically clear stale information from past tool calls, and a memory tool that lets Claude store and consult information outside its context window. Anthropic enforces usage tiers with spending caps that require deposits to raise limits, and teams at scale must plan capacity ahead of peak periods.

Google

Google's Gemini 2.5 Pro costs $1.25 per million input tokens and $10 per million output tokens for prompts up to 200,000 tokens, with pricing increasing to $2.50/$15 for prompts exceeding this threshold. Gemini 2.5 Flash-Lite, the most cost-efficient option, is priced at $0.10 per million input tokens and $0.40 per million output tokens. Gemini 2.5 Flash balances cost and performance with pricing between these two extremes.

All Gemini 2.5 models provide a 1 million token context window with multimodal capabilities supporting text, images, audio, and video inputs. Google AI Studio usage is free of charge in all available regions with rate limits, while the paid tier offers higher rate limits for production deployments. Context caching can save up to 75% on input token costs for repeated prompts, and batch mode offers 50% discounts for bulk processing.

Grounding with Google Search is charged separately based on requests that successfully return web results, with dynamic retrieval optimization available. The Vertex AI platform applies the same base token rates but adds enterprise features, including data residency options (the ability to choose which country or region your data is stored and processed in), **service level agreement (SLA)** guarantees, and consolidated Google Cloud billing. Vertex AI Model Optimizer provides dynamic pricing by automatically routing queries to the optimal model based on cost, quality, or balance preferences.

OpenRouter

OpenRouter is an API aggregator: instead of opening separate accounts with each provider, you can reach hundreds of AI models through a single endpoint that mimics the OpenAI API style, paying the same per-token rates the underlying providers charge with no markup on inference costs. The platform charges fees on credit purchases: 5.5% for card payments with a $0.80 minimum, and 5% for cryptocurrency purchases with no minimum. Users who bring their own provider API keys are charged a 5% usage fee deducted from credits.

The following figure shows the evolution of the most used models on OpenRouter. This leaderboard is a good way to find new models with more interesting cost-efficiency trade-offs:

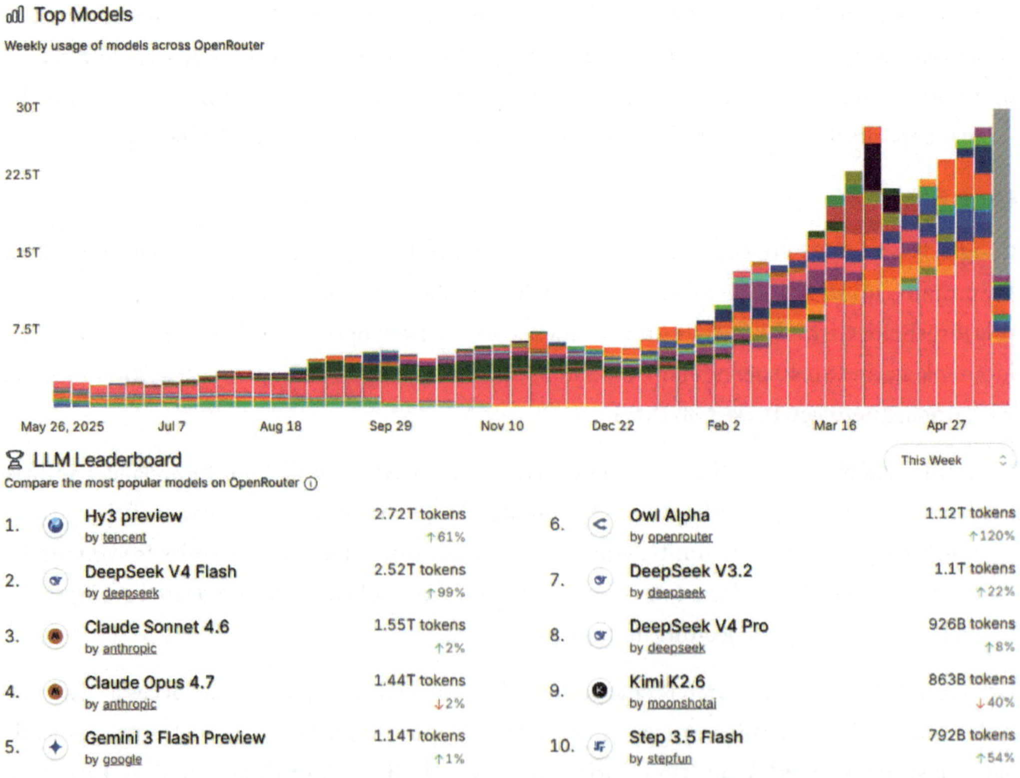

Figure 5.1: OpenRouter's leaderboard is a good indication of the most popular cloud models

OpenRouter offers routing variants, including `:nitro` for the fastest throughput routing and `:floor` for the lowest-price routing. The platform defaults to zero-logging mode, where prompts and responses are not stored unless users explicitly opt in. Zero Data Retention routing restricts requests to providers with no-storage policies, though this may reduce available models or affect latency.

Free models on OpenRouter have restrictive rate limits of 50 requests per day, increasing to 1000 requests per day after purchasing at least 10 credits. The effective total cost through OpenRouter includes purchase fees and optional **Bring Your Own Key** (**BYOK**) usage fees, making it slightly higher than direct provider access even when token rates match. As an aggregator, uptime and behavior can vary by upstream provider, though routing policies and automatic fallbacks help mitigate these issues.

Retrieval-augmented generation and agentic frameworks

Building AI applications beyond basic chatbots raises a fundamental challenge: coordinating multi-step workflows where the model decides what to do next, calls external tools, remembers what happened earlier, and occasionally hands control back to a human for review. Agentic frameworks provide the building blocks needed to handle all of this.

In *Chapter 4*, we described solutions for **retrieval-augmented generation** (**RAG**) and agentic systems from an outcome-based perspective. Now, we will take a tool-centric approach to explore what can be built with the two most popular frameworks: LangGraph and LlamaIndex.

LangGraph

LangGraph is a framework for building production-ready AI agents. It treats agent workflows as directed graphs, similar to a flowchart in which each box (a node) is one processing step and each arrow (an edge) shows where the agent can go next. Unlike more flexible frameworks like LlamaIndex that give agents more autonomy to call multiple tools or generate code dynamically, LangGraph prioritizes predictability and control. This is ideal for applications where you need to orchestrate specific sequences of actions with maximum control over agent behavior. LangGraph also integrates seamlessly with LangChain components, but can work independently.

Figure 5.2 shows a directed graph from start to finish for an email agent built with LangGraph:

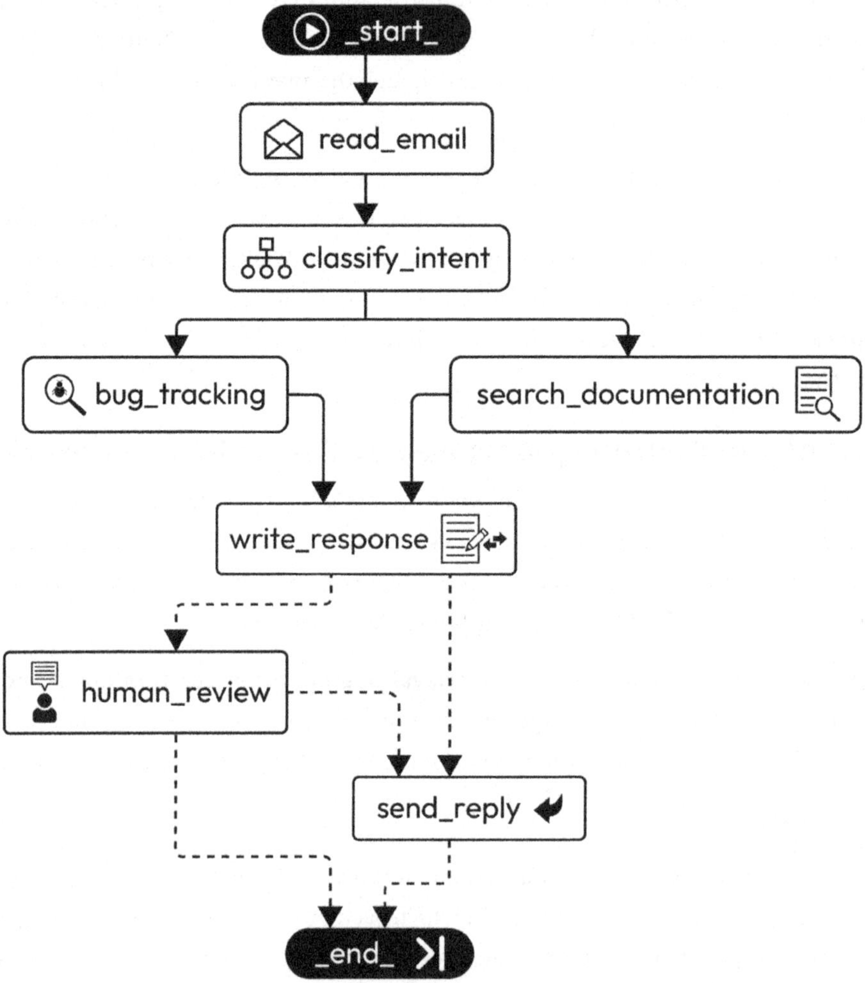

Figure 5.2: Flowchart of an email agent made in LangChain

LangGraph provides built-in state persistence, allowing agents to maintain context across multiple interactions and resume workflows after interruptions. Its human-in-the-loop features enable you to pause execution at specific points for human review or intervention, which is particularly handy for critical applications. LangGraph also offers a comprehensive observability layer (through its companion product LangSmith) that records every step the agent takes, which inputs it received, and which outputs it produced, making it much easier to debug agent behaviors and monitor performance. For readability, there is also a convenient visualization tool to generate diagrams of your agent's execution flow.

LangGraph is very general-purpose by design, which has pros and cons. While it can be used to develop most AI agents, it also has a steep learning curve and additional overhead with LangGraph-specific patterns you need to learn and operator overloading (redefining what familiar Python operators like `|` mean inside a LangGraph program). We recommend using it for the following use cases:

- SQL bots that transform natural language questions into SQL, find the right tables, write queries, fix errors, and enable employees to independently access data insights under appropriate permissions
- Document review assistants that analyze text, flag issues, and pause for human feedback while retaining all prior context
- Content moderation systems where an initial LLM node evaluates content for toxicity, and if confidence is low, conditional edges route to human moderators for review

Building agents with LangGraph follows a clear pattern centered around four core concepts. First, you define a **State** object: a structured bag of information that travels with the agent from step to step, holding inputs, intermediate results, and anything else the agent needs to make decisions. The state should be rich enough to drive every routing decision, but kept lean to avoid unnecessary bloat. Second, you implement **Nodes** as small Python functions: each one reads the current state, performs a specific operation (calling an LLM, using a tool, doing a calculation), and returns an update to the state. Each node represents a discrete step in the agent's reasoning process. Third, you create **Edges** that connect those nodes. An edge can be direct (always go from node A to node B) or conditional (pick the next node based on what the state currently looks like). Finally, you assemble these components into a **StateGraph**, compile it, and run it with an initial state to execute your agent workflow.

The typical LangGraph agent follows the ReAct (Reason-Act-Observe) pattern: the agent reasons about the task, decides which tool to call, observes the results, and repeats until the task is complete. This is implemented by creating an assistant node that calls an LLM with a list of tools, a tool node that executes the selected tools, and conditional edges that route between them. The assistant node checks if tool calls are needed, routes to the tool node when necessary, and the tools node connects back to the assistant, forming a loop that continues until the agent reaches a final answer.

Overall, LangGraph is a heavy framework that shines for particularly complex applications, involving human-in-the-loop or multi-agent systems. It provides many features (such as observability) that might not be needed for simpler applications. In this case, we recommend using LlamaIndex or a custom stack.

LlamaIndex

LlamaIndex is a comprehensive framework specifically designed for building data-augmented LLM applications, with a strong focus on RAG and agentic workflows. Originally created to connect LLMs to private or domain-specific data, LlamaIndex has evolved into an agentic framework. It provides a modular architecture built around **Components** (data loaders, embeddings, vector stores), **Tools** (capabilities agents can use), **Agents** (reasoning engines), and **Workflows** (event-driven execution patterns).

LlamaIndex provides native support for the complete RAG pipeline: loading data from hundreds of sources through LlamaHub (including web pages, PDFs, databases, and APIs), chunking and embedding documents with customizable strategies, storing vectors in various databases, and querying with various retrieval methods. Its `QueryEngine` component serves as a powerful RAG tool that agents can use, supporting multiple response synthesis strategies like tree summarization (where retrieved chunks are summarized in pairs, then those summaries are summarized again) and iterative refinement (where the model produces an initial answer from the first chunk, then updates it one chunk at a time as it reads the others). LlamaIndex's Workflow system provides an event-driven architecture where steps are triggered by typed events and can maintain state through contexts, offering more structure than pure agentic frameworks. Built-in evaluation tools help assess response faithfulness, relevance, and correctness, addressing a critical need in RAG applications.

Thanks to its focus on RAG, LlamaIndex is particularly well-suited for several categories of applications:

- Contract review workflows where document agents extract key clauses, cross-reference regulatory requirements, identify potential risks, and generate compliance recommendations
- Research assistants who search, analyze, and synthesize information from multiple sources and provide comprehensive answers with citations
- Finance industry applications to analyze client information and improve decision-making by simplifying data gathering from massive datasets
- Internal knowledge bases where employees need precise answers with custom retrieval pipelines tuned for specific use cases and integration with vector databases

Building agents with LlamaIndex typically begins with Components that handle the RAG pipeline: loading documents with `SimpleDirectoryReader` or specialized loaders from LlamaHub, creating nodes through an `IngestionPipeline` that chunks text and generates embeddings, storing these embeddings in a vector database like Chroma or Pinecone, and wrapping this in a `VectorStoreIndex` for retrieval. These components can then be converted into Tools. For example, `QueryEngineTool` wraps your RAG pipeline behind a simple interface so agents can search your data, `FunctionTool` converts any Python function into an agent capability, and `ToolSpecs` (from LlamaHub) provide pre-built integrations with services like Gmail or Google Drive.

For agent implementation, you have two main approaches: using the `AgentWorkflow` class, which automatically creates either a function-calling or ReAct agent (depending on LLM capabilities), or building custom Workflows where you define steps as async functions (decorated with @ step). This is highly use-case dependent. `AgentWorkflow` provides quick setup for standard agentic patterns, while custom workflows offer fine-grained control for complex applications with branching logic, loops, or specific orchestration requirements.

Compared to LangGraph, LlamaIndex is a lighter framework more suited for document-centric workflows involving parsing and proprietary data. They have some overlap in terms of features, but can also be combined, with LangGraph handling logic and decision-making, while LlamaIndex provides the data layer.

While these frameworks were originally designed to work with powerful frontier models, open-weight LLMs are also supported. In the next section, we will see the main tools and libraries used when working with local models to build more fine-tuned applications.

Building local applications

Open-weight models are language models whose trained parameters (the numerical values, or "weights", that determine the model's behavior) are published openly, so anyone can download them and run them on their own hardware. This is the opposite of closed models like GPT-5 or Claude, which are only accessible through an API where the provider runs the model on their servers. Open-weight models therefore allow you to directly control the engine that powers your AI applications. This can involve fine-tuning to improve the quality of the responses, adapt them to your specific use cases, and deploy models on premise or on device. In this section, we will explore the open-weight ecosystem, covering the Hugging Face Hub, inference tools, training frameworks, and evaluation frameworks.

Hugging Face Hub

The **Hugging Face Hub** serves as a central repository and collaboration platform for machine learning, hosting millions of models, datasets, and interactive applications. Originally launched to support the transformers library, the Hub has evolved into a comprehensive ecosystem to discover, share, and deploy models and datasets.

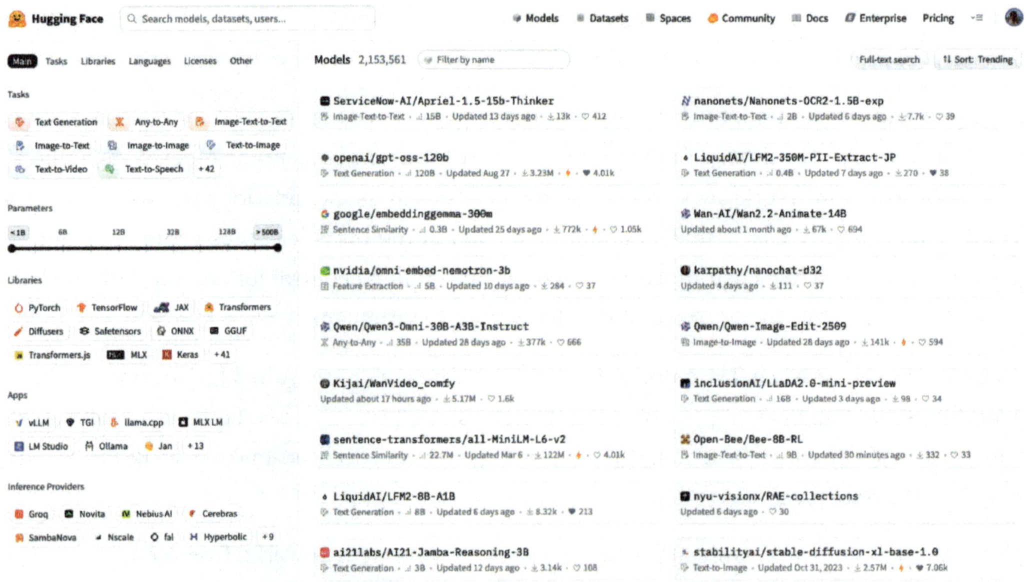

Figure 5.3: The model search page allows you to find trending models

Model pages provide essential metadata including the model's architecture, number of parameters, modalities, and more. It is often completed with a readme file with code examples and additional information about training, quantized versions (compressed copies of the model that shrink the size), and evaluation results. Models are organized with a tagging system that allows filtering by task (such as text classification, image generation, or speech recognition), framework (PyTorch, TensorFlow, JAX), language, and license. The model search is a good way to discover new popular models, based on the number of likes and downloads.

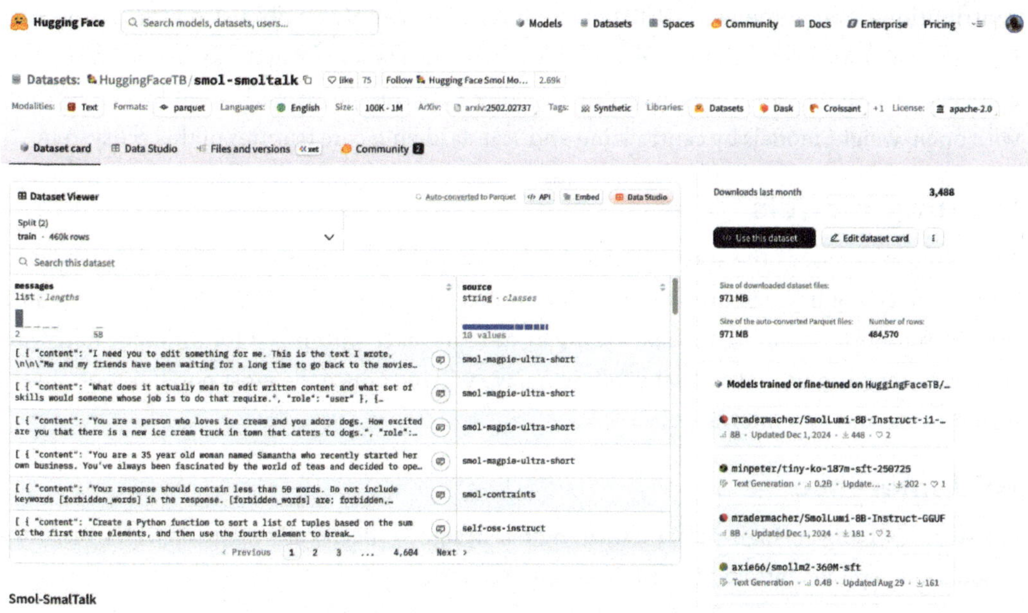

Figure 5.4: The smol-smoltalk dataset page shows samples and additional metadata

Dataset pages work in a similar way, with both metadata (like license and number of samples) and an optional description of the dataset, which can include the data generation process, sources, and more. The Hub's dataset viewer is particularly valuable. It renders tabular data directly in the browser, allowing you to explore sample rows, view statistics, and understand the schema before downloading. For instance, when examining a text classification dataset, the viewer displays columns in a spreadsheet-like interface, showing features such as input text, labels, and any additional metadata fields. This immediate visibility is particularly useful to assess the quality of a dataset.

Datasets on the Hub integrate seamlessly with the datasets library, which provides efficient loading, caching, and preprocessing capabilities. Many datasets support streaming, enabling work with large-scale data that exceeds local storage capacity. The platform also facilitates dataset versioning through Git-based infrastructure, ensuring reproducibility and allowing dataset maintainers to track changes over time.

Beyond models and datasets, the Hub hosts Spaces, which are interactive applications built with frameworks like Gradio, Streamlit, or static HTML. Spaces enable developers to create and share machine learning demos, tools, and visualizations without managing infrastructure. The platform also includes Organizations for team collaboration, pull request workflows for community contributions, and automated CI/CD through Actions. The Hub's discussion forums on each repository allow users to report issues, request features, or share insights about specific models and datasets. All these features make the Hugging Face Hub particularly useful when working with open-weight models by centralizing and standardizing core features of this ecosystem.

Running models

An inference engine is the software that loads a model into memory and runs it to generate outputs, deciding how computations are scheduled on your CPU or GPU. There are many such inference tools for running models locally or at scale, each optimized for different hardware configurations and use cases. In the following, we will introduce the most popular tools, based on hardware and user interfaces.

GPU inference

vLLM and **SGLang** are high-performance engines designed specifically to run on GPUs, targeting production deployments and high-throughput scenarios.

vLLM is the go-to choice for production environments demanding high performance at scale. Through clever GPU memory management and by grouping incoming requests so they share the same forward pass, it delivers up to 24x higher throughput compared to traditional inference methods. The engine can also split a single model across several NVIDIA or AMD GPUs, making it ideal for distributed deployments where the model is too large to fit on one card. Advanced features include streaming responses (sending tokens to the user as they are produced rather than waiting for the full answer), smart reuse of past computations to speed up follow-up tokens, and reliable handling of very long inputs under load. Choose vLLM if you operate a latency and throughput-sensitive API with spiky demand patterns and need predictable scaling characteristics.

SGLang differentiates itself through workload-specific optimizations that shine in real-world production scenarios. Its prefix caching dramatically reduces costs when many requests share the same opening text (for instance, a fixed system prompt or a common document retrieved by a RAG pipeline) by reusing the model's earlier work instead of redoing it. A smart scheduler overlaps CPU and GPU work to keep the GPU continuously engaged. SGLang is also up to 10x faster than alternatives at producing structured outputs like JSON, which matters when the model must return data in a strict, machine-readable format. The framework scales from single-GPU setups to cluster deployments and exposes the same API style as OpenAI for easy integration. Choose SGLang if you need excellent latency under concurrency, frequent prompt prefix reuse, or strict structured outputs.

CPU/GPU inference

llama.cpp and **Ollama** provide flexible inference across both CPU and GPU hardware, making them accessible for a wider range of deployment scenarios.

llama.cpp is a great tool to bring inference to the widest possible range of hardware. It runs efficiently on modern Intel, AMD, and ARM CPUs, on Apple Silicon Macs, and on NVIDIA and AMD GPUs, without requiring a Python environment or heavyweight dependencies. Its GGUF model format is also particularly popular: it packages the weights together with everything the engine needs to run them, and supports aggressive quantization down to as little as 1.5 bits per weight (compared to the 16 or 32 used during training), making it possible to fit large models on modest hardware with minimal quality loss. The engine can also split a model between system RAM and GPU memory, so models that would not fit on the GPU alone can still run by offloading some of their layers to the CPU.

Ollama is one of the most popular applications powered by llama.cpp. It streamlines the local inference experience with a simple model management system: each model is described by a short text file (called a Modelfile) that captures its settings, system prompt, and chat template in one place, making it easy to version, share, and tweak. Combined with GGUF packaging, this gives a clean approach to model configuration and sharing. Ollama also exposes the same API style as OpenAI, so code written for the OpenAI API can talk to a local Ollama with minimal changes. It runs as a background service that local tools, editors, and development environments can connect to without complex setup.

Inference frontends

LM Studio and **Jan** serve as graphical interfaces that abstract away the complexity of running local LLMs, making inference accessible to non-technical users.

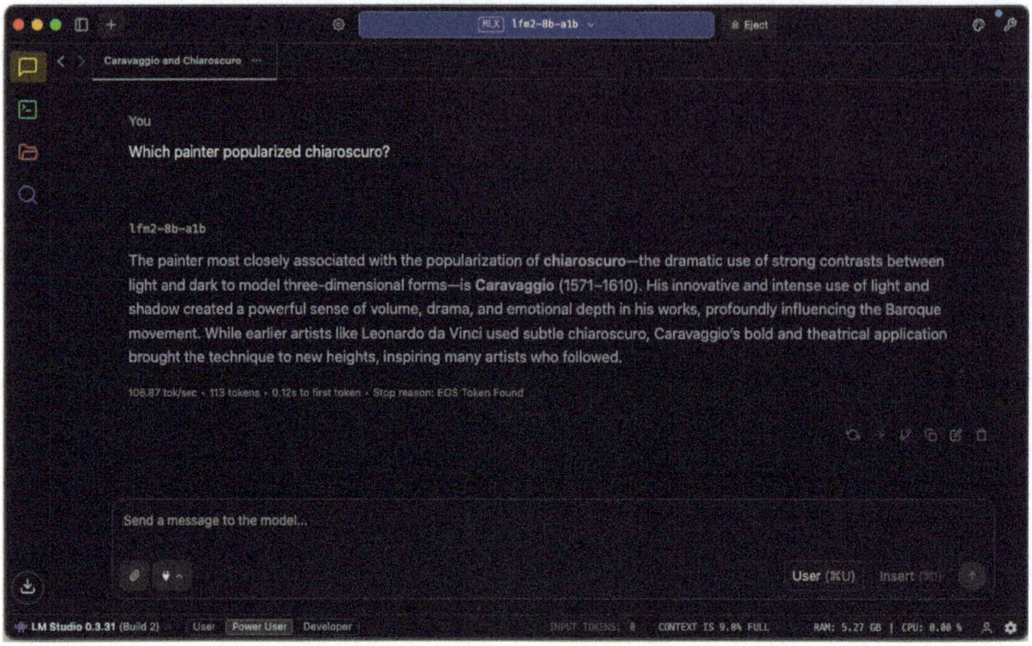

Figure 5.5: Example of LM Studio running on a MacBook Pro with over 100 tokens/sec

LM Studio is a desktop application featuring a graphical user interface that allows users to discover, download, and run local LLMs without any coding experience. It provides visual configuration for inference parameters (settings that shape how the model generates text, such as temperature, which controls randomness, and the maximum number of output tokens) and model management. The platform functions as a user-interface, API, and LLM engine that downloads GGUF models from Hugging Face and runs them on CPU or GPU, while also providing a local inference server with OpenAI-compatible API endpoints. LM Studio supports document chat with retrieval-augmented generation in a privacy-respecting environment and offers cross-platform SDKs in Python and TypeScript. Choose LM Studio if you want a friendly GUI combined with a local API for experiments, demos, and private document chat.

Jan is an open-source alternative that runs entirely offline on user devices, incorporating a lightweight built-in inference server called Nitro that supports both llama.cpp and NVIDIA's TensorRT-LLM engines. Jan's philosophical principles emphasize local-first and file-over-app approaches, with a Model Hub for easy installation of pre-configured models and support for importing models from Hugging Face or other local engines like Ollama. The open-source nature and Apache-2.0 licensing make Jan particularly appealing for users who value software freedom and community-driven development.

As shown through these examples, the choice of the best inference tool depends primarily on your target hardware (GPU vs. CPU) and use cases (command line interface vs. graphical user interface). There is a growing number of inference tools with unique trade-offs. However, many of them are short-lived or require additional maintenance because of breaking changes. For these reasons, we recommend adopting mature tools even when they don't provide the best possible performance.

Fine-tuning models

When fine-tuning open-weight language models, developers have several specialized frameworks to choose from, each optimized for different scenarios and constraints. The three most prominent frameworks (TRL, Axolotl, and Unsloth) take distinct approaches to making fine-tuning more accessible and efficient.

Transformer reinforcement learning

Transformer Reinforcement Learning (TRL) is Hugging Face's library for post-training foundation models using techniques like **Supervised Fine-Tuning (SFT)**, **Proximal Policy Optimization (PPO)**, and **Direct Preference Optimization (DPO)**. Built directly on the Transformers ecosystem, TRL provides trainers like SFTTrainer, GRPOTrainer, and DPOTrainer that integrate seamlessly with Hugging Face's tooling.

TRL supports training that spreads the work across multiple GPUs through two companion Hugging Face libraries, Accelerate and `DeepSpeed`. It also integrates with **Parameter-Efficient Fine-Tuning (PEFT)**, a family of techniques such as `LoRA` and its memory-saving variant `QLoRA`, which update only a small fraction of a model's weights rather than all of them and therefore allow fine-tuning on much smaller hardware. The framework also offers a command-line interface for quick fine-tuning without writing code.

The following code block shows an example of supervised fine-tuning using TRL. It requires a model, a tokenizer, a training dataset, and a validation ("eval") dataset. We first define a supervised fine-tuning config and pass it to the trainer with the relevant objects. This is an example of full fine-tuning, but it can be adapted to parameter-efficient fine-tuning techniques like `LoRA`. This code block is not designed to be executed, but you can find examples in TRL's official documentation:

```
from trl import SFTConfig, SFTTrainer

config = SFTConfig(
    output_dir="./output",
    num_train_epochs=1,
    per_device_train_batch_size=1,
```

```
    learning_rate=5e-5,
    lr_scheduler_type="linear",
    warmup_steps=100,
    warmup_ratio=0.2,
    logging_steps=10,
    save_strategy="epoch",
    eval_strategy="epoch",
)

sft_trainer = SFTTrainer(
    model=model,
    args=config,
    train_dataset=train_dataset,
    eval_dataset=eval_dataset,
    processing_class=tokenizer,
)

sft_trainer.train()
```

We recommend TRL for teams working within the Hugging Face ecosystem who need advanced post-training techniques like reinforcement learning from human feedback (RLHF) and DPO, or developers who want a well-documented, officially supported fine-tuning solution with tight integration to other Hugging Face libraries.

Axolotl

Axolotl is an open-source framework designed to streamline fine-tuning through a single YAML configuration file that covers dataset preprocessing, training, evaluation, quantization, and inference. The framework supports most models, with multimodal training capabilities for vision-language and audio models.

Axolotl includes performance optimizations like multipacking, Flash Attention, Flex Attention, Liger Kernel, sequence parallelism, and LoRA optimizations, along with multi-GPU support via **Fully Sharded Data Parallel** (FSDP) and DeepSpeed. It also supports sequence parallelism via Ring FlashAttention, enabling long-context fine-tuning by distributing sequences across GPUs.

Axolotl is recognized for its flexibility, ease of use, and rapid adoption of new open-source models, making it a strong choice for multi-GPU setups. The YAML-based configuration approach reduces the need for deep technical knowledge while maintaining broad compatibility with different model architectures and training techniques. Here is an example that includes parameters for supervised fine-tuning, as well as dataset preprocessing and model loading:

```
base_model: “LiquidAI/LFM2-1.2B”
xformers_attention: true
sample_packing: true  # 2-6x increase in tokens per micro-batch
chunked_cross_entropy: true
learning_rate: 0.00001
sequence_len: 16384
micro_batch_size: 1
gradient_accumulation_steps: 2
gradient_checkpointing: true  # tradeoff reduced VRAM for increased time
optimizer: “adamw_torch_8bit”
lr_scheduler: “cosine”
warmup_ratio: 0.2
float16: true
bf16: false
max_grad_norm: 0.1  # gradient clipping
num_epochs: 3
logging_steps: 5
output_dir: “./output”
chat_template: “tokenizer_default”  # use the model’s built-in chat
template
datasets:
  - path: mlabonne/FineTome-100k
    type: “chat_template”
    split: “train”
eot_tokens:
  - “<|im_end|>”
dataloader_prefetch_factor: 8  # dataloader optimizations
dataloader_num_workers: 2
dataloader_pin_memory: true
```

Axolotl is designed for developers who want a configuration-driven, user-friendly framework that abstracts away complexity. It is also a good choice for teams needing multi-GPU training capabilities or projects requiring long-context fine-tuning with sequence parallelism.

Unsloth

Unsloth is a lightweight library built to accelerate LLM fine-tuning by hand-optimizing the math behind training and rewriting the heaviest operations in Triton, a programming language for writing custom GPU code. The result is 2-5x faster training and up to 80% less memory usage compared to standard methods, with no loss in accuracy.

Unsloth is fully compatible with the Hugging Face ecosystem and can be used with TRL's entire trainer suite, including SFTTrainer, DPOTrainer, and PPOTrainer. The framework allows users to load 4-bit quantized models, fine-tune them, and merge them with the full model without exceeding limited GPU VRAM, making it possible to fine-tune large models on consumer hardware like laptops.

Unsloth's open-source version is designed primarily for single-GPU training, with multi-GPU and multi-node capabilities reserved for paid Pro and Enterprise tiers. Several optimizations target modern NVIDIA cards (Ampere generation and newer, which covers the RTX 30-series and later), so older hardware may not benefit from all performance improvements.

In terms of code, Unsloth extends TRL's features by wrapping trainers and adding utilities to preprocess datasets and quantize models. Let's revisit our supervised fine-tuning example for TRL with Unsloth:

```
from trl import SFTConfig, SFTTrainer
from unsloth.chat_templates import train_on_responses_only

config = SFTConfig(
    output_dir="./output",
    num_train_epochs=1,
    per_device_train_batch_size=1,
    learning_rate=5e-5,
    lr_scheduler_type="linear",
    warmup_steps=100,
    warmup_ratio=0.2,
    logging_steps=10,
    save_strategy="epoch",
    eval_strategy="epoch",
```

```
)

sft_trainer = SFTTrainer(
    model=model,
    args=config,
    train_dataset=train_dataset,
    eval_dataset=eval_dataset,
    processing_class=tokenizer,
)

trainer = train_on_responses_only(
    trainer,
    instruction_part = "<|im_start|>user\n",
    response_part = "<|im_start|>assistant\n",
)
```

The only change in this example is the `train_on_responses_only` function, which allows us to process the user prompts as context but only train on the assistant's answers (recommended for post-training).

Unsloth is ideal for individual developers or small teams with limited GPU resources (including free-tier Colab users), projects requiring maximum training speed and memory efficiency on a single GPU, or use cases where hardware constraints would otherwise make fine-tuning impractical.

The choice between these frameworks depends primarily on your infrastructure and workflow preferences. TRL offers the most comprehensive integration with Hugging Face's ecosystem and advanced post-training techniques. Axolotl provides the most accessible entry point through configuration-based workflows and excels at multi-GPU scenarios. Unsloth maximizes efficiency for resource-constrained single-GPU environments. All three frameworks support modern fine-tuning techniques and can be combined: for instance, using Unsloth's optimized models with TRL's trainers or leveraging Axolotl's configurations with various backends.

Experiment tracking

Effective fine-tuning requires systematic tracking of metrics, hyperparameters, and model artifacts across multiple experiments. Experiment tracking tools have become essential infrastructure for managing the iterative nature of model training, enabling teams to compare runs, reproduce results, and identify optimal configurations.

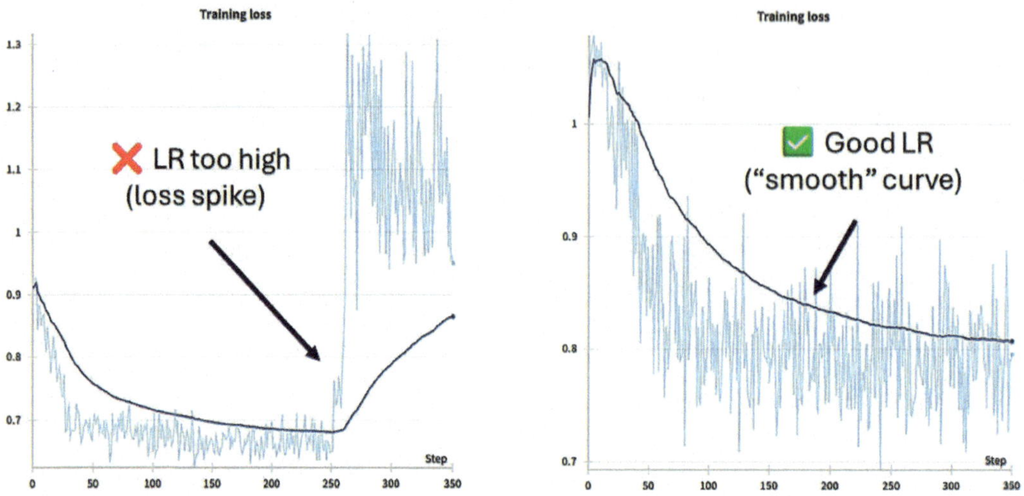

Figure 5.6: Tracking metrics like the training loss helps debugging the training parameters (here, we have the learning rate or LR)

Weights & Biases (**W&B**) has emerged as the leading experiment tracking platform in the machine learning community, offering comprehensive monitoring capabilities that integrate seamlessly with all major training frameworks. The platform automatically logs metrics, system resources, hyperparameters, and model artifacts in real-time, creating a centralized repository for all training runs. It can be easily integrated with any training framework via the `report_to="wandb"` configuration parameter.

However, several alternatives offer compelling features for specific use cases. Hugging Face's Trackio provides a lightweight, privacy-focused alternative with local-first storage and minimal dependencies. It's particularly suitable for teams working with sensitive data or those preferring self-hosted solutions without external service dependencies.

Neptune.ai emphasizes enterprise-grade features including advanced access controls, audit logs, and dedicated support for regulated industries. The platform excels at managing large-scale experiments across distributed teams and offers robust model registry capabilities for production deployment workflows.

Comet ML differentiates itself through strong model production monitoring capabilities that extend beyond training to inference performance tracking. The platform provides detailed experiment comparison tools and integrates well with CI/CD pipelines, making it attractive for teams focused on MLOps workflows.

MLflow stands apart as an open-source, vendor-neutral platform that can be self-hosted or used through managed services. Originally developed by Databricks, MLflow provides a complete lifecycle management platform covering experiment tracking, model packaging, and deployment. Its open-source nature and strong integration with the Python data science ecosystem make it popular in organizations with existing MLflow infrastructure or those prioritizing vendor independence.

Each of these tools integrates with popular training frameworks through Python APIs and typically requires only a few lines of code to begin logging. The choice between them often depends on organizational requirements around data privacy, existing infrastructure, team size, and whether production monitoring capabilities are needed beyond training metrics.

Evaluating models

Evaluating language models often requires frameworks to systematically assess performance across diverse benchmarks while minimizing implementation overhead. The evaluation landscape has matured to include specialized tools for different model types and use cases.

Academic benchmarks

Academic benchmarks are focused on reproducible tasks that target general-purpose capabilities, such as mathematical reasoning or knowledge. They are widely implemented in evaluation frameworks and serve as popular comparison points between models.

Eleuther AI's **Language Model Evaluation Harness** (or lm-evaluation-harness) is a unified framework for testing generative language models on a large number of evaluation tasks. It supports over 60 standard academic benchmarks with hundreds of subtasks and provides evaluation results with both exact matching and LLM-based answer extraction. The framework supports diverse model types through a unified interface, including local models via Hugging Face Transformers and vLLM, and API-based models from providers like OpenAI and Anthropic. The architecture ensures reproducibility through publicly available prompts and supports customized evaluations.

Hugging Face's **lighteval** is an all-in-one toolkit for evaluating large language models across multiple backends, supporting evaluation of models using Transformers, vLLM, Nanotron, and Hugging Face's inference providers. It can also evaluate large models in multi-GPU and multi-node settings, distributing the workload across several GPUs (or even several machines) when a single device would be too small.

VLMEvalKit is an open-source toolkit for evaluating large vision-language models, implementing over 200 different models, including proprietary APIs and open-source models, along with more than 80 multimodal benchmarks. To evaluate a model on multiple benchmarks, developers only need to implement a single `generate_inner()` function, while the toolkit automatically handles data downloading, preprocessing, prediction inference, and metric calculation. The framework hosts the OpenVLM Leaderboard to track progress in multimodal learning research and provides a comprehensive evaluation results database.

Custom evaluations

While academic benchmarks provide standardized metrics for comparing models, real-world applications typically require custom evaluations tailored to specific downstream tasks. Custom evaluations measure what actually matters for your use case, whether it's generating SQL queries from natural language, extracting structured data from documents, or providing domain-specific recommendations.

Designing and running custom evaluations is a difficult task with many pitfalls, such as overfitting on a single narrow use case, not comparing your fine-tune with the original model, and incorrectly parsing answers. To maximize the feedback signal you get from custom evaluations, we recommend the following best practices:

- **Define the ideal behavior of your system**: Before writing any evaluation code, define what "good" looks like for your task. If you're building a customer support agent, success might mean accurately identifying user intent and providing relevant solutions without hallucinations. If you're building a code assistant, it could be syntactically correct code that passes test cases. These criteria should be explicit, reflect real-world use cases, and get stakeholder alignment
- **Build a representative test set**: It's easy to convince yourself that your system works well on simple examples and vibe-checks. Make sure that your evaluation set reflects the actual diversity and complexity of real-world queries, including edge cases and failure modes. Aim for diversity across different difficulty levels, input formats, and domain-specific variations. Start with 100 examples for initial evaluations, prioritizing quality over quantity. Each example should include the input, expected output or behavior, and ideally metadata about why it's important (difficulty level, subdomain, common failure pattern). Consider incorporating actual production data when privacy and compliance allow

- **Multiple evaluation levels**: Efficient evaluation strategies involve different but complementary approaches like a combination of heuristics and LLM-as-a-Judge. Heuristics should be deterministic unit tests and assertions that run quickly, such as checking output format, required fields, prohibited content, or basic correctness rules. These catch obvious failures immediately without expensive LLM calls. Judge models capture nuanced assessments like relevance, coherence, or instruction-following. When using judge models, provide clear rubrics and validate judge agreement against human ratings on a subset of data. For more subjective assessments, you can also rely on human reviewers working from clear guidelines, with cross-checks between reviewers to ensure they agree on what counts as a good answer.
- **Iterate based on failures**: Treat evaluation design as an ongoing process, not a one-time delivery. Storing results in a user-friendly, readable way (like on the Hugging Face Hub) is essential to investigate whether an error is due to the model's capabilities or an error with the evaluation framework. Your evaluation will likely go through several iterations to increase the diversity and accuracy of the samples. Once it's finalized, it provides excellent feedback to understand what data is missing to improve your model.

While custom evaluations are inherently task-specific, these guidelines provide a foundation for designing high-quality evaluations. The key is establishing your evaluation framework early in development and automating it to track progress continuously. With reliable metrics in place, model improvement becomes a systematic process of rapid iteration with data generation, model training, and evaluations.

Summary

This chapter covered the essential tools for building AI applications, starting with major cloud providers like OpenAI, Anthropic, Google, and also the convenient aggregator OpenRouter. For building complex agentic applications, we detailed two popular frameworks. LangGraph provides a robust solution for creating controllable, predictable agent workflows as graphs, with state persistence and human-in-the-loop capabilities. In contrast, LlamaIndex is a data-centric framework optimized for building RAG pipelines, offering extensive tools for connecting LLMs to proprietary data sources.

We also discussed the open-source ecosystem, centered on the Hugging Face Hub as the primary repository for models and datasets. For local deployment, we covered different inference tools, from high-throughput GPU servers like vLLM and SGLang to flexible CPU/GPU tools like llama.cpp and Ollama, or convenient frontends with LM Studio and Jan. We detailed how fine-tuning these models is streamlined by frameworks such as TRL, Axolotl, and Unsloth with code examples. Finally, we highlighted the iterative process of working with open-weight models and fine-tuning when it comes to running and designing evaluations.

In the next chapter, we'll cover the key technical skills for the AI era: Python and essential programming languages, foundational machine learning concepts and frameworks, as well as prompt engineering.

Part 3

Building Your AI Toolkit – Skills and Strategy

Part 3 focuses on building the technical expertise, human capabilities, and career strategies needed to excel in the age of generative AI. You'll strengthen your foundation in essential technical skills, including machine learning fundamentals and prompt engineering, while developing the critical thinking, creativity, communication, and ethical judgment that set human professionals apart. The part concludes by helping you translate these capabilities into a successful career through practical guidance on upskilling, career transitions, and long-term professional growth in the rapidly evolving AI domain.

This part contains the following chapters:

- *Chapter 6, Mastering Hard Skills – The Technical Edge*
- *Chapter 7, Cultivating Technical and Human Skills for the Agentic AI Era*
- *Chapter 8, Strategic Career Moves – Entry, Transition, and Upskilling*

6

Mastering Hard Skills – The Technical Edge

"Mastering these hard skills does not require becoming an expert in every domain. Instead, it means developing enough depth in the areas most relevant to your path and enough breadth to collaborate effectively across the GenAI stack."

– Sadid Hasan

The global expansion of machine learning and generative AI reflects a simple truth: the people who can build, adapt, and operate these systems are now central to how industries evolve. Growth in the field is driven not just by what AI can do, but by professionals who understand how it works, who can reason about data, code, modeling, and the operational realities of deploying intelligent systems. For example, the rise of advanced code-generation models has not reduced the need for technical expertise; if anything, it has intensified it.

As more developers incorporate AI into their workflow, the ability to read, review, and refine machine-generated code becomes a core competency. AI can draft functions, but humans still decide whether the logic is sound (for example, a code review may catch a hallucinated API call or an off-by-one error—a small indexing mistake where a loop runs one step too early or too late—or a conditional branch that looks plausible but would fail silently in production), whether the system should be given agency, and how to monitor it once it is running. In this sense, programming has shifted from writing every line by hand to shaping the architecture around the model: the data pipelines that feed it, the retrieval layers that ground it, the tool interfaces that constrain it, and the deployment frameworks that keep it reliable. A useful analogy is to think of generative AI as a powerful appliance: prompting is how you choose the settings and tell it what you want, but technical skills are what let you understand what's happening inside, adjust it when something goes wrong, and keep it running safely over time. The people who can both direct the system and understand its inner workings will have the most durable and adaptable careers in the AI era.

This chapter offers a balanced exploration of the technical competencies that matter most. It explains what each skill is, why it matters, and how to develop it, whether you are a software engineer deepening your AI expertise, a healthcare researcher exploring computational methods, or a business professional seeking to understand how technology is reshaping your industry. The journey moves from foundational programming and data skills, through machine learning fundamentals and prompt design, into modern system patterns such as retrieval-augmented generation and evaluation frameworks, and finally into the interdisciplinary knowledge that gives innovators a distinctive edge.

In this chapter, we will cover the following topics:

- Foundational programming and data skills
- Machine learning fundamentals for generative AI
- Prompt engineering—the new technical literacy
- Tools, frameworks, and techniques shaping GenAI work
- Diverse technical backgrounds—interdisciplinary on-ramps
- From coding-only skills to human–AI collaboration

Foundational programming and data skills

Modern generative AI work depends on a practical foundation of programming and data fluency. Even as models automate more surface-level tasks, practitioners still need to verify outputs, debug model-assisted workflows, and maintain control over systems that can behave unpredictably. These capabilities form the baseline for every technical and semi-technical role in the GenAI ecosystem, which is why mastery of core tools like Python, SQL, and other essential languages and tools remains indispensable.

Python as the language of AI

Python has become the backbone of generative AI because it anchors the entire modern machine learning ecosystem (`https://www.secondtalent.com/resources/top-ai-programming-languages-by-usage-stats/`). For example, the dominant deep learning frameworks, TensorFlow and Keras for production-grade pipelines, PyTorch for research and rapid experimentation, and

Scikit-learn for classical ML are all built around Python as their primary interface. The same is true for the libraries that support today's generative AI systems; for example, model libraries like Hugging Face Transformers provide direct access to pre-trained models and the tools needed to load, fine-tune, and run them efficiently. In contrast, orchestration frameworks such as LangChain operate at a higher layer of the stack, helping developers build retrieval-augmented workflows, manage tool use, and coordinate multi-step agentic behaviors. This separation of models at one layer and orchestration at another illustrates the ecosystem depth that makes Python the natural environment for everything from data cleaning and feature engineering to fine-tuning models and deploying full agentic systems.

Its readability lowers the barrier for newcomers, while its flexibility allows experts to move quickly across the entire AI workflow. And even as code-generation models become more capable, Python remains essential because humans still need to review model-written code, shape the surrounding architecture, and ensure that systems behave safely and reliably. For anyone pursuing a technical or semi-technical role in generative AI, Python is not just another language; it is the foundation on which most real systems are currently built, and so mastering it is one of the most valuable investments you can make in your career.

SQL as the language of data

Similar to the Python language, SQL remains one of the most essential skills in generative AI because every model ultimately depends on high-quality data, and SQL is still the primary language for accessing, shaping, and validating that data (`https://aicareerfinder.com/blog/sql-for-ai-roles-why-it-still-matters-in-2025`). The rise of large language models has not replaced data fundamentals rather it has amplified them. SQL continues to be the main interface for relational databases, for example, cloud data warehouses such as Snowflake and BigQuery, and modern lakehouse platforms like Databricks. It shows up in the daily work of nearly every AI-related role. For example, machine learning engineers use it to engineer features directly in the database and monitor data drift; NLP and RAG practitioners rely on it to curate text corpora, filter document chunks, and manage metadata; AI product managers use it to query experiment results and compute model-level KPIs; prompt engineers use it to retrieve real-time contextual data that grounds model outputs; and researchers depend on it to curate clean, versioned datasets for experimentation.

What has changed in the generative AI era is not SQL's relevance but its accessibility. Natural-language-to-SQL tools now allow users to describe what they want in plain language and receive syntactically correct SQL in return (`https://learn.microsoft.com/en-us/microsoft-cloud/dev/tutorials/openai-acs-msgraph/03-openai-nl-sql`). This makes SQL easier to learn, use, and adopt across interdisciplinary teams. Newcomers can explore data without memorizing every clause or join pattern, while experts can offload boilerplate queries and focus on higher-level logic and system design. Instead of diminishing SQL, generative AI has made it more central by lowering the barrier to high-quality data work. If you wish to explore more and get started with NL2SQL, check this resource: `https://cloud.google.com/blog/products/data-analytics/nl2sql-with-bigquery-and-gemini`

> Natural-language-to-SQL tools still have important limitations: they may generate queries that are logically incorrect, inefficient, or insecure, and they can hallucinate tables or columns that do not exist. Because of these risks, practitioners treat NL2SQL as an accelerator rather than an authority, validating outputs through schema checks, query plans, and established verification workflows.

SQL also integrates seamlessly into the modern AI stack, showing up everywhere data needs to be accessed, transformed, or validated. For example, Python libraries such as SQLAlchemy and Pandas' SQL connectors allow developers to execute queries directly from scripts, making SQL a natural part of feature engineering, data exploration, and pipeline automation. In addition, modern MLOps platforms rely on SQL-backed stores for experiment tracking and pipeline metadata, and cloud AI services including major training and inference platforms store their data in SQL-compatible systems. This deep integration reinforces SQL as a core technical skill rather than an optional one.

Mastery of SQL also signals a shift in professional maturity: it marks the transition from someone who requests datasets to someone who designs data pipelines, builds feature stores, and owns the integrity of the data flowing into models. It is a foundational capability for roles that grow into technical leadership, whether that path leads toward a Tech Lead, ML Architect, or Head of Machine Learning role, because the people who understand the data most deeply are the ones who shape how intelligent systems behave in the real world.

Complementary languages and big data tools

Beyond the foundational languages that anchor modern generative-AI work, several additional technical competencies broaden your capability depending on your target role. Each language and ecosystem contributes something distinct to the modern AI workflow, and generative AI has only sharpened those boundaries. For example, **C++** remains essential for performance-critical AI systems where milliseconds matter. Self-driving cars processing sensor data in real time, high-frequency trading algorithms, and robotics systems all rely on C++ for levels of performance that interpreted languages cannot match.

GenAI is not built on a single language or tool. *Figure 6.1* illustrates the major technologies that contribute to the modern GenAI ecosystem and the roles they typically play.

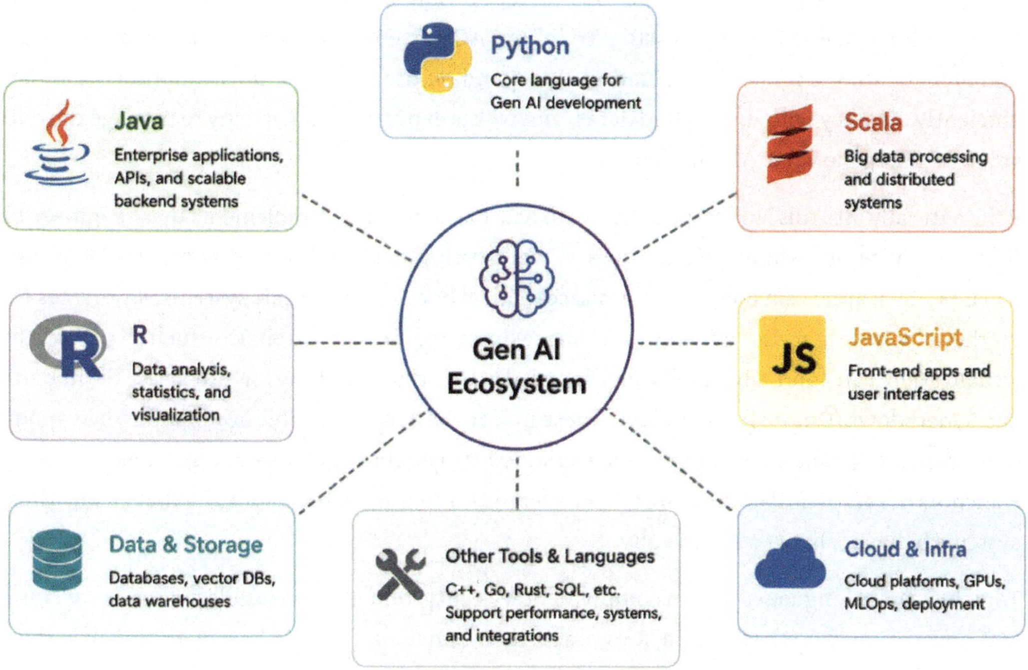

Figure 6.1: Key technologies in the GenAI ecosystem

Compiled languages like C++ run orders of magnitude faster than Python for CPU-intensive computation, which is why organizations building embedded or latency-sensitive AI systems often combine Python for rapid model development with C++ for deployment. Frameworks such as the TensorFlow C++ API, OpenCV for computer vision, and ONNX Runtime for cross-platform inference optimization anchor this ecosystem. In the generative-AI era, C++ increasingly powers the inference engines that run large models efficiently on edge devices and production servers.

Java continues to dominate enterprise AI deployments. Its platform independence, stability, and decades of adoption make it a natural fit for large organizations building chatbots, fraud-detection systems, or AI-powered CRM integrations. Libraries like Eclipse Deeplearning4j bring deep learning to the JVM ecosystem, and Java's strong tooling around security, observability, and distributed systems makes it a reliable backbone for production-grade generative-AI applications. As enterprises integrate generative models into existing systems, Java often becomes the glue that connects new AI capabilities to legacy infrastructure.

Scala plays a central role in big-data machine learning pipelines. As the primary language for Apache Spark, Scala is foundational for teams working with massive training corpora, enterprise-scale log processing, or distributed feature engineering. Generative AI has intensified the need for scalable data processing: training RAG systems, preparing multimodal datasets, and orchestrating large-scale evaluation all depend on the ability to move and transform data efficiently. Fluency with distributed data frameworks expands your capacity to manage the data volumes that generative AI now demands.

R fits naturally into this landscape as the statistical backbone that complements these engineering-heavy ecosystems. While Python drives model development and deployment, and languages like C++, Java, and Scala power performance-critical or enterprise-scale systems, R provides the methodological rigor that generative AI increasingly requires. Its strengths, such as ggplot2 for visualization, caret and tidymodels for principled ML workflows, Shiny for interactive dashboards, and R Markdown/Quarto for reproducible research, make it indispensable in domains where model outputs must be validated, audited, and explained. As generative AI accelerates experimentation, R anchors the statistical evaluation, causal inference, and transparent reporting that ensure those systems behave reliably and ethically.

Together, these languages form a complementary ecosystem. Python builds generative systems, SQL governs the data they rely on, R validates their behavior, C++ and Java operationalize these at scale, and Scala powers the distributed data pipelines that feed them. In a world increasingly shaped by generative AI, breadth across these tools expands your ability to design, evaluate, and deploy intelligent systems with confidence.

Machine learning fundamentals for generative AI

Programming languages give you the tools; machine learning gives you the logic. To work confidently with generative AI, you need a foundational understanding of how models learn from data, represent information, and produce outputs. Machine learning provides the mathematical and statistical principles that make generative systems possible, such as, how patterns are extracted, how relationships are encoded, and how models generalize beyond the examples they were trained on. Large Language Models (LLMs) are a prominent class of machine learning models trained on vast corpora of text to generate and interpret human-like language. By learning statistical relationships between words, phrases, and concepts, they can perform tasks ranging from text generation to sentiment analysis, summarization, question answering, and more. Their capabilities emerge from the same core ML ideas that underpin all generative systems: learning from data, optimizing objective functions, and representing meaning through high-dimensional embeddings.

Neural networks, deep learning, and the transformer revolution

Modern generative AI is built on neural network architectures that are essentially layered mathematical systems inspired loosely by how neurons connect and activate in the human brain. "Deep" neural networks contain many stacked layers, allowing them to learn increasingly abstract representations of data. Earlier modeling approaches such as convolutional neural networks (CNNs) for vision and recurrent neural networks (RNNs) for sequential data were grounded in intuitive analogies to human perception: CNNs mimic how the visual cortex detects edges and shapes, while RNNs emulate the way humans process information over time. *Figure 6.2* illustrates what deep neural networks look like:

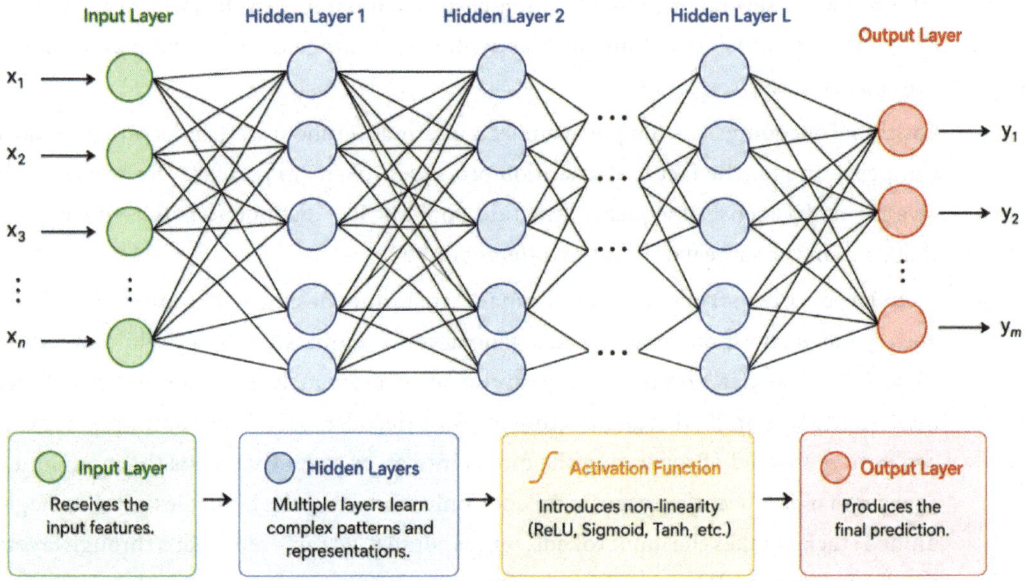

Figure 6.2: Deep neural network architecture

These architectures laid the foundation for today's generative AI models. The pivotal breakthrough behind virtually all state-of-the-art LLMs is the Transformer architecture (`https://en.wikipedia.org/wiki/Attention_Is_All_You_Need`). Transformers rely on attention mechanisms that allow the model to consider every token in a sequence simultaneously, rather than processing texts one word at a time as older recurrent models did. This parallelism is what enables the latest LLMs to handle long documents, maintain contextual coherence, and generate fluent, human-like text. The Transformer's efficiency, scalability, and ability to capture long-range dependencies made it the dominant architecture for modern generative AI. However, this design also introduces important tradeoffs: standard self-attention has a quadratic attention cost (computational cost that grows with the square of the sequence length), which limits how far context windows can scale. Recent optimizations, such as sparse attention (an attention pattern that computes only the most relevant token-to-token interactions), linear-attention variants (approaches that approximate attention in linear time), and block-wise or sliding-window mechanisms (methods that restrict attention to local segments to reduce computation), aim to reduce this cost while preserving model quality. Several Transformer-related concepts are especially important to understand:

- **Self-attention and multi-head attention**: Mechanisms that let the model evaluate the relevance of every word relative to every other word in a sequence. Self-attention allows each token to look across the entire sentence to determine what matters, while multi-head attention runs several of these attention patterns in parallel so the model can capture different types of relationships, such as syntax, long-range dependencies, or semantic cues all at once.
- **Positional encoding**: A technique that injects information about word order into the model, compensating for the fact that attention processes tokens in parallel. These encodings give the model a sense of sequence structure, enabling it to distinguish between sentences that contain the same words but in different orders.
- **Encoder–decoder structures**: The original Transformer design, where an encoder reads and represents the input and a decoder generates the output step by step while attending to both the encoder's representation and its own previously generated tokens; many modern LLMs simplify this architecture by using decoder-only stacks optimized for text generation. Instead of separating the model into an encoder that reads the input and a decoder that produces the output, a decoder-only model handles both roles within a single unified stack. It takes the input tokens, builds contextual representations through layers of self-attention, and then continues generating new tokens one at a time while attending to everything it has produced so far. This design is highly efficient for generative tasks because it removes the need for cross-attention between encoder and decoder, reduces architectural complexity, and allows the model to focus entirely on predicting the next token in a sequence.
- **Embedding layers**: Components that map discrete tokens (words or subwords) into continuous numerical vectors that capture semantic meaning. These vectors form the model's internal representation of language, allowing it to understand similarity, context, and relationships between words before any attention or higher-level processing occurs.

Being comfortable with concepts like embedding vectors, attention weights, and model parameters gives you a clearer sense of what an LLM is doing internally. This intuition strengthens your ability to troubleshoot unexpected outputs, design more effective prompts, and make informed decisions about model selection, fine-tuning, and evaluation. A working grasp of these ideas turns the model from a black box into a system you can reason about, guide, and optimize with confidence.

Training, fine-tuning, and transfer learning

Generative AI systems are built through a two-phase development process: large-scale pretraining on broad, general-purpose data followed by post-training, where the model is adapted or aligned for specific tasks or domains. Post-training includes fine-tuning but also encompasses a wider set of techniques used to shape model behavior. This approach of leveraging a powerful pretrained model and adapting it to a new, related problem is broadly known as transfer learning, and it dramatically reduces the data, compute, and time required to build specialized AI capabilities. Transfer learning is one of the key reasons modern generative AI is accessible to organizations of all sizes. You can explore more about transfer learning at: `https://en.wikipedia.org/wiki/Transfer_learning`

A wide range of post-training/fine-tuning techniques has emerged, each designed to optimize performance, efficiency, alignment, or reasoning ability:

- **Supervised Fine-Tuning (SFT)**: Trains the model on curated input–output examples to shape its behavior toward desired patterns; this is the foundation of most post-training workflows.
- **Instruction tuning**: A specialized form of SFT where the data is formatted as "Instruction → Response," enabling models to understand and follow natural-language instructions across diverse tasks
- **Reinforcement Learning from Human Feedback (RLHF)**: Aligns model behavior with human intent using preference rankings
- **Parameter-Efficient Fine-Tuning (PEFT)**: Updates only a small subset of parameters to reduce compute costs
- **LoRA (Low-Rank Adaptation)**:Injects low-rank matrices to approximate full fine-tuning, widely used for domain-specific adaptation. LoRA achieves this by inserting small, trainable low-rank matrices into targeted layers of a large model so that only these light-weight components are updated during training, while the base model remains frozen. This allows the adapters to learn the domain-specific shifts needed for high-quality customization without modifying the full parameter set, capturing most of the benefits of full fine-tuning at a fraction of the computational and memory cost.

- **QLoRA (Quantized LoRA)**: Combines LoRA with quantization to make post-training feasible on consumer GPUs. QLoRA extends the LoRA approach by running the underlying model in a quantized, lower-precision format that dramatically reduces memory usage, while still training the low-rank adapters in higher precision to preserve accuracy. This combination enables practitioners to fine-tune very large models on modest hardware, making advanced post-training accessible even on a single consumer-grade GPU.
- **LLM Distillation**: Transfers knowledge from a large model to a smaller one for lower-latency deployment.

Recent advances extend post-training even further:

- **Reinforcement Learning from Verifiable Rewards (RLVR):** Uses objective, automatically checkable signals to scale alignment and improve correctness
- **Reasoning-Model Training:** Strengthens long-horizon reasoning by optimizing models to generate extended chains of thought and explore solution paths
- **TinyLoRA and ultra-low-rank updates:** Achieve strong reasoning performance by training extremely small parameter sets
- **Self-training and synthetic-data bootstrapping:** Use high-quality model-generated reasoning traces to improve smaller or specialized models

Understanding these post-training techniques helps professionals design efficient, cost-effective generative-AI solutions. For example, an organization might start with an open-source pre-trained model and apply LoRA-based post-training to its proprietary data, creating a domain-specific assistant at a fraction of the cost of training from scratch. Knowing how to navigate the tradeoffs such as performance, compute, latency, alignment, and reasoning depth has become a valuable career skill.

Language modeling – how LLMs generate text

Large Language Models generate text by learning patterns in language and optimizing objectives that shape how they interpret context and predict tokens. Autoregressive and causal models, used in most generative systems today, predict the next token based on all previous tokens, enabling fluent long-form generation, coherent dialog, and strong performance on reasoning-style prompts. Masked language models take a different approach by predicting hidden tokens within a sentence, building a deep bidirectional understanding that excels at classification, retrieval, and semantic analysis. Newer models blend these ideas with hybrid objectives and reasoning-oriented training signals, but the core distinction remains as generative models rely on left-to-right prediction for natural text generation, while masked models specialize in understanding. Recognizing the objective of building a model helps practitioners choose the right tool and design prompts that align with the model's strengths.

ML and agentic frameworks – your workshop bench

Modern generative AI development relies on a small set of core frameworks that form a practical, end-to-end workflow, and hands-on proficiency with at least one deep learning framework is essential. Tools like TensorFlow and Keras enable scalable deep-learning pipelines, while PyTorch remains the preferred environment for experimentation and custom model development. Scikit-learn continues to anchor classical ML baselines, and Hugging Face Transformers makes it easy to load, fine-tune, and deploy state-of-the-art pretrained models. At the application layer, frameworks like LangChain help orchestrate model calls, integrate external tools, and build full GenAI products. The latest agentic frameworks, such as MAF, an open-source SDK and runtime, unify multi-agent orchestration by combining AutoGen's research strengths with the production foundations of Semantic Kernel. MAF lets developers experiment locally, deploy to Azure AI Foundry with built-in observability and compliance, integrate any API via OpenAPI, collaborate across runtimes with **Agent2Agent (A2A)**, connect tools dynamically using **Model Context Protocol (MCP)**, and orchestrate advanced multi-agent patterns. If you want to learn more about AI agents, check this resource: `https://microsoft.github.io/ai-agents-for-beginners/`.

Together, these frameworks give practitioners a complete bench of capabilities from classical ML to custom neural networks to production-ready generative AI and agentic applications.

Prompt engineering – the new technical literacy

Prompt engineering is the practice of designing clear, intentional prompts that guide a language model toward the response you want. At its core, it's the skill of communicating precisely with AI systems, where the clarity and structure of your request directly shape the quality of the output. Well-crafted prompts make requirements easier for the model to interpret, reduce ambiguity, and produce results that more closely match the user's intent. Specificity, context, and well-defined constraints consistently lead to better outcomes, whether the task involves analysis, writing, reasoning, or creative generation. Because these systems respond to natural language, prompt engineering has become a broadly applicable skill across roles, from content creation and research to customer support, product management, and data analysis. And while the mechanics are simple, the craft is not intuitive; it improves through practice, experimentation, and a growing understanding of how models interpret instructions.

Effective prompts share a simple principle: the clearer and more intentional the instruction, the better the model's output. Good prompt design focuses on expressing what you want with precision, such as, defining the role the model should take, stating the task in direct language, providing any background needed to ground the response, and specifying the format you expect so the output arrives in a usable form. The format of the prompt can matter as well: because LLMs rely on tokenization, the way you structure the instruction, whether in plain text, Markdown, XML-style blocks, or other structured sections can influence how the model parses and interprets it.

Plain text tends to be the most flexible and conversational, giving the model broad freedom to infer structure from context. Markdown introduces lightweight formatting cues, such as headings, lists, and code fences that help the model recognize boundaries, hierarchies, and task segments more reliably. XML-style blocks provide even stronger structure by wrapping instructions, examples, or constraints in explicit tags, which reduces ambiguity and makes it easier for the model to identify which parts of the prompt correspond to roles, inputs, outputs, or rules. More formal sectioned formats, such as multi-part templates or schema-like layouts, further constrain interpretation by giving the model a predictable pattern to follow. These differences matter because tokenization reflects not just the words, but the formatting symbols themselves, and the model's internal representation of those tokens can shift how it understands the task, the constraints, and the expected output. Adding examples, constraints, or small demonstrations can further reduce ambiguity and help the model match your style or requirements.

Modern prompting also emphasizes guiding the model through its reasoning, breaking complex tasks into steps, and shaping the structure of the response rather than leaving interpretation open-ended. And because no prompt is perfect on the first attempt, effective prompting is inherently iterative: start with an initial instruction, review the output, adjust the wording or context, simplify where needed, and refine until the result aligns with your goals. As you advance, techniques such as zero-shot prompting, few-shot prompting, chain-of-thought prompting, self-consistency prompting, ReAct prompting, retrieval-augmented prompting, and meta-prompting can expand what's possible via helping models reason more clearly, ground their answers in external information, or follow more sophisticated patterns of thought and action. In practice, prompt engineering is less about memorizing templates and more about communicating with clarity, structure, and deliberate refinement, an approach that consistently produces higher-quality results across creative, analytical, and operational work.

You can learn more about prompt engineering here: `https://www.ibm.com/think/prompt-engineering`

Tools, frameworks, and techniques shaping GenAI work

Generative AI development is shaped not only by model architectures but also by the expanding ecosystem of tools, frameworks, and techniques that make these systems practical to build, adapt, and deploy. As models grow larger and more capable, the surrounding infrastructure, such as open-source libraries, retrieval pipelines, orchestration frameworks, fine-tuning methods, and evaluation tools, has become just as important as the models themselves. These components form the operational backbone of GenAI work: they determine how developers interact with models, how organizations ground outputs in their own data, how systems scale, and how reliably they behave in real-world settings. Understanding this ecosystem is essential for anyone building or integrating GenAI systems, because each layer, from model access to retrieval to orchestration, shapes what the system can do and how effectively it can do it.

Open-source ecosystems

Open-source ecosystems such as Hugging Face have become a central pillar of modern generative-AI development, offering an open-source platform that makes advanced models broadly accessible. Its Transformers library provides simple, high-level APIs for loading, running, and fine-tuning state-of-the-art models across text, vision, and multimodal tasks, reducing what once required research-lab infrastructure to just a few lines of Python code. The platform's extensive catalog of pre-trained models dramatically lowers the barrier to experimentation, enabling developers to prototype, adapt, and deploy generative systems with minimal setup. When combined with orchestration tools like LangChain that manage model chaining, tool use, and memory, these open-source components compress complex workflows into approachable building blocks that support rapid iteration and real-world application development. Together, they form a practical foundation for anyone building modern GenAI systems, from early prototypes to production-ready solutions.

Retrieval-augmented generation – grounding AI in facts

Retrieval-Augmented Generation (**RAG**) has become one of the most important techniques for making generative AI systems factual, reliable, and grounded in real data. Instead of relying solely on what a model learned during training, which may be outdated or incomplete, a RAG system first retrieves relevant information from external sources such as documents, databases, or knowledge bases and then uses that retrieved content to generate a more accurate, context-aware answer.

In practice, these external sources are stored outside the model itself, typically in a vector database, document store, or enterprise data system, and the RAG pipeline retrieves them at query time. The model does not browse the raw files directly. Instead, documents are chunked, embedded, and indexed so the retriever can efficiently surface the most relevant pieces of information. Those retrieved chunks are then injected into the model's prompt, giving it grounded context that guides the final generation. This architecture allows organizations to keep their data fresh, secure, and under their control while still benefiting from the generative capabilities of large language models.

The RAG approach reduces fabricated or outdated responses, works well with specialized domains like medical or legal content, and eliminates the need to retrain a model every time new information becomes available. It can also incorporate user-specific or organization-specific data to produce more relevant outputs. In practice, RAG systems have shown substantial gains: implementations often improve accuracy dramatically, reduce hallucination-related errors, and offer a far more cost-effective way to keep AI systems current than repeated fine-tuning. By grounding generation in real, retrieved evidence, RAG provides a practical foundation for building trustworthy, domain-aware generative AI applications.

As introduced earlier, a RAG system is specifically built on a coordinated set of components that work together to ground an LLM's output in real evidence, as shown in *Figure 6.3*.

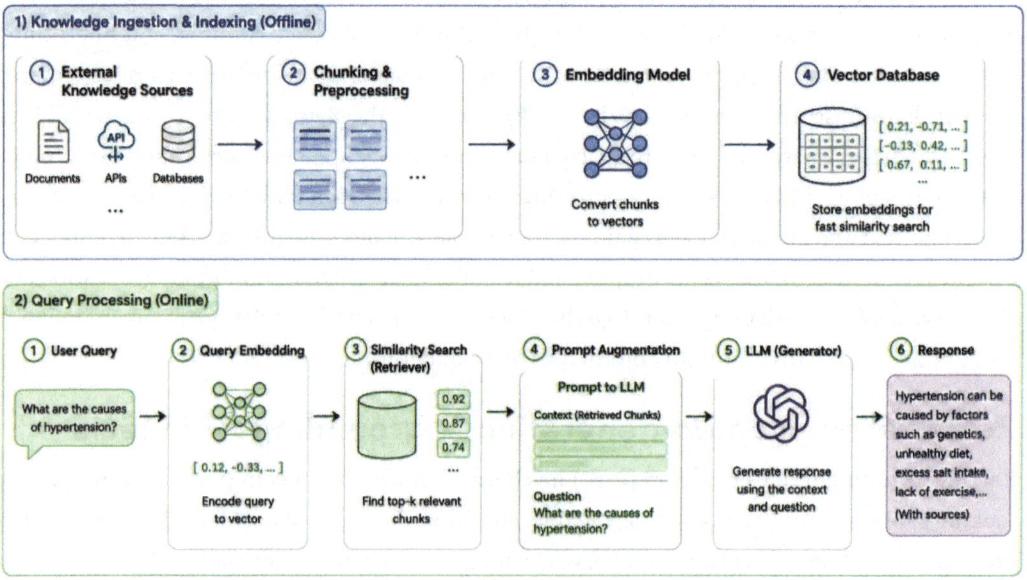

Figure 6.3: End-to-end workflow of a RAG system

It begins with an external knowledge source such as documents, APIs, or databases that hold the information the system can draw from. This content is broken into smaller, consistent chunks, and preprocessed so it can be searched efficiently. An embedding model then converts each chunk into a numerical vector (a list of numbers representing the meaning of the text in a high-dimensional space) that captures its semantic meaning, which is stored in a vector database (a specialized storage system designed to index and search these high-dimensional vectors efficiently) optimized for fast similarity search. When a user submits a query, it is encoded into its own vector (the same type of numerical representation used for documents) and compared against the stored embeddings to identify the most relevant pieces of information. A retriever selects the best matches, and a prompt augmentation layer weaves those retrieved chunks together with the user's question to give the LLM grounded context. The model then generates a response that reflects both the query and the retrieved evidence.

Retrieval strategies can vary, from pure semantic search to hybrid approaches that blend vector similarity with keyword search, reranking methods that reorder results using cross-encoders, or multi-query techniques that expand the search space for better recall. Together, these components form a pipeline that transforms raw knowledge into reliable, context-aware answers, making RAG one of the most practical architectures for building trustworthy generative-AI systems.

Vector databases form the infrastructure layer that makes RAG practical, providing the high-speed similarity search needed to match user queries with the most relevant information. Systems like Pinecone, Weaviate, Qdrant, FAISS, and Milvus each offer different strengths, such as managed scalability, hybrid search, fast filtering, in-memory performance, or enterprise-grade horizontal scaling, but all serve the same purpose: storing embeddings efficiently and retrieving the right context in milliseconds. These engines enable RAG pipelines to operate at production speed, ensuring that grounded, evidence-based responses can be generated without retraining models or slowing down applications. As organizations adopt RAG for reliable chatbots, intelligent search, and enterprise assistants, fluency in vectorization, retrieval design, and prompt augmentation has become central to GenAI architecture. Understanding how these databases power the retrieval layer is now a core competency for anyone building modern, domain-aware AI systems.

Choosing the right approach for grounding or improving an AI system often comes down to balancing cost, complexity, and the level of specialization required. Prompt engineering offers the simplest path, adjusting the input instructions to shape model behavior without modifying the model itself, which is ideal for quick, lightweight tasks where speed matters more than depth. RAG adds a layer of factual grounding by pulling in external information before generating a response, making it the preferred option when answers must reflect real-time or domain-specific knowledge. Fine-tuning goes further by retraining the model on curated, domain-specific data, producing highly specialized performance at a higher cost and with more operational overhead. At the far end of the spectrum, pre-training builds a model from scratch using massive datasets, creating a foundation for later customization but requiring substantial resources.

The tradeoff is straightforward: prompt engineering is the cheapest but least precise; fine-tuning is the most customized but also the most expensive; and RAG offers a practical middle ground, which is grounded, up-to-date responses at a moderate cost without the need for continual retraining. Understanding when to use each method has become a core skill for GenAI professionals designing reliable, scalable AI systems.

Evaluating generative AI outputs

Evaluating outputs is just as important as building the GenAI system itself, because the real measure of quality lies in how well the model's responses align with human expectations for clarity, coherence, relevance, factual accuracy, and fairness. Modern evaluation methods generally fall into three categories. Some approaches compare the model's output to human-written examples to assess how closely it matches expected phrasing or meaning. Others evaluate the output without relying on reference answers, instead checking whether the response stays consistent with the source material or avoids introducing unsupported claims. A third category uses large language models or agents as evaluators, scoring responses based on criteria such as correctness, completeness, or reasoning quality, though these methods can introduce their own biases and require careful calibration. Because the evaluator is itself a generative model, it may favor stylistic patterns, reasoning styles, or answer formats that resemble its own training distribution, leading to evaluator bias. When the model being judged is similar to the evaluator, or fine-tuned from the same base, there is also a risk of alignment drift, where the evaluator systematically over-estimates the quality of outputs that mirror its own preferences or weaknesses. These effects can distort evaluation results, mask real errors, and create feedback loops if the judged outputs are later used for further training. Mitigating these issues requires diverse evaluators, randomized prompt structures, and cross-model comparisons to ensure that judgments reflect true quality rather than model-to-model similarity.

While newer evaluation techniques often correlate more closely with human judgment, no single method is sufficient on its own; each captures a different aspect of quality and comes with tradeoffs. Developing the ability to interpret these signals, combine them thoughtfully, and critique model behavior is a practical differentiator for GenAI professionals. It moves you from simply using AI tools to understanding how to assess, debug, and improve them, which is an essential capability in any modern AI team.

Diverse technical backgrounds – interdisciplinary on-ramps to GenAI

One of the most powerful advantages in a generative AI career comes from having a diverse technical or interdisciplinary background. Modern AI systems increasingly draw ideas from multiple domains, and professionals who understand more than one way of thinking often bring insights that make these systems more capable, more responsible, and more aligned with real-world needs. Interdisciplinary knowledge strengthens everything from how models are designed to how they are evaluated, deployed, and governed, because it encourages broader perspectives on problem-solving, user experience, and societal impact. It also helps teams anticipate risks, design more inclusive solutions, and connect technical decisions to human outcomes. As generative AI becomes embedded across industries, the ability to bridge disciplines is no longer a bonus; rather, it accelerates learning, expands career pathways, and positions professionals to contribute meaningfully to the next wave of AI innovation.

Mathematics and statistics form the quantitative backbone of modern AI, shaping everything from how models learn to how their outputs are interpreted. When combined with computer science, these disciplines provide the analytical tools needed to work with large datasets, preprocess information, and train sophisticated systems. Contemporary AI architectures such as deep learning, reinforcement learning, or hybrid approaches are built through a synthesis of mathematical theory and empirical insights from fields like cognitive science. In practice, this means professionals with a strong grounding in linear algebra, probability, and statistical inference bring a distinctive advantage: they can evaluate models with rigor, detect bias through an understanding of distributions and uncertainty, design algorithms rooted in optimization principles, and structure experiments that meaningfully compare model behavior. These quantitative skills translate directly into GenAI product development, enabling practitioners not only to build systems but to understand why they behave as they do, a capability that consistently elevates the quality and reliability of AI solutions.

Neuroscience, cognitive science, and psychology provide essential foundations for understanding how to design AI systems that mirror aspects of human thought and perception. Neural networks themselves draw inspiration from the structure and signaling patterns of biological neurons, and many architectural ideas such as how models process visual information or handle sequences trace back to principles observed in the brain. Beyond architecture, insights from developmental psychology and cognitive science help explain how abilities emerge, adapt, and generalize over time, offering guidance for building models that learn efficiently, focus attention appropriately, and respond to changing environments. Professionals with training in these fields bring a unique intuition for how memory, attention, and learning operate in humans, which in turn informs how AI and agentic systems can be designed to complement human cognition rather than overwhelm it. This interdisciplinary perspective strengthens everything from model design to user experience, helping teams create systems that are technically capable as well as aligned with how people think, learn, and interact.

Physics, chemistry, and quantum computing are becoming some of the most exciting frontiers for generative AI, where advances in modeling meet some of the world's hardest scientific problems. In the physical and life sciences, generative models are already helping researchers explore vast design spaces via compressing complex molecular structures into compact representations, proposing new candidates with promising properties, and accelerating discovery cycles that once required months of manual experimentation. These approaches allow scientists to navigate chemical and materials landscapes more efficiently, identify patterns that are difficult to detect through traditional methods, and guide optimization in ways that blend theoretical insight with data-driven intuition.

On the computing side, progress in quantum technologies is opening new possibilities for simulating systems that are too large or too complex for classical hardware alone. Hybrid approaches that combine classical and quantum computation are beginning to show promise in areas such as chemistry, materials science, and optimization, pointing toward a future where quantum-enhanced workflows become part of mainstream scientific computing (`https://research.ibm.com/blog/what-s-next-in-computing-is-generative-and-quantum`). For career-minded professionals, expertise in fields like chemistry, materials science, and quantum physics places them at the intersection where generative AI is making some of its most consequential scientific contributions, an intersection where new discoveries, new computational paradigms, and new AI-driven methods are rapidly converging.

The interdisciplinary landscape of generative AI extends far beyond the technical sciences. As AI systems become embedded in everyday products and high-stakes decision environments, ethical, and legal perspectives have become essential complements to engineering. Ethicists help teams anticipate unintended consequences, identify sources of bias, and design safeguards that protect individuals and communities. Legal experts ensure that systems comply with evolving regulatory frameworks, from data-protection requirements to sector-specific standards, helping organizations navigate a rapidly shifting compliance environment. Together, these disciplines provide guardrails that keep innovation aligned with societal expectations and public trust.

Design, humanities, and social sciences contribute to another critical dimension. These fields bring a deep understanding of human behavior, culture, and communication, insights that shape how people interact with AI systems. Designers help translate complex capabilities into intuitive interfaces, ensuring that AI tools feel natural, accessible, and inclusive. Humanities perspectives broaden the lens through which AI is evaluated, highlighting cultural nuance, historical context, and the lived experiences of diverse communities. This combination leads to systems that are not only functional but also empathetic, respectful, and aligned with human values.

As AI adoption accelerates across industries, domain expertise from marketing, finance, business, education, and healthcare has become indispensable. Marketing professionals understand how people interpret messages, respond to personalization, and build trust, knowledge that directly informs how AI communicates with customers. Finance experts bring rigor in risk modeling, forecasting, and decision-making, enabling AI systems to support complex analytical workflows. Business leaders contribute operational insight, helping teams identify where AI can streamline processes, enhance productivity, or create new value. Educators bring expertise in learning science, guiding the design of AI-powered tutoring systems that adapt to student needs. Healthcare professionals provide clinical context, ensuring that AI tools are supportive and not disruptive to care delivery, patient safety, and medical decision-making. These domain perspectives ensure that AI solutions are grounded in real-world constraints and optimized for the environments in which they operate.

Linguistics and language expertise add yet another essential layer. As generative AI expands into multilingual and multicultural contexts, understanding how meaning is constructed across languages becomes critical. Linguists help teams design systems that handle ambiguity, idioms, dialects, and culturally specific expressions with greater accuracy. They guide the development of multilingual models, improve translation quality, and ensure that AI outputs remain clear, respectful, and contextually appropriate across regions. Their insights also strengthen evaluation and prompt design, helping models better interpret user intent and produce responses that align with linguistic norms.

Universities and research institutions are increasingly formalizing these intersections through interdisciplinary programs that blend technical training with social, behavioral, and domain-specific knowledge. These programs reflect a broader shift in the field: the recognition that building effective AI systems requires more than algorithms alone. It requires the combined strengths of multiple disciplines working together to create solutions that are technically sound, ethically grounded, and deeply adapted to the people and contexts they serve. For professionals entering or advancing in the field, interdisciplinary fluency is no longer optional; rather, it is a defining advantage that shapes both the quality of AI systems and the trajectory of AI careers.

From coding-only skills to human-AI collaboration

The evolution of technical skills in the generative-AI era reflects a profound shift in how people work with computational systems. For decades, being "technical" meant writing precise instructions that told a computer exactly what to do. The programmer's craft was rooted in control, determinism, and explicit logic. Today, that foundation still matters, but it is no longer the whole story. Generative AI introduces a new mode of problem-solving: one where humans guide, shape, and collaborate with models and agents rather than specifying every step. The work becomes less about dictating behavior and more about orchestrating it, via designing prompts, building retrieval pipelines, curating data, and constructing evaluation loops that steer an AI partner toward reliable outcomes. Coding remains essential, but it now sits alongside a broader set of skills that define modern technical fluency.

This shift expands the definition of what it means to be an engineer. Programming is still the backbone, but the role now includes understanding how models behave, how they fail, and how to structure interactions that produce consistent results. Instead of writing every algorithm from scratch, professionals increasingly write the scaffolding around AI systems: the APIs that call models, the pipelines that feed them context, the guardrails that constrain their behavior, and the evaluators that measure their performance. This is not a reduction of technical depth; rather, it is an expansion of technical scope. The most effective GenAI practitioners are those who can move fluidly between code, data, model reasoning, agentic orchestration, and human-centered design.

Data work has undergone a similar transformation. Traditional data management focused on querying databases, cleaning tables, and preparing features for classical machine learning models. In the GenAI era, data work includes building embedding pipelines, managing vector databases, curating retrieval corpora, and understanding how context windows shape model behavior. The quality of a generative system increasingly depends on the quality of the data that surrounds it, not just the data it was trained on. Professionals who can design these data flows, diagnose retrieval failures, and maintain high-quality knowledge sources play a central role in GenAI development.

Model understanding, once optional for many roles, has become essential. You don't need to train a model from scratch to work effectively with generative AI, but you do need to understand how these systems are structured, what their limitations are, and how to use them responsibly. Knowing how attention mechanisms work, why hallucinations occur, how underlying tokenization algorithms along with context windows influence reasoning, and how retrieval changes model behavior allows practitioners to design systems that are safer, more reliable, and more aligned with user needs. This conceptual literacy is now part of the core technical skill set.

Prompt design has emerged as a discipline of its own. It is not simply about writing clever instructions; it is about structuring tasks, defining personas, shaping context, and specifying formats in ways that produce predictable, high-quality outputs. Effective prompting requires clarity, precision, and an understanding of how models interpret language. It also requires the ability to translate domain knowledge into structured instructions that an AI system can follow. In many ways, prompt design is the new interface between human expertise and machine capability.

Evaluation and quality assurance have also evolved. Manual testing is no longer sufficient when models can generate thousands of variations in seconds. Modern GenAI workflows rely on automated evaluation pipelines that combine reference-based metrics, reference-free checks, and LLM-based judges to assess fluency, coherence, factuality, and safety. Professionals who can design these evaluation loops and interpret their signals play a critical role in ensuring that AI systems behave reliably in real-world settings. Evaluation is no longer an afterthought; it is a core engineering discipline.

Interdisciplinary knowledge once considered a *nice-to-have*, has become a competitive advantage. Domain experts who learn Python, SQL, and structured prompting can contribute to AI projects in ways that pure technologists cannot. They bring context, nuance, and real-world understanding that shape how AI systems are designed and deployed. Conversely, engineers who develop literacy in fields like design, linguistics, psychology, or business strategy gain the ability to build systems that are not only technically strong but also aligned with human needs and organizational goals. The most impactful GenAI professionals are those who build across multiple layers, not just the deepest one. This layered skill stack reveals an important career insight: growth in the GenAI era is not about abandoning your strengths but expanding around them. If you are already a strong coder, the next step is to deepen your understanding of model architectures, retrieval systems, and evaluation frameworks. If you come from a domain background, the most valuable investment is in foundational technical skills, such as Python, SQL, and structured prompting, which allow you to translate your expertise into AI-powered workflows. The professionals who cultivate breadth across layers along with strong technical depth in some will have the most durable and versatile careers in generative AI.

Ultimately, the shift from coding-only skills to human–AI collaboration marks a broader transformation in how work gets done. It is no longer enough to simply instruct a machine; you must know how to collaborate with one and do so with responsibility and purpose. The future belongs to professionals who blend technical fluency, model literacy, domain insight, and human-centered design with a commitment to responsible AI and the intent to use these systems for societal good. Those who pair skill with stewardship will shape the next generation of AI systems, and the organizations that deploy them.

Summary

The generative AI revolution is built on a foundation of hard skills that give professionals the ability to understand, shape, and guide intelligent systems. Programming, data management, and core machine learning concepts remain essential, forming the technical anchor on which modern AI workflows are constructed. To this foundation, a new layer of literacy has emerged: the ability to communicate with models through structured prompting, to design retrieval and orchestration pipelines, and to build evaluation loops that ensure systems behave reliably. These skills transform generative AI from an abstract capability into a practical tool, one that can be deployed, monitored, and improved in real-world environments.

Beyond these fundamentals, the modern GenAI toolkit includes the ability to operationalize ideas at scale. Professionals must understand how to integrate models into applications, manage context, and data flows, and evaluate outputs with rigor. They must be comfortable moving between conceptual understanding and hands-on implementation, knowing when to rely on model behavior and when to intervene with guardrails, retrieval, or evaluation. This blend of depth and adaptability is what turns prototypes into production systems and experimentation into impact.

Interdisciplinary backgrounds amplify this technical core. Insights from neuroscience, cognitive science, linguistics, physics, business, healthcare, and the humanities enrich the way AI systems are designed and applied. These perspectives help teams understand how people think, how organizations operate, how scientific discovery unfolds, and how cultural context shapes user experience. No single discipline can capture the full complexity of AI's impact; it is the combination of diverse expertise that accelerates innovation and ensures systems are grounded in real-world needs.

Mastering these hard skills does not require becoming an expert in every domain. Instead, it means developing enough depth in the areas most relevant to your path and enough breadth to collaborate effectively across the GenAI stack. The professionals who thrive are those who can open the hood of generative systems, understand the principles that drive them, and use that understanding to build, evaluate, and refine solutions that matter. They are able to translate between technical and non-technical perspectives, bridging gaps that once separated engineering, design, research, and domain expertise. In the chapters ahead, we will further explore how these technical foundations intersect with the strategic, creative, and interpersonal capabilities that define leadership in the AI age.

In the next chapter, you will learn the essential soft skills that complement AI expertise. These skills will help you work effectively with AI systems while providing the human judgment, creativity, and contextual understanding that machines cannot easily replicate.

7

Cultivating Technical and Human Skills for the Agentic AI Era

Because agents autonomously read untrusted data from emails, web crawls, and third-party documents, they are highly vulnerable to **Indirect Prompt Injection**...*Critical thinkers must master the* **Instruction Fidelity Auditing (IFA)** *mindset.*

– Dr. Ali Arsanjani

The transition from generative models to autonomous agents marks a definitive shift in software architecture. In this new paradigm, the model is merely the cognitive engine; the true technical edge belongs to engineers who can design, secure, and orchestrate the *operational scaffolding* that surrounds it. This is the domain of **Agent-Oriented Software Engineering (AOSE)** and **Harness Engineering**.

We need to be aware that as autonomous systems automate routine but complex and highly technical tasks, the human role transitions from *in-the-loop execution* to *above-the-loop strategic governance*. In this environment, uniquely human soft skills are not supplementary attributes; they are the primary mechanisms of system control and alignment. They will be your indispensable human advantage.

This chapter therefore brings these two dimensions together, exploring both the technical expertise required to build and orchestrate agentic systems and the human skills needed to govern them effectively. The first part covers some important technical aspects, and then we move on to the soft skills.

Specifically, in this chapter, we will cover the following key topics:

- Foundational systems and execution concepts
- Prompt optimization and structured reasoning
- Context engineering and agentic epistemic memory
- Harness engineering: Governance and boundaries
- Strategic oversight: Human-Above-the-Loop
- Redefining critical thinking: Instruction fidelity auditing
- Non-Human Identity governance and ethical judgment
- Privacy-preserving collaboration

Foundational systems and execution concepts

While Python remains the undisputed lingua franca of AI, the requirements for writing agent-compatible code have fundamentally evolved. Aspiring AI professionals must master the following modern execution paradigms:

1. **Portable, standardized scripting with PEP 723 and uv**: AI agents often dynamically generate or execute Python scripts to solve deterministic mathematical or data-processing tasks. To ensure these scripts execute seamlessly across heterogeneous environments without manual dependency intervention, the industry leverages **PEP 723 (Inline Script Metadata)**. Combined with fast package managers like **uv**, scripts declare their own isolated environments directly in their file headers:

```
# /// script
# requires-python = ">=3.11"
# dependencies = [
#     "pandas",
#     "scikit-learn",
#     "pydantic>=2.0",
# ]
# ///

import pandas as pd
# Agentic execution logic continues below...
```

When an agent invokes `uv run scripts/analyze.py`, the runtime automatically parses the inline metadata, instantiates an isolated virtual environment, installs the dependencies, and executes the script silently. This eliminates the "environment-rot" that frequently causes agent tools to crash in production.

2. **Asynchronous runtimes and multi-agent concurrency**: Because agents frequently wait for database queries, web scraping returns, and external API requests, synchronous execution causes severe performance bottlenecks. Practitioners must design agent runtimes using async frameworks (such as Python's asyncio or FastAPI). This allows agents to operate in parallel, passing messages via asynchronous event queues and avoiding blocking calls.

Having explored the technologies and execution paradigms that enable modern AI agents, let's now examine how these components come together to form the architecture and operational workflow of an agentic system.

The anatomy of agentic AI

To build or utilize an agent, you must understand its internal cognitive and operational loop. Unlike a stateless chatbot, an agent operates continuously on a standardized cycle:

$$\text{Sense} \longrightarrow \text{Reason} \longrightarrow \text{Plan} \longrightarrow \text{Coordinate} \longrightarrow \text{Act} \longrightarrow \text{Reflect}$$

Figure 7.1: Agentic AI operating cycle

Let's consider this standardized cycle in detail:

1. **Sense (Perception)**: Gathering data from the digital environment (APIs, system logs, vector databases) or physical streams (IoT sensors).
2. **Reason (The Brain)**: Leveraging high-reasoning LLMs to interpret sensory data, extract causal relationships, and align inputs with target goals.
3. **Plan**: Decomposing a complex, open-ended target (e.g., "Audit this portfolio's counterparty risk") into a serialized DAG (Directed Acyclic Graph) of sub-tasks.
4. **Coordinate**: Communicating with peer agents to delegate tasks, negotiate resources, and share state.
5. **Act**: Executing deterministic actions via API tool-calls, database mutations, or code execution.
6. **Reflect**: Critically evaluating the outcomes of completed actions against expected states, self-correcting mistakes, and committing insights to memory.

Prompt optimization and structured reasoning

Basic "persona prompting" has been replaced by programmatic optimization and structured reasoning frameworks that enforce logical accuracy.

Fractal Chain-of-Thought (FCoT) and self-correction

Rather than asking an LLM to "think step-by-step" in a single linear pass, **Fractal Chain-of-Thought (FCoT)** forces the model to recursively decompose its own reasoning. For every major step in its plan, the agent must spawn a sub-reasoning loop:

- State the proposed conclusion.
- Generate a counter-argument challenging that conclusion.
- Resolve the contradiction before proceeding.

This internal logical tension dramatically minimizes logical drift, ensuring that the agent does not latch onto an early reasoning error and amplify it across a long-horizon task.

DSPy and programmatic prompt compilation

Writing system prompts by hand is increasingly recognized as a brittle, "vibe-coded" anti-pattern. Frameworks like DSPy treat prompts as mathematical weights. Engineers write declarative modules (defining input and output schemas) and compile them over a set of training examples. The compilation compiler programmatically tests, bootstrap-prompts, and refines the instructions to optimize target evaluation metrics, turning prompting into a rigorous optimization discipline.

Context engineering and epistemic memory

An agent operating near the end of its context window suffers from severe reasoning degradation and omission hallucinations. **Context Engineering** is the discipline of managing an agent's focus and memory dynamically.

Figure 7.2 illustrates how epistemic memory is organized into two tiers: ephemeral memory for daily logs and append-only auditing, and durable memory for curated, persistent factual knowledge:

```
┌──────────────────────────┐
│ EPISTEMIC MEMORY         │
└──────────────────────────┘
                 │ │
┌────────────────┘ └────────────────┐
```

```
      ▼                                ▼
┌─────────────────────────────┐ ┌─────────────────────────────┐
│ EPHEMERAL MEMORY            │ │ DURABLE MEMORY              │
│ Daily Logs (JSONL)          │ │ Curated MEMORY.md           │
│ Append-only Auditing        │ │ Factual Belief States       │
└─────────────────────────────┘ └─────────────────────────────┘
```

Figure 7.2: Two-tiered epistemic memory

To prevent the agent's context from becoming bloated with conversational noise, modern architectures implement a two-tiered memory engine:

- **Tier 1: Ephemeral memory (Daily Logs):** An append-only JSONL transaction ledger that records the literal transcript of every interaction, action, and observation within a session. This is indexed for semantic search but rotated out of active memory.
- **Tier 2: Durable memory (MEMORY.md):** A curated, human-readable file containing the agent's updated belief states, core constraints, user preferences, and verified project facts.

Pre-compaction memory flush

When active session tokens hit a soft threshold (e.g., 75% of the context window), the runtime triggers a silent agentic turn, which is the **pre-compaction flush**. The agent is commanded to extract and write all critical, newly learned facts from the raw conversation history into its durable MEMORY.md file, before the runtime "compacts" (summarizes or truncates) the active transcript.

Hybrid search (Vector + SQLite FTS5)

Standard semantic vector search struggles to retrieve exact technical codes, variables, or unique IDs. High-performance agents may utilize a **70/30 Hybrid Search** approach, blending high-dimensional vector similarity with BM25 keyword matching via SQLite FTS5. This ensures the agent retrieves information accurately, whether the user refers to it conceptually or via an exact database key.

Harness engineering: Governance and boundaries

Harness Engineering is the operational layer that surrounds an agent, defining its capabilities, verifying its compliance, and restricting its blast radius.

As shown in *Figure 7.3*, the control plane enforces policy over the data plane, where the primary agent accesses tools through a gateway that blocks unsafe commands before execution in a secure sandbox:

```
┌────────────────────────────────────────┐
│ CONTROL PLANE
│
│ [Policy-as-Code] [IFA Supervisor]     │
└───────────────────┬────────────────────┘
│ Enforces Policy
▼
┌────────────────────────────────────────┐
│ DATA PLANE
│
│ [Primary Agent] ──▶ [Tool Gateway]│
└───────────────────┬────────────────────┘
│ Blocks Bad Commands
▼
[Secure Sandbox]
```

Figure 7.3: Standardizing tool integration with Model Context Protocol

Developed as an open standard, the **Model Context Protocol (MCP)** standardizes how LLM applications communicate with external data sources and tools. Instead of writing bespoke, brittle API wrappers for every database, repository, or service, developers build modular MCP servers. The agent client queries the MCP server's schema to dynamically discover available resources, tools, and prompts via a JSON-RPC interface. However, MCP does not enforce security principles at the protocol level. Implementors are responsible for establishing robust user-consent mechanisms, authorization flows, access controls, and data protections

Agent-to-Agent protocols and opaque execution

When multiple enterprise systems must collaborate, they utilize the open-source **Agent-to-Agent (A2A)** protocol. Under A2A:

- Agents advertise their capabilities, endpoints, and security requirements via an Agent Card (.well-known/agent.json).
- Agents negotiate tasks asynchronously over HTTP(S) using structured JSON-RPC.

- They enforce Opaque Execution: agents never expose their internal prompts, toolchains, or private memories to other agents; they only transmit well-defined tasks, inputs, and verified artifacts, preserving corporate IP and data privacy.

Containerized sandboxing and isolation

To prevent a compromised agent from executing destructive commands (e.g., recursive file deletion), the execution of code and tools must be isolated in the following ways:

- **WASM sandboxing:** Compiling community-built agent skills into WebAssembly runtimes, preventing them from accessing the host file system or network without explicit privilege delegation.
- **Ephemeral execution envelopes:** Restricting agents to isolated, short-lived Docker containers or MicroVMs that are completely wiped at the end of each task execution.

As covered so far, portable execution environments and asynchronous runtimes support reliable operation, while structured reasoning, context engineering, and epistemic memory improve decision-making and continuity. Harness engineering, MCP and A2A protocols, policy enforcement, and sandboxed execution further provide the governance boundaries required to control agent behavior and reduce operational risk.

However, technical expertise alone is not enough to ensure that agentic systems serve organizational and human goals responsibly. As people move from direct execution to strategic oversight, they must complement their engineering knowledge with critical thinking, ethical judgment, governance awareness, and effective collaboration. The next section explores these human capabilities and their role in supervising and governing effective agentic AI systems.

Strategic oversight: Human-Above-the-Loop

In the traditional *Human-in-the-Loop* model, human operators manually validate every small step of a process. This approach is slow, expensive, and fails to scale. In contrast, the **Human-Above-the-Loop (HATL)** model positions the human as a strategic supervisor:

- **Human:** Sets goals, establishes ethical policies, audits execution
- **AI agents:** Autonomously plan, invoke tools, handle exceptions
- **Guardian agents:** Monitor execution, enforce "kill switches", escalate alerts

◀———— HUMAN-ABOVE-THE-LOOP (HATL) ————▶

Humans define the objectives, write the core "constitutions", and audit completed trajectories. The autonomous agents execute the day-to-day coordination and tool work. When an agent encounters an action with catastrophic real-world risk (e.g., executing a high-value wire transfer), it triggers a **Human-in-the-Loop Mutation Gate** (e.g., ClawBands), requiring the supervisor to provide biometric confirmation (e.g., Face ID or hardware-token approval) before the action is executed.

To guide this strategic oversight, humans must wield the EPOCH framework (`https://papers.ssrn.com/sol3/papers.cfm?abstract_id=5028371`). EPOCH stands for:

- **Empathy:** Understanding unspoken user needs and customer contexts that structured data cannot capture
- **Presence:** Managing high-stakes, real-time human relationships and physical operations
- **Opinion:** Injecting authoritative, value-driven judgments on complex business scenarios
- **Creativity:** Out-of-the-box lateral thinking to devise brand-new business strategies
- **Hope:** Inspiring team purpose and vision in times of market disruption

Redefining critical thinking: Instruction fidelity auditing

In the agentic era, critical thinking is no longer just about checking facts; it is about auditing **systemic logical integrity**.

Because agents autonomously read untrusted data from emails, web crawls, and third-party documents, they are highly vulnerable to **Indirect Prompt Injection.** A malicious carrier manifest or a hidden line of white text on a website can command an agent to ignore its system prompt and exfiltrate sensitive credentials.

Critical thinkers must master the **Instruction Fidelity Auditing (IFA)** mindset with the help of the following steps:

1. Isolate data from instructions: Ensuring that the agent's core instructions are hard-anchored and unable to be overwritten by external inputs.
2. Verify provenance: Tracing every entry in an agent's memory back to a cryptographically signed source and a human decision, preventing Memory Poisoning attacks.
3. Evaluate causal trajectories: Inspecting the agent's execution log not just for a correct final answer, but for a valid, safe pathway of tool utilization.

Non-Human Identity governance and ethical judgment

Ethical judgment must now expand to cover the governance of digital autonomous workers. When an agent acts on behalf of an employee or enterprise, it must have a clearly defined **Non-Human Identity (NHI)**. The following are the core principles for establishing and governing NHIs:

- **Least-privilege scoping:** Scoping agent identities with granular tool permissions. Agents should never inherit a human user's master API key.
- **Risk-adaptive access control:** Dynamically adjusting an agent's security clearance based on its current operational context and risk score.
- **Short-lived credentials:** Utilizing rotatable tokens with short lifetimes (e.g., 24-hour TTL) to minimize the impact of a potential credential exfiltration event.

Privacy-preserving collaboration

Ensuring data sovereignty and privacy within multi-agent networks requires strategic implementation of **Privacy-Enhancing Technologies (PETs)**:

- **Confidential computing:** Running sensitive model inferences in hardware-isolated, encrypted processor domains (such as Intel TDX or NVIDIA secure enclaves), shielding proprietary data from multi-tenant cloud providers.
- **Differential privacy:** Injecting mathematical noise into shared agent memory stores or training sets to prevent agents from accidentally memorizing or leaking specific, private user transactions.

The following table summarizes the key soft skills required in the agentic era, explaining their significance and illustrating how they are applied in real-world AI systems:

Skill	Why it matters (in the agentic context)	Example application
Fidelity auditing and critical thinking	Evaluating multi-agent trajectories for logical drift, hallucinations, and indirect prompt injection attacks.	Auditing a logistics agent's proposed route to detect hidden prompt injections in carrier emails.

Above-the-Loop orchestration	Designing, managing, and evaluating complex multi-agent workflows while setting high-level strategic boundaries.	Re-architecting a brittle mortgage approval pipeline into a collaborative team of validation and underwriting agents.
Constitutional alignment	Translating human policies, ethical values, and regulatory compliance rules into machine-enforceable agent constitutions.	Embedding compliance constraints directly into an investment agent's prompt to prevent unapproved trading strategies.
Identity and NHI governance	Designing and managing secure credentials, tool access, and accountability models for non-human autonomous workers.	Implementing scoped OAuth 2.1 tokens to prevent a research agent from accessing sensitive employee HR directories.
Cognitive resilience and adaptability	Navigating rapid changes in model capabilities, tool protocols (such as MCP), and emerging security threats.	Upgrading an enterprise workflow from static APIs to standard MCP servers during an infrastructure modernization.
Inter-agent mediation	Resolving conflicts, data discrepancies, and coordination bottlenecks between specialized autonomous agents.	Mediating a deadlock where a logistics agent and a finance agent disagree on supply chain rerouting costs.

Table 7.1: Re-engineered soft skills for the agentic era

Summary

In this chapter, we explored the technical aspects of agentic AI, including portable and asynchronous execution, the agent operating cycle, structured reasoning, context engineering, epistemic memory, and hybrid retrieval. We also examined harness engineering, MCP and A2A communication, policy enforcement, opaque execution, and sandboxing techniques for building secure and reliable agentic systems.

We then focused on the human capabilities required to govern these systems effectively, including Human-Above-the-Loop oversight, instruction fidelity auditing, ethical judgment, Non-Human Identity governance, and privacy-preserving collaboration.

The key lesson is that effective agentic AI cannot be achieved through technical expertise alone. Building trustworthy systems requires engineers and leaders who can combine robust architectures with strategic oversight, ethical judgment, secure governance, adaptability, and human-centered decision-making.

In the next chapter, we will explore emerging agentic AI roles, career progression levels, and practical upskilling pathways for building a successful career in the evolving AI workforce.

8

Strategic Career Moves: Entry, Transition, and Upskilling

> *"Organizations are creating a new hierarchy of specialized roles focused on technical implementation, governance, security, and strategic leadership. For both graduates and transitioning professionals, upskilling should focus on building practical, auditable systems rather than static prompt experiments."*
>
> *– Dr. Ali Arsanjani*

Growth is the driving force behind both organizations and individuals, influencing decisions ranging from business strategy to personal career goals. From entry-level positions to highly specialized roles, career transitions and professional growth have always been central to long-term success. However, the rapid adoption of AI has accelerated this evolution like never before. As organizations redesign workflows and embrace intelligent automation, professionals are rethinking the skills they need and the career paths they want to pursue. While AI is changing the nature of work, it is also creating new opportunities for those prepared to adapt. After all, every technological revolution has rewarded those who learned to evolve with it.

The maturation of agentic systems has further transformed the workplace, disrupting traditional entry-level technical roles while creating entirely new categories of highly compensated, strategic positions. Rather than following a fixed career ladder, professionals must now continuously upskill, embrace lifelong learning, and understand where human expertise complements AI. Career planning in this new era requires a clear understanding of these emerging roles and a structured path to acquiring the skills they demand.

In this chapter, we will explore how this new career landscape is taking shape and what it means for professionals at every stage of their journey. You'll discover the emerging roles created by agentic AI, understand the skills they demand, and learn practical pathways to transition into them. Whether you are a student preparing for your first role, an experienced professional considering a career shift, or a leader planning the future of your workforce, this chapter will help you navigate the opportunities created by the AI era with confidence.

This chapter will cover the following key topics:

- Modern, emerging agentic AI roles
- Practical upskilling and transition pathways
- The AI professional's job leveling matrix

Modern, emerging agentic AI roles

As the adoption of agentic AI accelerates, organizations are creating a new hierarchy of specialized roles focusing on technical implementation, governance, security, and strategic leadership. The following agentic career ladder illustrates how professionals can progress from entry-level positions to leadership roles in this evolving ecosystem:

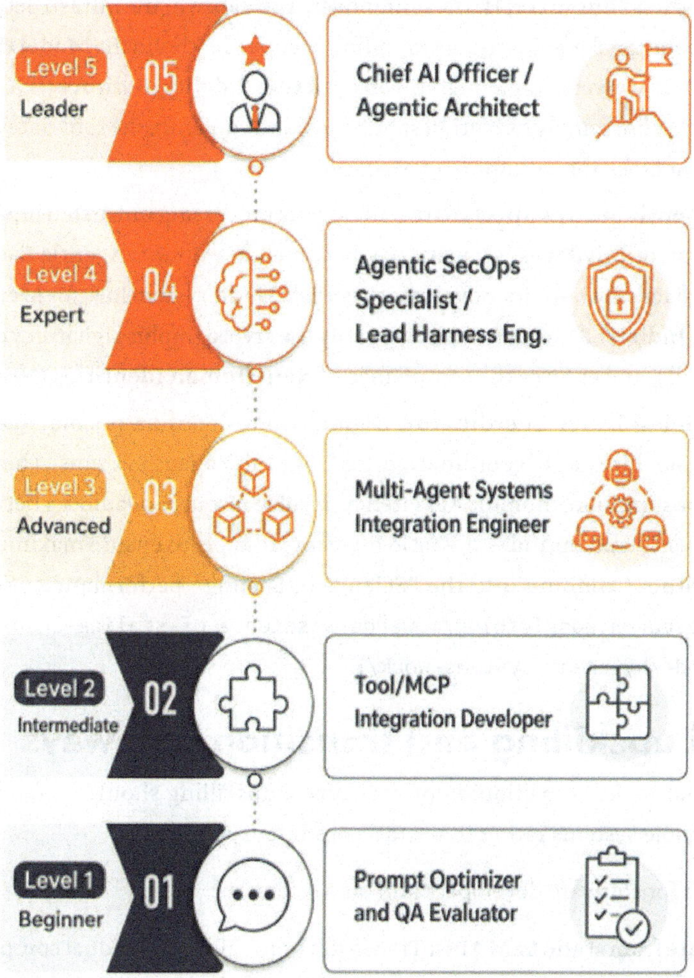

Figure 8.1: The agentic career ladder

The following roles represent some of the most prominent career opportunities emerging in the agentic AI industry. While each role has a distinct area of responsibility, they work together to design, deploy, secure, govern, and optimize autonomous AI systems in production:

- **AI Orchestrator/Agent Supervisor**: These professionals are the team leaders of the digital workforce. They do not write raw code; instead, they design agentic workflows, construct the instruction prompts, define role-specialized "agent crews," and audit agent performance. They are experts in human-agent collaboration patterns, configuring the ideal balance between autonomous execution and human-in-the-loop checkpoints.

- **Harness Engineer**: Harness Engineers specialize in the infrastructural security and operational boundaries surrounding agents. They build the **Model Context Protocol (MCP)** servers, implement the **Instruction Fidelity Auditors (IFA)**, enforce Docker or WebAssembly execution sandboxes, and configure the tool-gateway chokepoints that block rogue command execution.
- **Agentic SecOps Specialist:** With agents processing untrusted inputs and wielding system privileges, security has become paramount. Agentic SecOps Specialists proactively hunt for novel attack vectors, audit system logs for **Memory Poisoning** or **Indirect Prompt Injections**, verify the cryptographic signatures of installed agent skills, and enforce the compliance of **Non-Human Identities (NHIs)**.
- **Digital Labor Coordinator**: Digital Labor Coordinators manage the economics, scalability, and "coordination tax" of multi-agent systems. They analyze token consumption, monitor API latency, resolve resource deadlocks between competing agents, and optimize the ratio of agents to tools to ensure maximum business ROI without running into the "Science of Scaling" performance ceilings (`https://research.google/blog/towards-a-science-of-scaling-agent-systems-when-and-why-agent-systems-work/`).

Practical upskilling and transition pathways

For both graduates and transitioning professionals, upskilling should be focused on building practical, auditable systems rather than static prompt experiments.

Transition path for software developers and data scientists:

1. **Graduate from static LLM APIs:** Transition from calling individual completion endpoints to constructing stateful, multi-turn graphs using frameworks like Google ADK, LangGraph, or CrewAI.
2. **Master function calling and MCP:** Learn to expose internal databases and custom Python functions as secure, standard tools.
3. **Implement security containment:** Practice deploying your agents in isolated, rootless container environments, configuring API rate-limiting, and managing scoped IAM roles.

Learn more about Google ADK by referring to the official documentation: `https://adk.dev/`.

Browse the official documentation for more information on LangChain: `https://docs.langchain.com/oss/python/langgraph/overview`.

Get guidance on building collaborative AI agents, crews, and flows that are production ready: `https://docs.crewai.com/`

Transition path for non-technical professionals:

1. **Develop systemic thinking:** Learn to write clear, unambiguous standard operating procedures (SOPs). In the agentic era, a well-written SOP is easily compiled into an agent skill.
1. **Master no-code/low-code builders:** Leverage platforms like Vertex AI Agent Builder or Google AI Studio to build functional, goal-oriented personal productivity agents.
2. **Become an expert evaluator:** Learn to design "golden datasets" of ideal outputs, evaluating agentic reasoning trajectories, and validating compliance.

The AI professional's job leveling matrix

The following leveling matrix outlines the skills and competencies required across the career spectrum of Agentic AI:

Career Path	**Level 1: Beginner**	**Level 2: Intermediate**	**Level 3: Advanced**	**Level 4: Expert**	**Level 5: Leader**
Agent/ Harness Engineer	Basic Python scripting Writing structured prompts	Developing MCP servers Implementing basic tools	Building stateful agent graphs (ADK, LangGraph) Configuring sandboxes	Designing dual-model IFA supervisors Developing custom WASM compilers	Architecting enterprise agentic infrastructure Scaling A2A deployments

AI Orchestrator / Project Manager	Understanding agent capabilities Mapping business processes	Designing single-agent tools Coordinating prompt versions	Managing role-specialized agent crews Tuning HATL gates	Optimizing tokenomics and cost per query Managing model and workflow drift	Formulating organization-wide digital labor strategy Aligning with the Chief AI Officer (CAIO)
Agentic SecOps Auditor	Basic OWASP awareness Traditional IT logging	Managing rotatable credentials Implementing basic input filtering	Auditing for indirect prompt injection attacks Sandboxing tools	Defending against memory poisoning attacks Enforcing RBAC+ for NHIs	Defining global agentic compliance standards Implementing multi-mesh defense strategies

Table 8.1: The AI professional's job leveling matrix

Based on what we learned in the chapter, here are your action items:

- **Establish your sandboxed development lab:** Clone a local-first repository, set up uv, and write standard Python tools utilizing inline metadata. uv is a Python package and project manager developed by Astral (`https://docs.astral.sh/uv/`).
- **Build your first MCP server:** Standardize your local database or file connections using the Model Context Protocol.
- **Draft an agent constitution:** Practice writing an immutable system prompt utilizing **Fractal Chain-of-Thought** (**FCoT**) and audit its execution paths.

Summary

In this chapter, you explored how the rise of agentic AI is reshaping careers and creating new opportunities across the workforce. You learned about the emerging roles that are defining the next generation of AI-enabled organizations, the skills required to succeed in them, and practical pathways for transitioning into these careers. You also examined how continuous upskilling has become an essential part of professional growth.

Beyond understanding individual roles, you were introduced to the job leveling matrix, a framework that helps map career progression from foundational to advanced levels of expertise. Together, these concepts will help you navigate the new roles that are part of the workforce, enabling you to make informed career decisions and build the skills needed to thrive in the age of agentic AI.

In the next chapter, we will examine industry use cases to see how GenAI and multi-agent systems are being applied to solve real-world challenges.

Part 4

The Gen AI Landscape: Understanding the Revolution

Part 4 explores how generative AI is transforming industries such as finance, healthcare, software development, marketing, education, and supply chain management through real-world applications. You'll also learn the end-to-end process of building and deploying LLM-powered applications, including model development, evaluation, integration, and multi-agent systems, enabling you to design practical AI solutions for diverse business scenarios.

This part contains the following chapter:

- *Chapter 9, Applied Generative AI: Industry Use Cases and Multi-Agent Systems*

9

Applied Generative AI: Industry Use Cases and Multi-Agent Systems

> *AI could potentially anticipate customer needs even before they explicitly state them and proactively reach out to the customer via different channels to offer help and take care of an issue.*
>
> *– Leonid Kuligin*

The overall landscape in the tech industry is becoming more competitive than it has been during the last decade. Excellent tech skills do not guarantee landing a job quickly anymore. In *Chapter 7*, we discussed the importance of mastering soft skills; now, we're shifting to another aspect. When an organization is looking to hire a generative AI engineer, it is often seeking someone who understands the overall landscape and can lead (or co-lead) the corresponding business changes across the organization. Candidates are expected to drive business transformation and not only be technical leaders, but also become strategic partners for business, capable of contributing to the company's long-term strategy and vision besides contributing to its code base. Such abilities might become your key differentiator in interviews and on the job.

So, what does it mean in practice? You might expect questions like these:

- What do you think about the recent GPT-5 model released by OpenAI?
- What is your view on MCP or A2A protocols?
- What do you think about how generative AI is disrupting the finance sector?
- Looking five years into the future, what do you believe will be the most significant societal or economic impact of generative AI in the construction industry?
- Will we reach the AGI next year?
- What do you consider the biggest non-technical risk for a company deploying a customer-facing generative AI tool?

These questions might not be directly relevant to evaluating your technical skills, nor directly related to the job. However, a good answer might help set you apart from other candidates, and this aspect is sometimes overlooked during interview preparation.

In this chapter, we'll look at some tips for interview preparation and discuss some examples of how different industries are transforming with generative AI.

The following key topics will be covered in this chapter:

- Mastering strategic thinking about generative AI impact
- How generative AI is transforming industries
- Multi-agentic systems

Mastering strategic thinking about generative AI impact

The ability to bridge the gap between technical possibilities and business realities is what truly sets you apart as a candidate and helps you to position yourself as a future leader who can navigate the evolving landscape of artificial intelligence and drive innovation. Combining a broad generative AI expertise with your domain experience and field experience might be a great boost for your career. That means you need to master your strategic thinking about the industry on top of your hard skills. We suggest including three aspects in your preparation:

- Master answering (and thinking about!) business-centric questions.
- Be prepared to have a meaningful conversation about how generative AI would transform software development (or another) industry you are expert at. For software engineers, it's important to be opinionated on what generative AI changes in the software development industry.

- Be prepared to talk about how generative AI would affect the industry in which the company you're applying to operates.

We'll begin by looking into the first topic, then we'll discuss potential changes in the software industry, and give you a few examples of how you could reason about other industries. Keep in mind that there are no right or wrong answers to such questions. You should be able to express your ability for strategic thinking and analytic skills, your deep understanding of industry trends, your broad outlook, and your ability to communicate clearly on complex topics. And of course, such work goes beyond preparation for the interview. Regular analysis of key trends helps you prepare yourself to drive the transformation across an organization. Hence, if you want to build a successful career in this field, we highly recommend that you go beyond mastering your technical skills. Of course, generative AI in general is a very large area, and you can't become an expert in all related topics, but growing your horizontal expertise will be a good investment of your time and effort.

Let's dive into preparation tips. Your goal is to understand the "why" behind the technology, not just master the "how." This starts with investing time weekly in reading high-quality business and strategy content. You need to cultivate a specific mindset and breadth of knowledge. We suggest a few tools that you can add to your toolset.

First, pay attention to broad trend reports. Focus on quality over quantity. Spend 1-2 hours each week reading and analyzing, keeping a backlog of truly valuable reports to study. Resist the hype and be selective. Invest your time only in genuinely worthwhile assets. When a new report comes out, give it a quick scan to judge its importance and decide whether it's worth adding to your queue for a deeper dive.

You can find here a few examples of high-quality reports published in 2025 (but do not be limited by them, check for the latest report available or explore other providers):

1. AI Index 2025, a more than 450-page-long report published by the Stanford Institute for Human-Centered AI (`https://hai.stanford.edu/ai-index/2025-ai-index-report`)
2. Mary Meeker, an American venture capitalist, was writing Internet Trends reports back in the day, and in 2025, she and her team came back with the AI Trends report: `https://www.bondcap.com/report/tai/`
3. Another famous report is the State of AI, regularly produced by AI investor Nathan Benaich and Air Street Capital: `https://www.stateof.ai/2024`

You can continue this list and add reports from McKinsey, Nvidia, and other top consulting and industrial companies. What else? Consider subscribing to the blogs of top industry players. Companies such as OpenAI, Anthropic, Google (Google Research), and others often publish important research papers and technical reports in their tech blogs. You don't necessarily need to deeply read each of them, but at least scan and grasp a quick idea of what is discussed.

Another great source of insights is podcasts. Research which podcasts CEOs and top researchers of top generative AI companies and venture funds (Anthropic, Google, DeepMind, OpenAI, Perplexity, Y Combinator, Sequoia, and so on) visit. Subscribe to these podcasts and listen selectively to the episodes that are interesting to you. Podcasts often provide a lot of insights into how these people think about the future, what their bets and beliefs are, and what the reasoning behind them is. You do not need to agree with everything being said, but it would help you to build your own line of arguments.

It might sound obvious, but it's sometimes overseen by engineers working at large companies. Try the most recent foundational models and different products around them. Understand what OpenAI, Google, Anthropic, and others are releasing, and develop your own view on Perplexity, ElevenLabs, and so on. Read tech reports, look at the recent API changes, and invest some time into trying these products and APIs yourself. Look at the startup ecosystem, especially in the industry you're working in. Try their early products, look at the most recent funding rounds, and what large VCs believe in.

Last but not least, utilize social networks. Many AI researchers still use X extensively, so it might be a good idea to start with LinkedIn and X. Research people and accounts you'd like to follow, and try to train your feed by giving it explicit feedback on the posts you'd like to see (upvoting, downvoting, or commenting on certain posts). Your feed should become a constant source of important signals and updates to you.

These days, the key challenge is not finding information. It's about filtering out noise and focusing on what's important and valuable. You need to find a delicate balance between being overwhelmed by all the information flow that exists and taking the time to study, analyze, and decompose important industry trends and developing a big picture. To summarize, you might include the following sources in your picture:

- Industry reports
- Tech blogs from leading tech companies and venture funds such as Anthropic, Google Research, OpenAI, Y Combinator, and so on
- Podcasts with CEOs and top researchers from these companies

- New products and announcements (changes in the foundational models, APIs, and consumer products) from these companies and trending startups in your industry
- Tuned newsfeed on X, LinkedIn, and other work-related social networks

Of course, feel free to add additional tools to this toolset that you find fit (such as newsfeeds, Substack, contributing to open source, online courses, etc.). First, invest time in collecting useful signals and building your own system to filter out noisy signals. Once you develop a source of high-quality information, start investing 1-2 hours a week into building up your strategic vision and intuition behind the changes that are happening in the industry. Disruptive times demand a lot of learning and staying open-minded.

How generative AI is transforming industries

Generative AI is impacting almost every industry, from video production or supply chain management to education, insurance, and retail. We're going to discuss five examples (software development, marketing, customer relationship management, finance, and healthcare) with slightly different perspectives. I also suggest a simple framework that helps you to think about any other industry, and you can apply the learning to the industry you're particularly interested in.

Software development

We will start by discussing how generative AI might reshape software development. Just to reiterate, I don't think I can give you a final prognosis, but that's not what is expected from a candidate. You should be able to understand the polarities of different forecasts and articulate your own position. Your reasoning, broad outlook, and your readiness to take calculated bets are what matter. Nobody knows whether your answer is right or wrong. But why do you believe something might happen? What are alternative hypotheses? How do you articulate your beliefs? And how do you update your beliefs based on the new evidence?

Software development might become the first industry truly disrupted by generative AI. According to the Stanford 2025 AI Index report, more than 13% of enterprises surveyed by McKinsey in 2024 mentioned code creation as a generative AI use case of interest. According to another study, "*Navigating the generative AI disruption in software,*" published by McKinsey in 2024, software development would account for approximately 40% of enterprise spending on generative AI, accounting for the largest share. Why? First, there's plenty of training data that represents code in different programming languages. Second, developers of LLMs and services based on LLMs are engineers themselves; hence, they understand very well various aspects of the job and incorporate this knowledge when training LLMs. Third, the software development flow is often well-suited for agentic workflows since, for most of the tasks, no real-time answer is required, and an agent can run simulations in the background.

How are LLMs' code capabilities being evaluated? These are three of the most popular benchmarks:

- Human Eval is a benchmark introduced by OpenAI in 2021. It includes >150 well-structured programming problems crafted by humans. You can find the leaderboard at `https://evalplus.github.io/leaderboard.html`.
- The SWE-bench dataset was presented at the ICLR 2024 by C. Jimenez et. al., and it includes more than 2,000 real-world software engineering tasks (a GitHub issue and a corresponding pull request in Python) that were sampled from real code repositories. You can explore the SWE-bench leaderboard at `https://www.swebench.com/`, compare foundational models versus more complex agents, and see an impressive gain in performance over time.
- The latest Polyglot benchmark (introduced in 2024) is not only Python-based, but it also includes >200 difficult coding problems in various languages originating from the educational platform Exercism, and you can explore the leaderboard here: `https://aider.chat/docs/leaderboards/`.

Last but not least, LLMArena (`https://lmarena.ai/leaderboard`) crowd-sources anonymous comparisons between various LLMs by collecting feedback from volunteers, and there are two separate coding-related benchmarks: WebDev (which includes web development problems related to HTML, CSS, and JavaScript) and Copilot (which includes tasks related to understanding and generating code).

When exploring leaderboards, keep in mind performance across different foundational models: proprietary versus open-weighted, large (with longer inference time and inferred costs) versus small (fast inference, low cost of ownership), prompting foundational models directly versus complex agents.

Code generation is the first function that comes to mind when thinking about how generative AI might influence the software development industry, but in fact, there are multiple ways that you can imagine:

- Improving developer productivity with fast code-aware autocomplete incorporated in the IDE (and Jupyter or Colab can also be treated as a Python IDE).

- Helping software engineers by solving "boring" tasks such as writing unit tests, migrations, and refactoring. Coding agents work asynchronously on given tasks (or they identify bottlenecks themselves) and raise pull requests that are reviewed by humans. The key distinction in this case is that such agents can follow multiple paths, try to compile their written code and recover from failures, and simulate various options since they are not limited by time.
- Real-time assistance for software developers with writing code when working on specific tasks. Coding agents act as a copilot to a human developer, when humans task them with specific prompts and provide real-time feedback, and agents are aware of the code base on the other side.
- Acting as an assistant for software engineers and architects to help them find solutions for tricky questions, generate documentation, co-develop solutions, and design software. Like any intellectual work, software engineering can benefit from using LLMs (grounded on the web or the company's knowledge bases) used in "classical" ways.
- Code-aware generation assistance (question-answering, generating documentation and examples, etc.) helps people across the organization to better understand how their systems work, generate feature requests, and debug customer issues. OpenAI Codex, Claude Code, Gemini Code Assist, and other coding agents have these capabilities.
- Democratizing access to the data across the entire organization by using text-to-SQL agents and other agents that can develop visualization, reason, and answer complex questions based on the organization's business data. For example, business teams can potentially analyze sales, investigate sudden spikes and declines, and do modeling and forecasting using AI agents without the need to involve data analysts or data scientists.
- Developing quick prototypes through vibe coding using agents, such as Cursor, Lovable, and others.

> Vibe coding is an approach that allows you to develop code by using a natural language interface (just prompting LLMs or dedicated software development agents).

Let's put together in a table key scenarios, relevant technologies, and other aspects of how GenAI influences software development:

Scenario	Relevant technologies	Audience	Examples
Code-aware autocomplete	Context-aware text (code) generation	Developers	JetBrains Mellum AI, Gemini Code Assist, GitHub Copilot
Asynchronous work on tasks or improving the existing code base	Agentic workflows with environment feedback, Tree-of-Thoughts, Monte-Carlo Tree Search, multi-agentic systems	Engineering teams	Codex, GitHub Copilot
Vibe coding	Same as above	Engineering and business	Lovable, Cursor
Real-time assistance in code generation	RAG, code generation agents with a feedback loop	Developers	Cursor, Claude Code, Gemini Code Assist, Gemini CLI, local open-weighted LLMs
Real-time assistance in complex tasks (not code-related)	Question-answering, web grounding, multi-modal generation, reasoning	Developers and architects	OpenAI, Gemini, Anthropic Claude, local open-weighted LLMs
Code-aware text generation	RAG, code generation	Engineering and business	Codex, Gemini Code Assist, GitHub Copilot
Data analysis	Code generation, text-to-SQL, reasoning models	Engineering and business	BigQuery Studio, Cursor, Claude Code, QueryGPT

Table 9.1: Key user journeys in software development being transformed with generative AI

If you are interested in a real-world example, I would recommend checking the *Real-world engineering challenges: building Cursor* blog post (`https://newsletter.pragmaticengineer.com/p/cursor`) from Gergely Orosz, which provides an overview of how the Cursor architecture looks and what the main engineering challenges are to build such an assistant.

Software engineering is an especially challenging industry since the issue of how to estimate engineering productivity has been open for decades. On the other side, LLMs or coding agents assist developers in generating material artifacts (such as generated code or documentation). There have been multiple controlled studies performed by companies such as Microsoft (GitHub), McKinsey, Amazon, and others that demonstrate substantial productivity gains from AI code development tools. Interestingly, researchers looked at different success metrics, such as the following:

- GitHub reported in their *Unleashing developer productivity with generative AI* study that developers with GitHub Copilot demonstrated the ability to **complete tasks** up to 55% faster, and completion rates were also higher (78% versus 70% in a controlled group without GitHub Copilot). McKinsey reported similar numbers in their study across multiple task categories, such as writing new code (up to 35-45% productivity gain), documentation generation (up to 45-50% productivity gain), and code refactoring (up to 20-40% productivity gain).
- GitHub also reported that developers' satisfaction with their job improved, and they made a point that it's one of the key aspects of developers' productivity. They asked such questions as whether they felt less fatigue when completing tasks, if they felt more fulfilled with what they were doing, and the amount of time they spent in the flow during their working hours.

Is the overall picture really that rosy? When evaluating the generative AI's effect on a given industry, I always recommend researching side effects. Many people use generative AI tools for research tasks these days, especially Deep Research features that Gemini, Perplexity, and other assistants offer (and if you haven't used them, we hope you'll start doing so after reading this book)! Please remember that the quality of such an assistant's answer depends on the prompt. Hence, I recommend also running a separate prompt that focuses on critique, negative, and side effects. Prompt AI to provide supporting evidence, such as research papers, controlled studies, and other trusted sources, and carefully review such evidence.

Let's briefly discuss the main concerns that experts raise with respect to the application of generative AI to software development. First, strictly speaking, from a mathematical point of view, in a static, well-defined system, a lot of small improvements (such as AI code suggestions) lead to a better state. But the global optimum is still not guaranteed. To illustrate an analogy, imagine that you're traveling up the hill in the fog. If you're always going upwards, you will eventually reach the top. But because of the fog, you might overlook a higher hill nearby, hence you might end up not on the highest hill in the area. Real-world software systems are even more complicated than such a simple example.

There might be some overlooked consequences, and good-looking changes might fundamentally change the system and lead to disastrous, unintended consequences. I myself have seen systems with a high proportion of AI-generated code (or even fully vibe-coded) that stopped functioning well, and making any change became almost impossible because of very complicated, unreadable, and heavy-to-maintain code that was auto-generated earlier. Such anecdotal evidence has been reported multiple times, and the industry still needs to design a better benchmark oriented on the long-term stability and maintainability of software systems. Every senior developer knows that the biggest challenge is not to implement a particular feature but managing future complexity and making systems easy to extend. The biggest challenge software engineers experience is typically in the integration of various systems. As a matter of fact, we don't have good benchmarks to evaluate AI on such tasks yet; all we test is its ability to solve puzzles and simple tasks. So, the point raised by some of the senior folks in the industry is a valid one, and it has to be studied. Multiple studies have demonstrated that the gain in developers' productivity was smaller than expected, or even negative. For example, a non-profit called **Model Evaluation & Threat Research** (**METR**) published a study in July 2025 on the impact of AI on developer productivity in open source, and they found that "*when developers use AI tools, they take 19% longer than without AI.*"

Second, some concerns are raised around potential security vulnerabilities. I'm not saying these risks cannot be addressed; there's a high likelihood that existing coding agents could be improved on this side, or other generative AI agents that help with security could be introduced. But these risks are there. The **Center for Security and Emerging Technology** (**CSET**) at Georgetown University published an extensive report on the cybersecurity risks of AI-generated code. They identify risks around coding assistants generating insecure code and being vulnerable to attacks from the outside. They demonstrated that 48% of snippets generated by coding assistants in their study had vulnerability risks. Multiple other studies confirm these risks at the current level of coding assistants.

We will look at a few other industries that could potentially be disrupted by generative AI. But before switching to that, let's briefly summarize the approach I propose to research the impact of generative AI on a given industry.

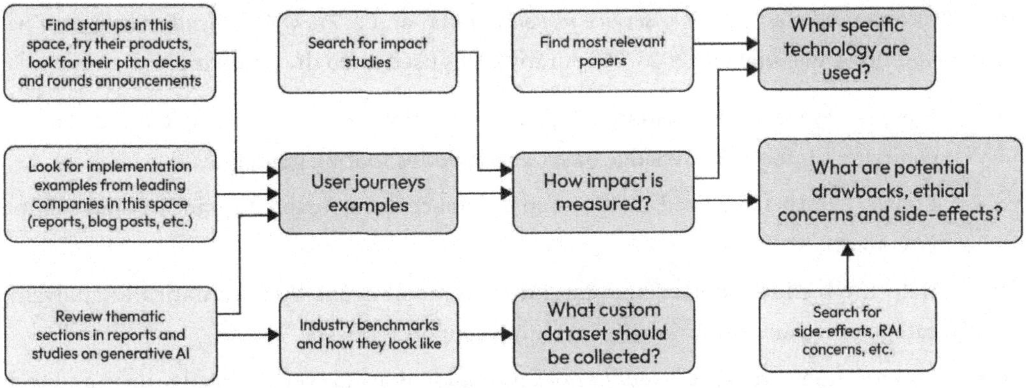

Figure 9.1: Analyzing the impact of generative AI on a given industry

You will find some actions (in green) in the preceding flowchart, and I think you could start by answering the following:

- Examples of user journeys that can be addressed (partially or fully) with generative AI
- Industry-specific benchmarks, performance of open-weighted versus proprietary LLMs, requirements on dataset collection and evaluation
- Specific technologies (for example, agentic architectures) can be used to address the user journeys. What kind of engineering skills and talent are needed?
- Success criteria and the ways to measure the impact of real-world implementations
- Potential drawbacks, ethical and responsible AI concerns, and side effects to consider

Now, let's use the same approach and take a look at a few other industries.

Customer relationship management

Customer support is an important function of almost any business. To think a little bit more broadly, we should discuss **customer relationship management** (**CRM**) in general, which covers all aspects of a company's interactions with customers.

CRM is one of the fields where generative AI adoption is growing rapidly, and it's far beyond prototypes. Chatbots, assistants for human customer support agents, and other solutions are rolled out across multiple organizations. HubSpot, one of the leading US providers of customer service solutions, mentioned in their *2024 State of Service Trends Report* that "*92% of CRM leaders say AI has improved their customer service response times*" and "*77% of CRM leaders believe AI will handle most ticket resolutions by 2025.*" Generative AI is used to do the following:

- Provide support to the customer 24/7 via a text or voice chatbot, being grounded on the company's internal knowledge bases and troubleshooting guidelines
- Provide more personalized answers and assistance to the customer, going beyond a simple FAQ solution
- Help the business better understand customers' needs by automatically analyzing, categorizing, and summarizing incoming support requests
- Give a customer more self-service options (and thus avoid even the need to open a support ticket) and provide true omni-channel coverage across the phone, website, social media, messengers, and so on

Organizations start by building more intelligent chatbots and virtual assistants on top of existing solutions to automate customer support, but with generative AI, they can take a further step and shift to proactive customer care. AI could potentially anticipate customer needs even before they explicitly state them and proactively reach out to the customer via different channels to offer help and take care of an issue.

When evaluating generative AI's impact on CRM, enterprises look at metrics such as customer satisfaction and customer churn, time to resolution, cost of support, and the ability to scale support with the company's growth.

Some engineering aspects of CRM applications

There are a few aspects that an engineer should take into account when preparing for a conversation or an interview:

- Implementing text and voice chatbots with short-term and long-term memory: Think about what frameworks you would use and how your architecture would look; look into such engineering aspects as streaming, web sockets, what speech-to-text and text-to-speech solutions to use, how to generate a "native" voice, how to handle multilingual conversations, and so on.
- Implementing a chatbot with RAG solutions and grounding answers on custom knowledge bases: What indexing and retrieval strategies would you use, how would you implement and evaluate retrieval, and what vector databases would you recommend? But besides that, keep in mind that knowledge in organizations is often represented across multiple unstructured sources (for example, support tickets, internal wikis, multiple documents in various formats – scans, videos, and so on).

- Adding multimodal input to chatbots (for example, a customer could send photos or videos illustrating their issue, and an AI assistant would use them for troubleshooting).
- Balancing latency and quality: what role fine-tuning of smaller and/or open-weighted models plays, how you can blend small and large foundational models, and how to manage the costs of the solution
- Security guardrails to prevent the unintentional use of a chatbot and any harm to users or the brand that could be caused by its answers.

Evaluating text and voice chatbots is still a developing area with a lot of unsolved challenges. The industry is still looking for good and reliable ways to measure performance across such pillars as conversation quality (such as brand values alignment, emotional intelligence, and understanding underlying intents in multi-turn conversations), accuracy and trust (whether AI was grounded on appropriate data, hallucination rates), and the ability to resolve an issue successfully (driving a high containment rate, which means AI was able to handle the conversation from the beginning to the end without the need to escalate it to a human, and a high resolution rate, which means that the customer's issue was successfully resolved). You should be prepared to speak about key challenges in evaluation, what you would suggest to solve them, and how you would collect and organize evaluation datasets.

To reiterate on the importance of evaluation, Klarna, a Swedish fintech company offering **buy now, pay later** (**BNPL**) services, was one of the first large enterprises that scaled customer support based on OpenAI models, back in 2023. It was handling more than 75% of support tickets with generative AI in more than 35 languages, and short-term metrics such as time to resolution and costs looked impressive. Nevertheless, in 2025, they admitted that fully automated support doesn't necessarily meet their service standards, and they increased the role of human agents in customer care.

Marketing

Marketing is another industry that has been undergoing a significant transformation with generative AI. According to the Salesforce State of Marketing Report 2024, around 32% of marketing organizations "*have fully implemented AI in their workflows, and an additional 43% are experimenting with it.*" By 2025-2026, these rates are expected only to increase. Adobe 2025 Digital Trends Report mentions that 86% of senior executives expect generative AI "*to significantly increase content speed and volume.*"

Marketing, especially in the social media era, is about generating content, and that's the most natural task you can imagine for generative AI. Generating content at unprecedented volumes with low costs allows better personalization of advertisements and product offerings to various groups of customers. For example, think of a furniture retailer that can now generate dozens of various interiors for each item they're selling. Modern image generation models have become so advanced that by the end of 2024, people had difficulties distinguishing actual photos of human faces from AI-generated ones.

Let's take a look at key user journeys in marketing influenced by generative AI:

- Create novel and personalized content in multiple formats: text, images, video, audio. Video generation is still a frontier for LLMs, but models from OpenAI (Sora), Google (Veo), Stability AI, and other providers demonstrate impressive capabilities in video creation. In their "2025 Digital Video Ad Spend & Strategy," (`https://www.iab.com/insights/video-ad-spend-report-2025/`) IAB estimates that around 30% of all digital video ads were created by generative AI in 2024, and this share is expected to reach 39% by 2026 (note that the adoption rate is even higher for small and medium businesses). Such automation significantly cuts costs for producing content, allowing brands to experiment more, and reach a higher level of engagement and personalization. Another direction is the development of digital twins of human models and celebrities (of course, with their consent) and using these digital twins for a fast and scalable production of thousands of marketing videos. For example, H&M launched such a campaign in July 2025 based on 30 digital twins (`https://www.just-style.com/news/hm-ai-digital-twins-denim/`).
- Virtual try-ons of various sorts that provide a different level of experience for customers choosing specific products. For example, Sephora SA, a French retailer of beauty and personal care products, introduced a Virtual Artist app that allows customers to try makeup virtually (`https://www.sephora.sg/pages/virtual-artist`).

  Nike introduced Nike Fit, a tool that allows a user to scan their feet with a phone's camera and map foot morphology to the shoe size (`https://www.forbes.com/sites/andriacheng/2019/05/09/this-new-nike-fit-feature-could-be-a-game-changer/`).

- Marketing is a data-driven area with a lot of effort spent on cleaning, unifying, and analyzing data on various campaigns from different data sources. Low-code tools utilizing generative AI and text-to-SQL capabilities can reduce the routine and help marketing specialists with the creative and most rewarding part of their job. This aspect is similar to software development, so refer to the corresponding preceding section if you're interested in more details.

- **Generative search optimization** (**GSO**) is a new area that comes on top of well-known **Search Engine Optimization** (**SEO**). Why is it an emergent trend?

Generative AI has fundamentally changed how users find and interact with information. We are moving from a paradigm of searching and clicking to one of asking and receiving. It's difficult to predict what share of users will switch to this new way of consuming information, but the audience is definitely getting big enough. ChatGPT has more than 700 million active weekly users (as of August 2025; `https://www.cnbc.com/2025/08/04/openai-chatgpt-700-million-users.html`). And according to TechCrunch, Google AI Overview (an AI-generated answer on top of search results provided for some queries) has more than 2 billion monthly users (`https://techcrunch.com/2025/07/23/googles-ai-overviews-have-2b-monthly-users-ai-mode-100m-in-the-us-and-india/`). That means you might want your relevant links and information about your product and services to be included in AI-generated content. It is not enough that your website is ranked high enough in some list of links; you need to optimize a brand's entire digital footprint to ensure its content is selected, summarized, and cited within AI-generated search results. In particular, you need to make your web content available for corresponding crawlers, optimize your pages for LLM understanding, and run other experiments to improve your visibility.

Some engineering aspects of marketing applications

Since marketing use cases are mainly focused on image and video generation, it might be a good idea to understand how diffusion models are different from transformer-based LLMs, and what the video generation workflow could look like (a model creates an initial starting point and tries to gradually improve it while running the generation pipeline). Take a look at recent image and video model capabilities and the specific API they offer. The basic aspects include questions such as what video generation length various models support, or what resolutions for generated images and videos they offer. But often such models offer advanced capabilities beyond "vanilla" image generation – for example, Imagen from Google allows editing an uploaded image using a user-defined mask (or without it).

Take a look at industry-specific benchmarks and the quality of recent-generation models, specific prompting techniques used for image and video generation, and evaluation aspects for specific use cases.

Marketing use cases often require a multi-step agentic flow to solve the task. For example, generating a viral video advertisement includes multiple steps and foundational models (text-generating, image-generating, and video-generating) as shown in *Figure 9.2*:

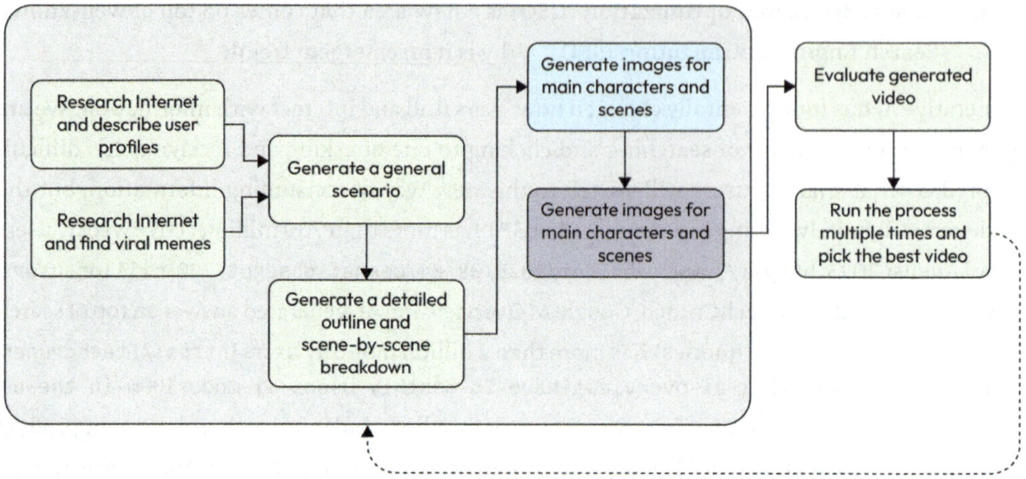

Figure 9.2: An example of agentic flow to generate a video ad

Think about 1-2 agentic flows that you might suggest for a specific use case, or take existing use cases reported by industry players and try to imagine how they could solve a problem, and only then search for technical details of their implementation. That might help you train your system design skill very quickly.

Finance

As the next example, let's look at the finance industry. Finance in general, and banking and investment banking in particular, is, in essence, the business of information arbitrage. Its core function is to process all the available information in any form and identify opportunities to efficiently allocate capital. Generative AI's ability to understand and generate natural language is a paradigm shift in how finance operates.

User journeys include the following:

- Automating and augmenting knowledge work and helping humans to discover new and subtle nuances from the large amount of structured and unstructured data (such as financial reports, meeting transcripts, customer feedback, etc.), including such aspects as report generation, compliance checks, financial and investment analysis, preparing pitch decks, discovering trading signals, and so on. For example, Morgan Stanley uses a generative AI-powered chatbot to enhance its 16,000 wealth managers and financial advisers by giving them easier access to internal data and research (`https://www.cnbc.com/2023/03/14/morgan-stanley-testing-openai-powered-chatbot-for-its-financial-advisors.html`).

- Improved operational efficiency and productivity by touching such areas as customer care, client communications, sales, and software development.
- Improving risk management and compliance by analyzing customer and transactional information at scale to improve financial crime and **anti-money laundering** (**AML**) models. For example, HSBC mentions in their *Harnessing the power of AI to fight financial crime* report (2024) that the new *Dynamic Risk Assessment* model allowed them to identify "*two to four times more financial crime than we did previously*" and at the same time, false positive rates declined by 60% (`https://www.hsbc.com/news-and-views/views/hsbc-views/harnessing-the-power-of-ai-to-fight-financial-crime`).
- Developing a new generation of trading algorithms and price predictive models. For example, JP Morgan used an LLM to analyze speeches and public communications from central banks (including the Federal Reserve) to predict whether interest rates would be raised or decreased (`https://www.bloomberg.com/news/articles/2023-04-26/jpmorgan-s-ai-puts-25-years-of-federal-reserve-talk-into-a-hawk-dove-score`). Nubank, a major neobank in Latin America with more than 100 million customers, trained its own model to predict price signals and get better product recommendations. You can read their paper "*Your Spending Needs Attention: Modeling Financial Habits with Transformers*" to get more details on how they transformed transactional data into transformer-based representations and used them to train their model that performed better than their previous extensively tuned XGBoost-based one (`https://arxiv.org/abs/2507.23267`).

Besides new opportunities and a dramatic increase in productivity, generative AI also brings significant threats to the financial industry. Bad actors use its capabilities to generate fake videos and messages, and mimic personalities at scale for fraudulent activities, and financial institutions have no other choice but to use AI to fight back against attackers.

Some engineering aspects of financial applications

When talking about generative AI in finance, we should start with RAG. Start with the "classic" RAG and aspects of building retrievals on large amounts of unstructured data, including hybrid search, informational retrieval, query expansion, and so on. Go beyond that with architectures such as agentic RAG or graph RAG (to analyze connected sources and entities). Look into multimodal capabilities of modern LLMs and use long context (an ability of modern LLMs to handle very long inputs, from 128K to 2M tokens) to process a large context. Financial data typically contains a lot of tables, and often it's a PDF, Excel, or a scan, so it's important to understand advanced parsing and chunking of such data (for example, to preserve the table structure, heading, and context of the chapter, etc.). Last but not least, factuality is very important in this industry, so you need to master aspects of LLM grounding and output verification.

Next, think about how you can utilize all financial data, including transitions, in your generative AI applications. Financial analysts often require data modeling, and that includes SQL generation, exploration of source metadata, advanced visualizations, and generating scripts for financial modeling (which brings us back to the applications of generative AI in software development we discussed in the previous section).

One additional aspect to look into is using **large models (LMs)** for time-series data. On one side, you can transform sequential numerical data into a text sequence and use existing or fine-tuned foundational models for forecasting. Multiple specialized large transformer-based models were trained on vast amounts of sometimes unrelated time-series data and can perform zero-shot time-series forecasting. Examples include TimesFM from Google, with 200 or 500 million parameters, Chronos from AWS (with up to 710 million parameters), and MOIRAI (with up to 311 million parameters) from Salesforce.

Healthcare

Current challenges in healthcare are related to rising costs, staffing shortages, demographic shifts, and the increasing complexity of medical knowledge. Generative AI is well-positioned to address some of these challenges and help human professionals meet the rising demand for medical care. On the bright side, Generative AI can assist doctors and nurses, increase their operational efficiency, and let them focus on the most complex aspects of their jobs.

The ability of modern LLMs to pass complex medical exams is well documented, especially since recent versions can deal with multimodal input (such as X-ray images or photos). Of course, this reminds us how well medical exam benchmarks (most of which are multiple-choice questions) represent the actual ability of an LLM to assist a medical professional, but first implementations demonstrate good results. Applications of generative AI vary from assisting with note-taking and information retrieval to specialized clinical decision support systems that go through clinical trials. For example, **Helsinki University Hospital (HUS)**, the largest healthcare provider in Finland, rolled out an AI assistant that helps doctors with translations, retrieving information on internal medical guidelines, and preparing reports (`https://www.tietoevry.com/en/success-stories/2024/generative-ai-pilot-assists-clinicians-at-new-childrens-hospital/`). Clinical decision support systems are still in development and simulated testing, only slowly proceeding to clinical trials. For example, researchers at Yale evaluated GutGPT, a **clinical decision support system**

(CDSS) to help doctors with the treatment of acute upper gastrointestinal bleeding management (`https://www.nature.com/articles/s41746-025-01896-5`), and researchers at the School of Medicine and Health at TUM demonstrated the benefits of using generative AI to assist with the treatment of rare gynecological tumors (`https://www.nature.com/articles/s41746-025-01810-z`).

Let's look at examples of some user journeys:

- *Therapy adherence* represents the patient's ability and willingness to follow a prescribed treatment plan.

  Modern medical treatment approaches often are pretty complex and difficult to grasp for somebody not trained as a medical professional, and clinical recommendations meet real-world human behavior and physiological aspects. It is well documented across finance, medicine, and other use cases that, in some cases, human behavior is not fully rational, especially if we, as humans, lack domain knowledge on a subject. The more time medical professionals can devote to explaining details behind therapy to the patients, the higher the adherence rates are, and the better decisions humans make (when, for example, choosing a treatment option such as a surgery). The problem is, as usual, that the time a doctor can devote to a patient is often very limited. Generative AI could act as a cost-effective coach that enhances the doctor and explains to patients details of their treatment, helps them cope with difficult news, provides psychological support, and provides detailed answers grounded in curated sources such as patient handbooks and treatment plans (escalating difficult cases to humans). For example, Epic Systems, a US company that develops large-scale **electronic health record (EHR)** software systems, developed an assistant called MyChart AI, which drafts replies and messages to patients (beyond many other tasks) (`https://www.fiercehealthcare.com/ai-and-machine-learning/epic-touts-new-ai-applications-streamline-charting-and-bring-research`). A US healthcare start-up, Neru Health, develops an LLM-based voice AI solution to keep patients engaged with Obstructive Sleep Apnea therapy and improve their therapy adherence (`https://www.neruhealth.com/blog`).

- Research assistants significantly accelerate drug discovery.

  For example, traditionally, the process of determining the 3D structure of proteins was an expensive and time-consuming manual process that required actual laboratory experiments and measurements. Google DeepMind developed AlphaFold, an AI-based solution that can predict a protein's 3D structure from its amino acid sequence with accuracy close to that of the laboratory. Isomorphic Labs, a company within Alphabet, is preparing to start clinical testing of drugs developed with AI (`https://fortune.com/2025/07/06/deepmind-isomorphic-labs-cure-all-diseases-ai-now-first-human-trials/`). Another related example is Coscientist, an "*artificial intelligence system driven by GPT-4 that autonomously designs, plans, and performs complex experiments*" (`https://www.nature.com/articles/s41586-023-06792-0`) developed by researchers at Carnegie Mellon University.

According to McKinsey, operational overhead accounts for up to 25% of total US healthcare costs (`https://www.mckinsey.com/industries/healthcare/our-insights/ai-ushers-in-next-gen-prior-authorization-in-healthcare`).

Generative AI can help increase operational efficiency and assist insurance companies in better and faster handling of healthcare claims. For example, Prudential uses LLMs to analyze documents (such as diagnostic reports or invoices) supporting claims and assist human agents to process claims faster and more accurately (`https://www.prudentialplc.com/en/news-and-insights/all-news/news-releases/2024/24-10-2024`).

Wearable devices are becoming more and more popular, and they collect plenty of signals that can be used for preventive medical care. I already mentioned LMs specialized in time-series forecasting when we were talking about the financial industry. The same type of LMs can be applied in healthcare. An example is a *Gluformer*, "*a generative foundation model for continuous glucose monitoring (CGM) data that learns nuanced glycemic patterns and translates them into predictive representations of metabolic health*" (`https://arxiv.org/abs/2408.11876`).

Some engineering aspects of healthcare applications

What engineering aspects should you focus on when thinking about applications of generative AI in healthcare? You can start with "classical" and multimodal RAGs, grounded on custom knowledge bases, working with long context, image understanding, voice AI, and chatbots, guardrails, regulatory, safety, and ethical aspects of using foundational models. Many medical use cases are based on voice AI, and voice chatbots still utilize a pipeline that converts voice to text, sends it to an LLM, and generates voice based on its answer. Hence, look at the quality of speech-to-text and text-to-speech models, what customization does voice generation allow, and so on. Be able to provide the cons and pros of such a "classical" approach versus tasking a multimodal foundational model to generate speech based on voice input directly. Another aspect is multilingual support, especially when covering the use cases oriented to patients. How well do LLMs perform in non-English languages? How can your system support many languages with high quality?

There are plenty of custom (proprietary and open-weighted) AI models: MUSK for precision oncology, Radfound for radiology, and many others. Look at the landscape of these models, details on their performance, cost-effectiveness, and, of course, what public data is available. From the architecture side, take a look at how diffusion models and **large vision-language models (LVMs)** are different from "classical" transformer-based LLMs. And, of course, medical imaging still remains one of the most important real-world applications of ML in diagnostics (according to Stanford HAI, around 80% of FDA-cleared ML software is related to medical imaging).

Many medical organizations prefer to use self-hosted foundational models, so you should be able to present the pros and cons of such decisions, including aspects of performance, benchmarking, compliance, and legal.

Multi-agentic workflows are another important topic. Researchers have demonstrated that multi-agentic flows work well for complex diagnostic cases. For example, according to Microsoft, their AI Diagnostic Orchestrator (MAI-DxO) was able to diagnose up to 85% of case records published by the New England Journal of Medicine. It performed better and was more cost-efficient than a group of experienced physicians (`https://microsoft.ai/news/the-path-to-medical-superintelligence/`). Be prepared to present some multi-agentic architectures (supported by research publications) and explain why they work well for a given use case. Another example is a virtual AI lab introduced by Stanford to advance biomedical research (`https://www.nature.com/articles/d41586-024-01684-3`), which includes LLM-based agents with different roles collaborating.

Evaluation is another really important aspect that we should keep in mind when discussing applications of generative AI in healthcare. How would you proceed with evaluation and simulations on a given use case? How would you design a clinical trial? What guardrails would you implement? What are the key ethical and operational risks to address when designing such a system? Development of healthcare AI systems often requires synthetic data, so take a look at this topic, including aspects such as privacy preservation.

Of course, a very interesting aspect is that biology and biochemistry are two of the few domains where start-ups are training tailored foundational models. Foundational models trained on DNA, RNA, amino acids, and other types of sequences help to study genes and genetic mutations, understand proteins' functions, and design molecules that target specific proteins, study cell types, their interactions, and their response to specific treatments. Hence, you might cover some aspects of this setup and how generative AI can be applied in the field of personalized medicine, bioengineering, and drug discovery.

Multi-agentic systems

Developing **multi-agentic systems** (**MAS**) is a controversial but important aspect of generative AI applications. Traditionally, enterprises tend to develop large, centralized systems focused on solving a specific complex problem or automating a given business process. When we developed an ML-based solution, such an approach involved collecting datasets specific to each narrow use case, training tailored ML models, and improving the performance of the system step by step.

In contrast, MAS are composed of multiple, often smaller and more specialized, AI agents that collaborate to achieve a common goal. Each agent can be thought of as an independent entity with its own set of skills and knowledge. Why do we need multi-agency at all? Let's start looking at some of the assumptions behind agentic workloads in general.

First, generative AI benefits from scaling laws. In general, models trained on large amounts of weights and large amounts of data get emergent capabilities, and in general become better if we increase these amounts (of course, we can also optimize the architecture and training process, but the general trend still holds). Since there is not enough data to train foundational models for narrow use cases, we need to tune foundational models trained on general data in different ways: with prompt engineering, agentic workflows, or fine-tuning. In other words, even for very specific enterprise use cases, we typically still use LLMs trained for general purposes, and agentic workflows are one way of customizing these LLMs.

Secondly, it has been demonstrated that generative AI workflows benefit from collaboration and task decomposition. Specialized agents working on subtasks might be based on the same foundational model but use various customizations (as mentioned previously). So, our workflow starts using multiple specialized agents collaborating with one another.

Last but not least, in most industrial use cases, generative AI agents need to interact with the external environment (it is often referred to as *tool calling*). In short, a *tool* is an API that has a description of when and how to use this tool, which includes a description of its schema (often in OpenAPI format). An LLM is very good at generating tokens that represent the name of the tool to be called (when appropriate), a valid payload for this tool, and a final answer for a user based on the previous tool calls. So, we provide an LLM with a set of tools that it should use to solve a specific task, and they use tools to explore the environment, gather new information, improve their reasoning, validate a solution, or even act on behalf of a human to complete the task. We are not going into details on engineering aspects of designing MAS, but please, feel free to take a look at the additional sources suggested in the *Further reading* section.

Now, let's take it a step further. What if we give our agentic workflow an even larger degree of freedom? Let's expose all tools and agents available within our enterprise to an LLM that is the "brain" behind the workflow. An LLM could itself pick the most appropriate tool to solve the task or a subtask, and different agents could find their own way of collaborating on a task, without the need for a predetermined control flow. This is the idea behind the **Model Context Protocol (MCP)**, an open industry standard introduced by Anthropic in 2024. The official definition states that MCP "*standardizes how applications provide context to LLMs.*" In other words, it's a client-server architecture that allows the easy connection of LLMs with external data sources and tools. It aims to simplify the development, scalability, and interoperability of MAS. You can go beyond integrating a single agent with tools. Agent-to-agent, or A2A, is an open standard introduced by Google in 2025 that allows communication and collaboration between independent AI agents, and it facilitates discovery, task delegation, and coordination among different agents.

Finch, a financial AI agent developed by Uber for their financial teams, is a real-world example of a MAS (`https://www.uber.com/en-DE/blog/unlocking-financial-insights-with-finch/`). Financial analysts needed to analyze complex financial data. Identifying the right source and writing SQL queries often became a bottleneck for financial teams, and it's a boring and time-consuming task anyway. Finch is integrated directly into the company's Slack environment, and it allows asking questions in natural language. A supervisor agent interprets the query and routes it to the most appropriate specialized sub-agent (for example, an SQL writer agent, which is responsible for constructing and executing an SQL query).

So, how nice would it be to give a very smart LLM full freedom to explore all options (such as tools, data sources, and specialized agents available within your enterprise), so that it finds a way to utilize them in the optimal way to solve a complex problem. This is the North Star of MAS, and its proponents highlight increased scalability, efficiency, and flexibility that such systems would bring. On the contrary, there's a rising critique that highlights performance and security risks associated with MAS. Some researchers demonstrated that multi-agentic workflows fail on up to 40% to 60% of benchmark examples (`https://arxiv.org/pdf/2503.13657`), and this rate might be even higher on vertical enterprise use cases. Enterprise use cases require high reliability and accuracy, and multi-agentic workflows suffer from coordination breakdowns and misalignment across specialized agents, specification errors, infinite loops, redundant work, and context loss.

Another big issue is safety and jailbreaking. It has been demonstrated that MAS are vulnerable to jailbreaks, including so-called *infectious jailbreaks* when a single compromised agent leads to the whole system being compromised in an uncontrolled way (`https://arxiv.org/abs/2402.08567`, `https://arxiv.org/abs/2309.15817`).

It's difficult to predict how quickly we will be able to solve these problems and how widely MAS will be adopted in the real world. The issue of evaluation and ensuring the reliability and safety of agentic workflows is still an unsolved challenge in the industry. But that makes it even more important and interesting, and maybe you might contribute to solving this challenge if you plan your career in the generative AI space.

Anyway, almost everybody working in the generative AI space should follow the development in the agentic field. What new benchmarks will be developed? How do LLMs perform on existing benchmarks (such as GAIA, RE-BENCH, Berkeley function-calling leaderboards)? What new agentic architectures will be introduced? What evaluation approaches will be adopted? How could agentic workflows be guardrailed? How can the reliability of such workflows be improved? What new safety and security risks are identified?

Summary

In this chapter, we talked about the evolving landscape of the tech industry and why technical skills alone are no longer sufficient in many cases. We touched on the importance of generative AI engineers possessing strategic thinking, business acumen, and the ability to drive organizational transformation. Now, you should be better prepared for strategy-focused interview questions by suggesting a three-pronged approach: mastering business-centric questions, understanding generative AI's impact on software development, and analyzing its effects on the target company's industry. We also discussed the need for continuous learning and a broad outlook, recommending various resources such as industry reports, tech blogs, podcasts, hands-on product trials, and curated social media feeds to stay informed and develop a strategic vision.

Then we dived into specific industry transformations, starting with software development, which is identified as a prime candidate for disruption due to abundant training data, developer-centric LLM design, and suitability for agentic workflows. We discussed how generative AI can enhance developer productivity through code generation, intelligent autocomplete, assistance with "boring" tasks, and real-time support. However, we also critically examined potential drawbacks, such as challenges in long-term code maintainability, the difficulty of evaluating complex system changes, and security vulnerabilities associated with AI-generated code.

Later, we explored the impact of generative AI on **CRM**, marketing, finance, and healthcare. In CRM, we looked at examples of how AI is revolutionizing customer support with chatbots, personalized assistance, proactive care, and improved self-service options, while also touching upon engineering aspects such as RAG, multimodal inputs, and evaluation challenges. Then we discussed such marketing examples as content generation, personalization, virtual try-ons, and the emerging field of **GSO**, with a note on the engineering considerations of diffusion models and video generation workflows.

In finance, we looked at how generative AI is presented as a tool for automating knowledge work, enhancing operational efficiency, improving risk management, and developing new trading algorithms, with RAG, time-series analysis, and factuality being key engineering concerns. Finally, we discussed AI's role in assisting medical professionals, improving therapy adherence, accelerating drug discovery, boosting operational efficiency, and leveraging wearable device data, with a strong emphasis on RAG, multimodal capabilities, guardrails, and MAS for complex diagnostics. Throughout these discussions, we consistently highlighted the importance of evaluating both the benefits and the potential side effects, ethical concerns, and engineering complexities of generative AI adoption in each sector.

The next chapter explores the journey from prototype to production for generative AI applications, focusing on reliability, maintainability, and evaluation. It also explains how production AI systems differ from traditional software, assuming LLMs are consumed through external APIs rather than trained or hosted by the reader.

Further reading

To learn more about the topics that were covered in this chapter, look at the following resources:

1. Andrej Karpathy, *Software Is Changing (Again)*: https://www.youtube.com/watch?v=LCEmiRjPEtQ&ta
2. Ben Auffarth, Leonid Kuligin, *Generative AI with LangChain: Build production-ready LLM applications and advanced agents using Python, LangChain, and LangGraph*, Packt, 2025

Part 5

Landing Your Role and Sustaining Growth

Part 5 focuses on transforming your technical expertise into long-term career success in the generative AI era. You will learn how to build a strong professional brand, leverage AI responsibly to enhance your online presence and job search, and prepare for interviews with confidence using practical strategies and AI-powered tools. The part concludes with expert career advice, guidance on avoiding common pitfalls, and actionable recommendations for continuous learning, community engagement, and sustained professional growth in the rapidly evolving field of AI.

This part contains the following chapters:

- *Chapter 10, Building and Deploying LLM Applications*
- *Chapter 11, Crafting Your AI Identity – Personal Branding for Impact*
- *Chapter 12, Conquering the AI Job Market – Strategic Search Techniques and Interview Tips*
- *Chapter 13, Expert Insights and Sustaining Growth – Building a Career That Compounds*

10

Building and Deploying LLM Applications

If you have a good evaluation mechanism, it not only gives you confidence in the performance of your solution but also allows you to confidently improve your solution and roll out new updates.

– Leonid Kuligin

Developing a prototype is a difficult task since you need to find an impactful use case, inspirational examples, put together a working solution, and tell a story. This is not easy. But there is a long way to production after you attract attention with your prototype and secure investment in developing a solution.

In this chapter, we will look into the major steps that you will need to take on your way to bringing your generative AI application to production. We're going to briefly discuss the main phases that explain how a prototype is different from production deployment, and what steps you should consider on the path to production to increase the reliability and maintainability of your application. We will see how important evaluation is, and why it is often underestimated, and we'll discuss how generative AI applications are different from "classical" software applications we've been used to (the ones that require us to program a deterministic algorithm to solve a task).

To make it clear, we're not going to talk about training or serving LLMs. The assumption in this chapter is that you and your team are going to use an API provided by a vendor who is in the business of LLM inference or the platform team. We will briefly touch on some considerations related to what tradeoffs you should consider when thinking about open-weight (i.e., with the weights openly released that make it available to host an LLM on your own device) LLMs yourselves.

We will cover the following main topics:

- Application development
- Evaluation
- Is developing generative AI solutions the same as application development?
- From prototype to production
- Integration and deployment

Application development

These days, developing generative AI applications is not about building from scratch, but about shaping powerful pre-trained foundational LLMs or **large vision models (LVMs)** that mainly process vision data. Of course, first you need to make a *build versus adapt decision*. You might use a general-purpose API (such as Claude, Gemini, GPT-4, etc.) or use a self-hosted open-weight model (such as DeepSeek, Gemma, Llama, etc.). Of course, you have some options between these two polarities, such as using an open-weight model hosted by the cloud provider in a pay-as-you-go way.

When choosing a model, you typically balance across multiple pillars, such as:

- Cost of inference (including cost of owning and maintaining your own hardware). There is a common misperception that self-hosted models are cheaper, but it depends on the throughput and traffic distribution. If you have uniform traffic and you can utilize your GPUs over time, it might make sense to use your own infrastructure since you'll be able to achieve a high utilization.
- Quality and performance (for example, latency) on your own tasks. Of course, a thorough evaluation of your specific use case requires effort and collecting a labeled dataset. Larger and more sophisticated models typically offer better quality, but it comes at a cost, such as latency and inference costs.
- Capabilities such as tool calling, controlled generation, multimodal input and output, context length limitations, LORA fine-tuning, etc. Some applications (or specific architectures that you may need to develop your applications) might require specific capabilities that open-weight models still do not possess.

We are not going to discuss in detail the technical aspects of developing a generative AI application and tuning it to the specific domain and task. In short, you have a large number of tools at your disposal. Let us just quickly summarize various options:

Options	**Examples**	**Data needs**	**Development effort**
Low-code tools	Google Conversational Agents, Claude AI Agents, n8n, Retell AI	Small	Small
Prompt engineering	Chain-of-thought (CoT), one-shot, and few-shot, dynamic examples retrieval	Small	Small
Retrieval-augmented generation (RAG)	Retrieval-based, query expansion, re-ranking, hybrid search	A custom knowledge base and a small number of labeled examples	middle
Real-time agentic workflows	Decomposition, reflection, swarm, supervision, tool calling	small	middle
Offline simulations via agentic workflows	Tree-of-Thoughts, **Language Agent Tree Search (LATS)**, AlphaEvolve	small	large
Parameter-efficient fine-tuning (PEFT)	LoRA fine-tuning	middle	middle
Post-training	Full post-training, distillation, training a custom model from scratch	large	large

Table 10.1: Overview of common approaches to building generative AI applications, with indicative data needs and development complexity

Of course, these options can be nested. For example, when developing an agentic workflow, you still need to work on your prompts for your agent's steps (and it's prompt engineering!). But in general, understand the whole landscape, the data needs, the efforts, and the potential gains from different architectures you can use to build generative AI applications. We've briefly touched on data needs, so let us now briefly discuss the importance of evaluating your applications.

Evaluation

Your application performance is critically dependent on clean, well-structured, and relevant training data (even if you use only a small number of examples in your few-shot prompts). Your training dataset should include the evaluation dataset.

Why does evaluation matter? In machine learning, **generalization** is a model's ability to accurately adapt and perform well on new, unseen data. When you train an ML model, you don't want it to memorize the training data, but to learn the underlying pattern in this data. That means it should be able to make correct (or good enough) predictions on the data it has not encountered before. Hence, your ultimate goal is to develop a model that generalizes well. Typically, poor generalization is caused either by *overfitting* or *underfitting*. Overfitting is a situation where your model has memorized training data too much, including some random noise. You can say that the model has become too complex relative to the dataset provided. It works very well on the data it has seen, but it fails on unseen data. On the other hand, underfitting means that the model has not learned all the patterns presented in the data, hence its poor performance both on the seen and unseen data.

When we develop a prompt to tailor an LLM (or build a more complex multi-step agentic flow), we're going through a similar process. In a certain way, we're training a model by selecting specific natural language instructions that would be passed to an LLM, and we aim to achieve better performance on the specific task. If we have only a small number of examples, we are facing the same risk of poor generalization. The prototype looks great, but when put in front of actual users, it doesn't meet their expectations.

Either our solution (in a simple example, the prompt we prepared) lacks all the details needed, or we have added too many specifics tailored to the limited number of examples we observed. In other words, if you have a few examples in front of you and you change the prompt (or an agentic flow) to achieve better performance of an LLM, you can't guarantee it will work well for *all* examples if you haven't introduced an appropriate evaluation routine.

Let me emphasize once again, please. Evaluation of any ML and AI solutions is crucial, and generative AI is no exception. When thinking about the operationalization of a complex solution, evaluation is one of the most underestimated topics in terms of effort and importance. If you have a good evaluation mechanism, it not only gives you confidence in the performance of your solution but also allows you to confidently improve your solution and roll out new updates.

Why is evaluation a difficult topic? You need to collect a representative evaluation dataset, agree on evaluation criteria and metrics that correspond to your business goals, and implement the evaluation routine itself. Since LLMs are non-deterministic by design, your evaluation routine is subject to random noise, and simulating end-to-end performance might be difficult. Imagine you have a chatbot with actual users calling by phone, and your chat is subject to signal delays, interruptions, and other distortions. Simulating such a chat and evaluating its performance on a complex flow is not easy, and that explains why we observe many startups trying to solve the problem of evaluating generative AI applications.

To summarize, from my observations, many teams consistently underestimate the unique challenges posed by non-deterministic and complex systems (this is sometimes referred to as the *evaluation gap*). Let's briefly look at how we can address this gap.

How to evaluate your application

As we have seen, evaluation is an extremely important and broad topic. We could have written an entire book on evaluation only (and there are some great examples out there!). When thinking from a high-level perspective on evaluation topics, I believe there are three important aspects to keep in mind:

1. Being able to articulate the importance of evaluation itself to your stakeholders. What kind of challenges do you need to overcome? What resources do you need to allocate? What aspects to consider? What data should you collect? A generative AI leader in an organization should become an advocate for developing reliable and repeatable evaluation routines across the enterprise. From my observations, the aspect of communication and expectations management is often overlooked, especially by great engineers who want to be focused on technical work.
2. Data collection. In 2006, almost 20 years ago, Clive Humby, a British data scientist, said, "*Data is the new oil*". This saying became very famous, and it still holds true in the generative AI era. No, you don't need such massive datasets to train your models as we needed in the

classical ML era, but you still need a labeled dataset tailored for your use cases and your domain. The problem is that not all data would be equally valuable. Carefully evaluate your data needs, and try to answer the following questions:

- What kind of labeled data can you collect?
- What data would move your solutions forward? Developing code has become relatively easy these days, especially given the availability of vibe coding tools. Custom evaluation methods and labeled datasets designed for specific use cases can become a competitive advantage for your organization.
- What does it mean that your solution *works well*? On what scales should you evaluate your solution? It's a tricky question that typically sounds easy to answer, but when you start thinking about it, a lot of questions arise. Imagine you're developing an HR bot assistant for your employees. What is a good answer? Should it be factual, helpful, easy to grasp, grounded in the enterprise data, concise, or grammatically correct? You might want all of it, but how would you include all these (and many other) aspects in a single rating? How much would such a united rating tell you about an actual problem? Or should you evaluate separately on every scale, and what do you do if scales move in different directions?
- How can you collect this data? What context do you need to bring to an LLM? What additional logging routines or interface elements (i.e., what additional data you need to collect, such as user behavior or the environment's state, and how you need to adjust the UI of your application to gather such data) do you need to incorporate into your user-facing product? That's another difficult question since you need to avoid training-serving skew, or a discrepancy between the performance of the model during the testing phase and when it's used in the real world. Imagine you developed a chatbot that is grounded on the enterprise data, and your prompts have specific instructions on how to handle the context retrieved from the internal knowledge base. If one day the underlying knowledge base changes its format, your prompts might start misleading an LLM, and the end-to-end quality drops.
- What additional annotation needs do you have, and where can you get a pool of annotators? Are you going to use in-house annotators or scale crowd-sourced ones?

> An **annotation** is a process of labeling an input example. In other words, a human creates a desired output that an ML model (or agentic workflow) should produce. In "classical" ML, we use these annotations to train and evaluate a model. In the world of generative AI, we don't train the model in the classical sense (although we might fine-tune one, and we need a labeled dataset for that). But we still need to evaluate our agents to pick the best prompt, LLM parameters like temperature or output_tokens, choose agentic architecture, and, at the end of the day, to make sure it's working well on a large variety of inputs. And that's why we still need labeled datasets, and in most cases, we don't have ones out of the box (since we use agents to assist humans on complex tasks that don't necessarily have examples of inputs and desired outputs). Hence, we need to create such labeled datasets by asking SMEs to provide examples of outputs given the inputs (and maybe we don't even have examples of the inputs, so we need help with that as well). You can recruit humans, or SMEs, who do the annotations, from in-house (and that's definitely a good way to start), but if you need to scale your annotations, you sometimes can recruit part-time specialists on crowdsourcing platforms (such as Scale.ai, Appen, Toloka, etc.).

- How can you validate the job of human annotators? How to make their evaluations consistent so that they agree with each other? What does the evaluation itself look like? Coming back to the HR bot example provided above, should you evaluate its response on a scale from 0-100, use a scale from 0 to 5, do binary evaluations (*good* or *bad* answer), or anything else?
- What size of datasets do you need? Should you try to decrease the cost of data collection? Can you use synthetic data somewhere in the process?

3. Last but not least is ongoing work on improving the metrics you're using. You need validated metrics and corresponding evaluation routines that you can use both for offline and online experiments. That means, you first evaluate a new version of your solution without putting it in front of the users, i.e., you're re-simulating the behavior with historical data and evaluating some metrics that are proxies of your business ones. Then you deploy the solution to the users, and validate that it's performing better than the previous version (for example, through A/B testing). As a generative AI leader, you should be able to suggest potential metrics, understand what metrics are typically used for similar use cases, and lay out the strategy for A/B testing in the organization.

These days, a lot of dedicated tools have emerged to help with the systematic tracking, automated metrics, and human-in-the-loop analysis of generative AI applications. You still need human **subject matter experts (SMEs)** to help with evaluation, and you need to define your evaluation strategy first (your metrics, sampling evaluation examples from the entire collected dataset, evaluation frequency, guidelines for annotators, etc.), but such tools make it easier to organize your evaluation at scale. You can take a look at end-to-end platforms for the entire LLM application lifecycle, including logging, debugging, tracing, testing, and continuous monitoring, such as LangSmith or LangFuse. On the other hand, you can use open-source libraries such as Ragas or DeepEval that help you define and compute metrics for specific types of LLM applications (such as RAG or agents).

Now, let's take a look at how else generative AI solutions differ from classical application development, besides a large need for evaluations

Is developing generative AI solutions the same as application development?

On the one hand, developing generative AI solutions is closer to application development than people sometimes think. At the end of the day, it looks like most of the work that we do when developing an RAG or an agent is stitching multiple APIs together. For example, to build a RAG, we need to export the knowledge base, transform it (by parsing, chunking, merging multiple sources, and enriching chunks with metadata, etc.), insert it into a vector database, implement an efficient retrieval mechanism, pass context to an LLM, and then present results to the user. That looks like classical application development work. Same thing, many agentic patterns are relatively easy wrappers on top of calls to an LLM (such as planning or reflection). We observe this in the industry, since more and more application teams are quite successfully incorporating LLMs in the products they are building.

On the other hand, implicit non-determinism and difficulties with the evaluation arising from it are what make developing generative AI applications quite different from "classical" application development. With this new type of software product, it's difficult to make an incremental change.

Like with any ML solution, it's not straightforward to fix a bug anymore. A user complains about a specific behavior, but you can't just update an ML model to make it work on this example. You need to collect a large amount of similar examples, include them in your training dataset, and re-train the model. With generative AI, it might seem that it is simpler to fix the behavior on one particular edge case, since it looks like you can always modify a prompt and make it work. You are not re-training the underlying model, are you? But this is a delusion that is very easy to fall into! If you just take one non-working example and adjust the prompt to make it work, there's no guarantee that your overall performance has improved (since you might decrease the performance on other examples).

Holistic evaluation is the key to iterations on your applications, and implementing such evaluation is a difficult challenge. Hence, when you introduce generative AI features to your product, you need to start changing the way you think about development and be closer to an ML development lifecycle:

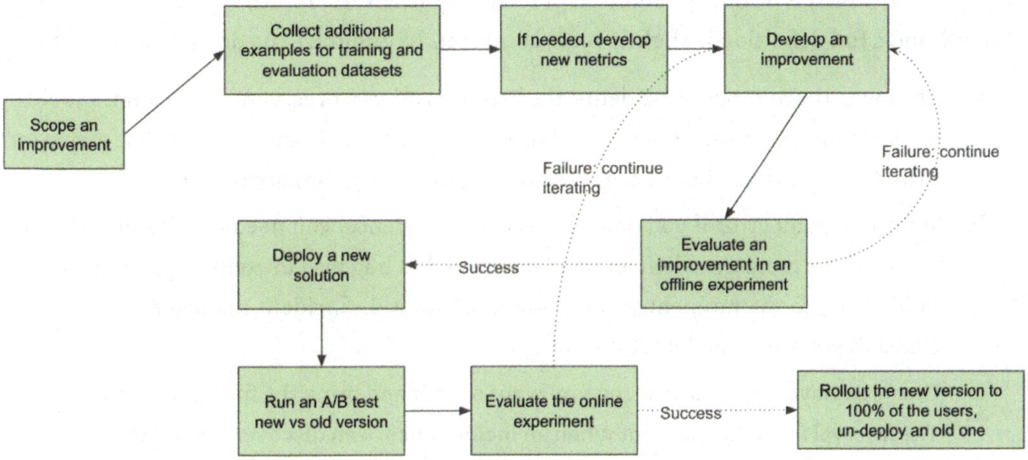

Figure 10.1: ML development lifecycle

You constantly iterate, from data to a solution candidate that is evaluated first offline and then online. Simply put, the quality of your solution depends on the quality of your data, and this is the reason we speak so much about evaluation in this chapter on building generative AI applications.

From prototype to production

We've been speaking for quite some time about evaluation, but I can't emphasize enough its importance. A robust evaluation is the main issue that lies between a prototype and a production-ready application. Often, a prototype is a proof-of-concept and demonstration of the feasibility of the solution that works well on a small number of curated examples. You can't expand it and move forward to production without an evaluation dataset and evaluation routines.

But now let's look at other aspects that you should keep in mind when preparing for production. It might sound familiar to software engineers, but these aspects are often overlooked by data scientists who become responsible for products enabled by generative AI. If you have an ML and data science background and you're driving generative AI adoption in your organization, you might soon find out that you and your team are responsible for quite a few applications that are daily used by internal or external users. This changes your responsibilities and routines.

When moving to production, your focus shifts to maintainability and reliability of your application. To keep it simple, it should work well *almost always* for *most* of your users. Why almost always? Because applications fail: there are bugs, hardware failures, and other unexpected problems. This, unfortunately, happens all the time. However, we want to minimize the downtime of our applications, which is a simple definition of reliability (there are multiple aspects to reliability, though, and a full definition is slightly more complex). To minimize the downtime, we need:

a. The lower the number of incidents, the better. In other words, your application should be stable, and when a developer introduces a change, they should feel safe that they won't introduce additional bugs because of the application's complexity.
b. You can't fix an error if you don't know it exists. Hence, you need to minimize the time between the moment when an incident started (a bug was introduced, a hardware has failed, etc.) to the moment you found out about it. In incident management, it's often called **mean-time-to-detect** (**MTTD**).
c. Once you have detected an error, you want to fix it and bring the fix to production quickly. The interval from the moment when an incident has been discovered until the moment it has been mitigated is often called the **mean-time-to-resolve** (**MTTR**). Low MTTR requires certain tooling and processes.

Let's now look at these three pillars one by one.

Reliability of your application

Why do applications fail? There are two main reasons. First, new edge cases occur that developers have overlooked when developing an application. It is a well-known problem in software development that how *we think customers will use our products* differs from *how customers really use our products*. That means, we constantly discover new failures, or bugs, that we need to fix, or new feature requests that we need to fulfill. Hence, software changes are inevitable. However, often when we introduce a new change, an application fails. That's why we want our production applications to be easy to maintain.

What does ease of maintenance mean? It implies that it's both easy and safe to make a change to an application. The code should be well-organized, easy to grasp, and relatively easy to extend. That requires a thoughtful design of an application; you should introduce a proper hierarchy of classes and modules, follow the code style, use readable naming of the variables, etc. There are a lot of good guidelines on how a production-ready code should look in the "pre-generative AI" era. Try to develop your own opinion on what software development best practices you would advise your team to use, how to ensure the code quality and readability remain high with a wide use of vibe coding, how to organize the hierarchy of classes and avoid code duplication when developing agents, etc.

Of course, a big component of the maintainability of your application is testing and continuous integration and delivery (CI/CD). Tests help both the readability of your code (looking at tests often helps to grasp the details of what's going on) and the maintainability of your application (if you have good tests, they incorporate all the nuances of your business logic, and that makes it safe for a developer to change something). On the other hand, unit tests capture nuances of business logic, and allow for introducing new changes quickly and in a safe manner, minimizing the risk of breaking an intended behavior.

If you are an experienced software engineer, you're well aware of the importance of a good testing strategy. I'd suggest you think about two aspects, though. First, generative AI applications typically stitch together multiple underlying services and APIs, such as foundational models, retrievals, and databases, and tools. Think about how to mock all such dependencies in unit tests in a reusable and easy-to-use manner. Second, ask yourself what integration tests mean in the genAI context. Such systems have a lot of internal non-determinism, and you should not only test that everything works together well (in other words, you get an output that looks valid), but also that this output is valid from the

If you have little experience in software engineering, consider reading one or two books on the basics of software engineering and design. It would help you to better prompt your coding assistants and develop better applications in general. For example, testing is often omitted in data science, but if you're a data scientist in transition to genAI builders, think about how you could benefit from testing in your area of expertise, and then apply it to the generative AI applications you're developing.

Detecting incidents

You need to detect that things went wrong quickly; otherwise, you can't start fixing it. Extensive monitoring, dashboards, and alerting systems help you with that. But building a good monitoring and alerting system is difficult, and how we define monitoring has changed for generative AI applications.

Why is that? Because these applications are non-deterministic by design. That means it becomes difficult or close to impossible to define what the behavior of an application looks like. In a "classical" world, we could rely on the amount of HTTP errors, CPU consumption, and metrics like that. Nowadays, it might seem that an application is behaving normally, but its outcomes are not relevant anymore. Hence, we need to inspect and rate additional aspects of its behavior and be able to detect when predictions are not relevant anymore (while the application itself is working fine), and to distinguish between a random failure and an outage where a substantial portion of incoming requests is impacted.

To solve this problem, we use tools like extensive user feedback and real-time business metrics (such as success or escalation rates, repetitive calls, etc.), run shadow evaluation, etc. There are two ways to organize evaluations. Evaluations take a long time to proceed, and they might be expensive in terms of token consumption and other resources. Hence, we might not be able to run them on every commit as we do with integration tests. Typically, you trigger offline evaluation only on major changes, and run them on schedule to check that there's no regression (i.e., degradation of the service quality). But as mentioned above, such evaluations won't make you aware of a training-serving skew. For example, users might start asking you new types of questions, and since these questions are not part of the evaluation dataset, you would never know that the systems fail on them.

Of course, it increases the costs of development, maintenance, and monitoring itself, so we need to carefully balance them with the value provided.

Resolving incidents

Now, once an incident has been detected, the team can finally start working on it. The faster they fix it, the lower the downtime caused by this incident. It's easier said than done. First, you need to find a root cause, and that requires having appropriate tools for observability and debugging. If you have an agentic flow, you need to trace everything that happens at every step: what is sent to an LLM? What do prompts look like after all substitutions? What kind of context is retrieved from other systems? What tools are called and how?

Answering these questions fast and efficiently requires you to use dedicated observability platforms like LangSmith, LangFuse, etc. When you have found the root cause, you need to fix it quickly without introducing new bugs. That's why the readability of your code and test coverage are important.

Finally, you need to deliver these new changes or roll back the bad changes that caused an error quickly. That requires the adoption of CI/CD tools and a well-established release process. It won't come as a surprise to you, but generative AI applications are again quite different from *classical* ones. Pretty often, an application is not just code anymore, but it includes data. For example, for a RAG application, you need an indexed knowledge base, a fine-tuned embeddings model, etc. If there's a bug in a new version, you might need to roll back not only the code changes, but the data changes associated with it. It complicates your release and rollback setup, and your team should be prepared to address these issues.

So far, we have discussed various aspects of bringing your generative AI to production such as ease of maintenance and increased reliability. Now, let's briefly discuss some aspects of deploying your application to the production environment.

Integration and deployment

A frequently asked question is "How should I deploy my generative AI application?" From my perspective, concerns with the deployment of an application are often overamplified. At the end of the day, it doesn't differ too much from deploying a "classical" web application that has storage, backend, and frontend layers. Your backend might have slightly more integrations than you might be used to, and hence require slightly more effort both in the design and implementation phases. You need to integrate all the APIs (LLMs, tools that you're going to use, etc.), and take care of issues such as authentication. In a nutshell, you wrap your application with a FastAPI or Flask, and deploy a web application that exposes an API to your frontend or other components that invoke your app. In other words, you take your working application as a program and expose an HTTP API for users or upstream applications (for example, you can incorporate a customer success chatbot into an existing mobile app). Your agentic logic is encapsulated behind the well-defined interface (an API) that you provide, and you can use existing frameworks to run and manage the server that hosts such an API.

What is still different, and what aspects should you consider as a generative AI lead? You might need specific components and building blocks that generative AI applications require, such as short-term and long-term agent memory.

Permission management

If your agent is acting on behalf of a user, you should carefully think about how you preserve the permissions. Let's imagine you're developing a RAG on top of an enterprise knowledge base like an internal wiki or Confluence. You exported all the articles, chunked them, encoded, and now you're retrieving a context. But there's a problem! Originally, different users had different access levels to various documents. Let's add metadata tags to chunks to check for an access right during retrieval. If you have dozens of thousands of employees in your organization, the size of your metadata might explode. It might actually negatively influence the recall of your retrieval (or how well you find the corresponding documents). Since you need to first filter by permissions and then rank the documents based on their utility relative to the input query, vector databases do not necessarily perform well on such access patterns. Of course, you might not have such issues with your evaluation dataset; hence, you can't even measure how well you perform.

The problem might become even more difficult. Imagine that User A is not allowed to see the document D1, but they are allowed to see documents {D2, D3, D4}, and you need to preserve these permissions. The source knowledge management systems often have a sophisticated way of managing permissions. For example, access can be both granted or denied based on indirect membership in groups, or it can have an expiration date. Hence, exporting such permissions to a third-party system might become a complicated task, and you would need to sync changes close to real-time (and, again, not all vector databases can handle such an update efficiently).

Do you need a custom API for every agent?

In the section above, we discussed that when deploying an agent, you wrap it with a web development framework such as FastAPI or Flask to expose a backend service. However, that means you need to develop an API specification and align with all downstream services that consume it. Ask yourself, do you really need a custom API schema for your agent? Having a custom schema allows you to design an API tailored to the very specific behavior of an agent, but at the same time, it requires additional effort and coordination, slows down the development, and decreases the portability of your agents. What if you're developing and maintaining multiple agents for different use cases? Could you use a unified API for all of them?

Having a shared API schema for different agents is the core idea behind managed platforms like LangGraph Platform, Vertex AI Agent Engine, and others. A unified API is a single, aggregated interface that provides a standardized method for developers to connect with multiple, similar software applications using one connection. Such an approach reduces complexity and promotes reusability of your agents. It also makes it easier for agents to communicate through protocols like A2A.

Hosting an open-weight LLM yourselves

As a generative AI leader, you should have an opinionated view on hosting open-weighted LLMs yourself. This question comes up in discussions with the business more often than you might think. Why would a business want to host an LLM instead of using it from a vendor as an API? The main rationale behind it is typically staying vendor independent, minimizing the costs, and privacy concerns. For instance, a healthcare provider might choose to self-host a fine-tuned model using vLLM for data privacy, while using a managed GPT-4 API for administrative automation tasks. Let's address pros and cons one by one.

First, keep in mind the need to carefully evaluate the quality of the open-weighted model of your choice. Not all models have the same performance on various tasks and the same set of features, such as controlled generation, long context window, reasoning, etc. Open-weighted models typically lag behind the proprietary ones in terms of quality and additional functions supported (but so far they have been able to close the lag in 3-6 months after a frontier proprietary model has been released). On the other side, for some business tasks you don't need state-of-the-art performance. Hence, we are back to the topic we've discussed at the beginning of this chapter, or evaluations. The most advanced state-of-the-art LLMs typically originate from Anthropic, Google, OpenAI, and other large providers, and open-weighted models catch up with a certain delay. Having said that, not all tasks require the most state-of-the-art LLMs, but you need to benchmark them for your own dataset. On the other hand, you don't really get true vendor independence given the speed of advances in this field at the current moment. When you start using an open-weighted model, you depend on the community or model's provider to continue improving the model to stay on par, and the license that is associated with this specific model (for example, to what extent the commercial use is allowed).

Another important topic is costs. Again, sometimes people think that hosting a model themselves is the cheapest option, but that might not be the case. Large vendors actually have state-of-the-art hardware, specialized datacenters, and optimized software stack for a low-latency and high-throughput LLM inference. Take into account the true cost of ownership that would include maintenance, support, ensuring redundancy (what if your GPU fails), etc. Of course, consider your load. If you can ensure a uniform load to keep your hardware highly utilized over time, you might actually see some cost savings. On the other hand, if you have spiky consumption, that would mean that most of the time your GPUs would be idle, and you might be more cost-effective with a pay-as-you-go model. Last but not least, consider whether inference costs really play a large role in your applications, since often costs of related infrastructure (data processing, storage, retrieval, and so on) are actually higher than LLM inference.

Finally, carefully understand the privacy and security risks presented to you. We're not going to dive deep into it, but often an open collaboration with compliance and security teams eliminates their concerns and opens a door to use LLM providers for your use cases. On the contrary, if you use an open-weight LLM, there's also a certain risk that it might be trained on a compromised dataset.

Nevertheless, if you have leaned toward using an open-weighted model, take a look at different frameworks (like vLLM, TGI, Ollama) that you might use for inference. Carefully consider whether you need real-time inference (since it would incur higher costs) and how you would handle the spikes in requests. Modern LLM inference frameworks have a lot of built-in options to improve inference performance, so you might need to run some load tests and experiments to find the best inference options that fit your use case and your hardware.

To summarize, I don't think there's a universal answer to whether to host an LLM or to consume it through an API from a vendor. As usual in software engineering, it depends on requirements and assumptions, and different use cases might require different solutions. Your role is to be able to gather these requirements and make a rational decision based on facts and calculations, not on emotions. You might discover that there is strategic value in a hybrid approach that involves using quick, cost-effective APIs for low-volume, non-sensitive, or seasonal workloads, and reserving self-hosted or secure LLM deployments for core, high-volume workloads that require maximum data privacy, guaranteed low latency, or deep fine-tuning. This blended strategy allows organizations to leverage the speed and convenience of managed services while retaining control and cost-efficiency where it matters most.

Summary

In this chapter, we focused on the journey from a prototype to a production-ready generative AI application. We looked into the distinction between a prototype and production, with the latter demanding significant effort in reliability, maintainability, and robust evaluation. Developing generative AI applications often involves shaping pre-trained foundational LLMs, requiring a balance of cost, quality, performance, and capabilities when choosing between general-purpose APIs and self-hosted open-weight models. Various tools and architectures like prompt engineering, RAG, and agentic workflows are available for this purpose.

Then we discussed the importance of developing a robust evaluation mechanism. Evaluation is paramount for generalization and ensuring the application performs well on unseen data, a process that is often underestimated and requires collecting representative datasets, agreeing on metrics, and implementing robust routines, especially given the non-deterministic nature of LLMs. The development of generative AI solutions aligns more closely with an ML development lifecycle than traditional application development, emphasizing continuous iteration from data to solution candidates, with both offline and online evaluation.

Finally, we looked at various aspects of moving to production, and how the team's focus shifts to maintainability and reliability, aiming to minimize downtime through stable applications, quick incident detection (MTTD), and fast incident resolution (MTTR). Monitoring generative AI applications presents challenges due to their non-deterministic nature, necessitating the inspection of outcomes and real-time business metrics beyond traditional system metrics. Efficient incident resolution requires observability tools for debugging agentic flows and a robust CI/CD pipeline capable of handling both code and data changes for rollbacks. While deployment is similar to classical web applications, it may involve specific generative AI components like agent memory and careful consideration of permission management in RAG systems. The decision between a custom API for each agent or a unified API schema should consider reusability and simplified communication. The choice to host open-weight LLMs versus using vendor APIs involves evaluating quality, true cost of ownership, privacy concerns, and the strategic value of a hybrid approach.

In the next chapter, we'll talk about various aspects of creating your personal brand to advance your career.

11

Crafting Your AI Identity – Personal Branding for Impact

> *"We live in a culture of instant gratification. We check likes within minutes. We measure success in notifications. But personal branding doesn't work that way. It's a long game disguised as a series of small, unremarkable actions."*
>
> *– Andreas Horn*

Much of professional success comes down to one deceptively simple skill: persuading others to recognize your value. You do it when applying for a job, pitching for promotion, seeking investment, or even writing a dating profile. In a world where every career is increasingly mediated by digital platforms, everyone has become, whether they like it or not, a brand. The difference between stagnation and acceleration often depends on whether you cultivate that brand deliberately or let others define it for you.

Personal branding is not about vanity, selfies, or constant exposure. It is, at its core, about making your skills, ideas, and contributions visible in a noisy, competitive environment. For many, the term feels uncomfortable or artificial, but reframing it as *professional visibility* shifts the equation. Branding is simply the mechanism by which others come to understand your expertise and trust your perspective.

The good news is that personal branding has never been more accessible. With the rise of generative AI tools, anyone can amplify their reach, clarify their message, and build networks. You don't need to spend hours online or master design and copywriting. AI makes it possible to *ship* content consistently, refine your voice, and target your audience with precision. In other words: if you can learn to work with AI, you can learn to build a brand. This shift is visible across many professional communities.

Personal branding systems can be studied and applied across LinkedIn, newsletters, and professional communication. The lessons in this chapter are practical, repeatable, and focused on helping professionals build clearer visibility around their work. They are not reserved for the few. They are available to anyone willing to commit to a process.

This chapter introduces a practical framework for building a durable personal brand in the AI era. It explores how to position yourself effectively, craft a strong professional profile, and set up a strategic content system. It also covers what to do and what to avoid along the way.

Think of this chapter not as advice, but as a playbook: a way to design your *AI identity* in a world where visibility, credibility, and adaptability matter for professional success.

This chapter will cover the following topics:

- Why personal branding matters now
- Why LinkedIn is the most underrated stage
- Getting started on LinkedIn
- Finding your mission
- Writing your first LinkedIn post
- Creating a content strategy and content plan
- The hidden side of LinkedIn
- Using AI for personal branding
- AI tools for LinkedIn

Why personal branding matters now

The 21st-century job market is being reshaped by forces that few previous generations have faced at this scale. AI, generative AI, and especially the rise of large language models are changing how many organizations operate—although the pace and impact vary significantly across industries, business models, and regulatory environments.

These shifts are not only influencing how work gets done; they are also changing how people are discovered, evaluated, and trusted in the market. Nobody can predict the future with certainty, but the signals are becoming impossible to ignore. "65% of the jobs that will exist in 2030 don't exist today," according to a recent WEF study (`https://www3.weforum.org/docs/WEF_FOJ_Executive_Summary_Jobs.pdf`). This does not mean that entire professions will simply disappear overnight. In enterprise environments especially, change often happens through task recomposition: parts of a role are automated, augmented, redesigned, or moved into new workflows.

McKinsey estimates that generative AI could add between $2.6 trillion and $4.4 trillion in annual value across the global economy (`https://www.mckinsey.com/capabilities/mckinsey-digital/our-insights/the-economic-potential-of-generative-ai-the-next-productivity-frontier`). The point is not that every job will be replaced. The point is that nearly every professional will need to understand how their work, skills, and visibility change when AI becomes part of a new operating model.

The outlook is a paradox of challenge and opportunity. On one hand, entry-level positions are shrinking, a trend recently confirmed by Stanford researchers in a large-scale study of the U.S. labor market (`https://digitaleconomy.stanford.edu/wp-content/uploads/2025/08/Canaries_BrynjolfssonChandarChen.pdf`). Tasks once reserved for junior employees are increasingly automated, and career ladders that were once predictable now resemble shifting sand.

For those just starting out, finding a foothold is harder than ever. On the other hand, new fields, roles, and industries are opening up at a historic pace (such as outlined in *Chapter 3, Mapping Your Path – Roles and Roadmaps in GenAI* of this book) – offering unprecedented chances for those who can adapt and position themselves effectively. At the same time, automation, digitalization and LLMs have introduced another paradox. Content, communication, and even professional profiles are starting to look and sound the same: polished and, in many cases, artificial. That *sameness* creates an opportunity: differentiation through personal branding. Your brand is the human signal in the algorithmic noise. It is what makes your work, expertise, and judgment easier to recognize when everything else begins to blur together. But visibility alone does not create impact. In enterprise environments, differentiation still comes from outcomes, trust in delivery, and deep domain expertise. A strong personal brand amplifies those signals. It helps the right people see, understand, and remember the value you already create.

This is why personal branding is no longer optional. It is the differentiator that positions you as visible and valuable in an AI-driven world. Whether you're pursuing a deeply technical role, a more business-oriented one, or a hybrid one, building your brand is both parachute and superpower. If markets tighten, your reputation and visibility help you land softly. If opportunities arise, they help you accelerate quickly. And make no mistake: people don't buy into resumes—they buy into people. They buy into values, stories, and the *why* behind your work. If you're not showing up (digitally or in person) as the human face of your expertise, you are leaving opportunity on the table.

It's important to be clear: personal branding is not vanity. It is distribution and proof of work. In practice, it doesn't mean chasing likes or trying to amass followers at all costs. It means creating a coherent online presence—where your profile, your projects, and your content consistently answer one question: What do you stand for?

A blog, for example, can serve as a portfolio, a place to demonstrate expertise, and a training ground for your own thinking. A LinkedIn profile can be more than a digital CV; it can be a stage for conversations that show your unique perspective. A YouTube channel can take this further, turning your ideas into visual stories, tutorials, or interviews that reach people across the globe and help them connect not only with what you know, but with how you think. Each post, article, or contribution becomes both a signal of competence and an invitation to connect.

The mindset shift is simple: think conversations, not content. Don't write to sound smart. Write to start a dialog. Share what you've learned from failures, pivots, or real projects. Add personal touches that humanize your expertise: an early mistake or a behind-the-scenes look. These elements don't diminish professionalism; they build trust.

The encouraging truth is that personal branding is not a talent. It's a system anyone, regardless of background, can apply through a structured, repeatable approach. The platforms may vary (LinkedIn, X, Substack, personal blogs) but the principle is constant: in a world where AI can automate much of the visible work, your brand carries the human behind it.

Creating a strong personal brand follows three simple steps:

- Finding your vision
- Building an online presence
- Creating a repeatable system

First, define who you are and what you stand for. Next, shape your identity with consistent visuals, messaging, and platforms. Finally, share it widely to create visibility and trust.

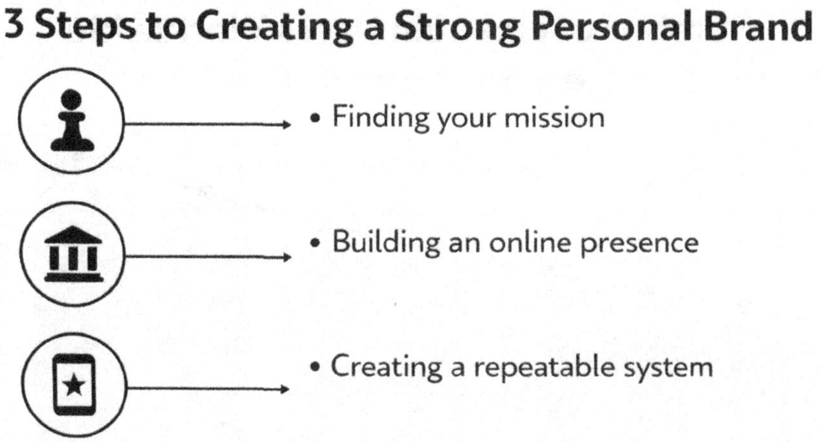

Figure 11.1: The three elements of personal branding

In the rest of this chapter, we'll look into these three steps and focus on LinkedIn, which is one of the most relevant platforms for professional visibility and career discovery, especially in AI-adjacent fields. Most of the advice, however, can be applied to all other platforms as well.

Why LinkedIn is the most underrated platform

LinkedIn can be an effective channel for building professional credibility at scale. Decision-makers and recruiters are present, search intent is high, and the feed rewards clarity and utility. Of course, credibility is never built on one platform alone. In enterprise and technical roles, it is also shaped by outcomes, domain expertise, architecture leadership, customer-facing work, GitHub contributions, and conference visibility. But LinkedIn amplifies these signals in a way few other platforms can. LinkedIn has a very large global professional user base, and only a small share of users publish consistently. According to publicly available platform estimates, the network has more than one billion members (`https://resourcera.com/data/social/linkedin-users/`). Other engagement figures vary by source and should be treated as directional. That creates room for professionals who can share useful, credible insights.

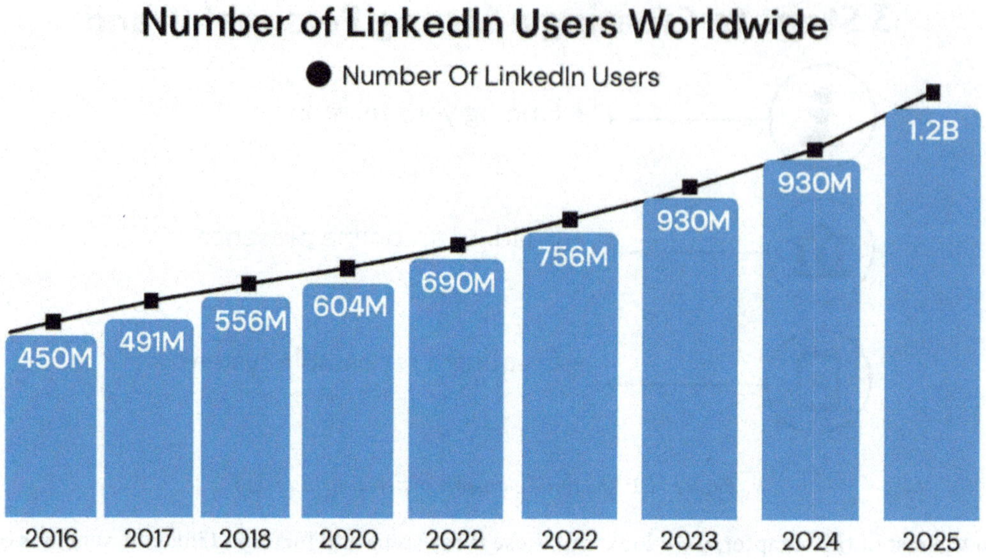

Figure 11.2: Overview of LinkedIn users worldwide and growth

Seventy-five percent of job seekers now consider an employer's brand before applying (`https://www.glassdoor.com/blog/most-important-employer-branding-statistics/`). The reverse is also true: employers, clients, and collaborators evaluate your personal brand before they decide to engage. That said, enterprise hiring decisions also rest on more structured signals—referrals, system design interviews, and internal calibration loops. Brand awareness opens the door; it does not close the offer. Many recruiters and hiring managers will check your online presence before deciding whether to engage. Your LinkedIn presence has become your professional storefront.

However, most professionals still see LinkedIn as a résumé warehouse, a static recruiting platform. They couldn't be more wrong. LinkedIn is a distribution engine for credibility. Post here, and you're not competing with memes or dance challenges. You're competing with silence.

That's what makes LinkedIn unique:

- Instagram is highly visual
- TikTok favors short-form video

- X moves quickly through news and debate
- LinkedIn is structurally closer to professional learning, career discovery, and industry discussion

For many corporate careers, LinkedIn is a highly relevant place to build visibility and credibility. And here's the hidden truth: most of the people who will shape your career won't like, comment, or engage publicly. They're watching silently. Some professional opportunities, such as speaking invitations and meaningful conversations, often come from people who have quietly followed someone's content over time. So if you're getting started, don't obsess over the numbers – focus on the potential behind them.

Getting started with LinkedIn

Before you post a single word, you need to set the stage. Your LinkedIn profile is your digital handshake. It's what people see before they decide whether to take you seriously. If it feels sloppy or half-empty, the rest of your content won't land the way you want it to.

The first thing you should do after creating an account is to update your profile. Here are eight things you must do to get started with your profile the right way:

1. **Professional photo:** First impressions matter. Use a clear, professional headshot – not a blurry selfie or a vacation snapshot. Dress for the industry you want to be in, not just the one you're in today. AI makes this easy: take a simple selfie against a neutral background, then run it through a leading model like Flux or Nano Banana with a prompt such as "create a corporate headshot from this picture."
2. **Headline:** This is the first line people see when your profile pops up in a comment, a recommendation list, or a profile visit. Don't waste it on just your job title. Use it to show the value you bring. "Helping companies scale AI responsibly" is more specific than "Consultant at a tech firm."
3. **Custom URL:** LinkedIn gives you a generic profile link by default. Change it. A clean URL with your name makes you easier to find, easier to share, and shows you care about details. For example: `linkedin.com/in/[yourname]`.

4. **Engaging summary (about section):** This is your story. Skip the clichés ("hard-working, motivated professional"). Write in the first person. Share what drives you, what problems you solve, and where you're headed. Make it human.
5. **Detailed experience:** Don't just list responsibilities – show achievements. Use numbers, outcomes, and impact. "Improved a recurring onboarding workflow by documenting the process, identifying bottlenecks, and introducing automation support" is better than "Responsible for AI implementation."
6. **Featured section:** Pin your best work. Articles, keynote recordings, whitepapers, even strong LinkedIn posts. This is your highlight reel and people will watch this first before they skip to your latest posts.
7. **Skills and endorsements:** Select skills that align with where you're going, not just where you've been. Get colleagues to endorse them. Small signal, but it adds credibility and helps you get found by recruiters.
8. **Recommendations:** Ask for 2–3 genuine recommendations from colleagues, clients, or managers. Social proof builds trust faster than any headline.

And always remember to audit your profile regularly. Treat your profile like a live product – revisit it every few months. Update achievements, tweak your headline, refine your summary. A stagnant profile sends the wrong message.

Once you've done these 8 things, your profile stops being a static resume. It becomes a platform – a stage for your ideas, your credibility, your story. And once the stage is set, you post with much more confidence, knowing that when opportunity comes, you'll look ready. A well-maintained profile already puts you ahead of many passive or incomplete profiles.

Finding your mission

A mission is the primary problem you choose to be known for solving, for the audience you most want to serve – expressed in one sentence. For senior or cross-functional professionals, this does not mean reducing your work to a single narrow lane. You may serve multiple stakeholders and operate across evolving problem spaces. The point is to define your center of gravity: the main theme that connects your expertise, your experience, and the value you bring to others.

It must also match your profile. If your headline says "AI Consultant" but your posts scatter across unrelated topics, such as quantum computing, productivity hacks, and startup investing, you create dissonance. Draft it, publish around it for a month, then refine. Mission evolves with evidence, not mood.

When many professionals start posting on LinkedIn, they often lack a clear mission. One week they share a project update, the next a certification, and later a reflection from an industry event. Each post may be useful on its own, but together they can create a fragmented story. The audience does not know what to expect, and the contributor often does not either.

This is a common mistake. Many professionals treat LinkedIn like a digital notepad – a place to record whatever comes to mind. Don't get me wrong: it is always good to be active and to share valuable things. Posting a few times a month with genuine insights is far better than disappearing altogether. But if the long-term goal is to build a recognizable presence, *activity* alone will not be enough. The problem is that the market does not reward randomness. Both algorithms and audiences look for consistency. They want to know: Who are you? What do you stand for? Why should I listen? Without a clear mission, your voice gets lost in the noise.

Having a mission is not about becoming a content creator. It is about professional strategy. In an environment where careers and reputations are increasingly shaped online, your mission provides the anchor. It is the through-line that connects your expertise, your experiences, and the value you deliver to others.

Mission works like product positioning. A product that tries to be everything to everyone rarely succeeds; the same applies to personal brands. Mission brings focus. Focus builds recognition. Recognition opens doors.

A practical framework to find your mission

There are 5 key questions you should ask yourself:

- What problems do I naturally solve that others struggle with?
- Which topics energize me enough that I could talk about them every week without running out of ideas?
- If people remembered me for one thing in 12 months, what would I want that to be?
- On what topic could I talk for 10 minutes straight without preparing?
- What unique perspective or expertise do I love to search for and share with the world?

How to apply it:

- **Block 20 minutes.** No distractions, just you and a blank page.
- **Answer all 5 questions in one go.** Don't polish, don't Google, don't ask friends. First instincts only.
- **Scan for patterns.** Circle any words, themes, or answers that show up 2–3 times. That's your signal.
- **Pressure-test it.** Imagine you have to post once a week for the next 6 months on this topic. Does it feel exciting or exhausting? If exciting → you're in the right zone. If exhausting → refine it.
- **Draft your mission statement.** Use this template: "I help [audience] achieve [outcome] by sharing [topic/expertise]."
- **Make it real.** Add it to your LinkedIn headline, About section, and first pinned post.
- **Stress test in the wild.** Post 3 times in the next week around this mission. Watch what resonates. If it lands, double down. If it doesn't, adjust wording—not the mission itself.

Examples:

- **Justin Welsh** – *Mission:* Help solo entrepreneurs and professionals build a one-person business and grow on LinkedIn. *How it shows:* Every post ties back to solopreneurship, content systems, or revenue growth without employees.
- **Sahil Bloom** – *Mission:* Demystify business, finance, and personal growth through simple storytelling and mental models. *How it shows:* Consistently shares frameworks that make complex ideas practical and easy to digest.
- **Simon Sinek** – *Mission:* Inspire people to find their "Why" and build organizations that put purpose at the center. *How it shows:* Books, talks, and posts all reinforce the theme of leadership through purpose and clarity. His message is consistent across platforms: great leaders start with "Why."

A mission isn't a long essay. It's one problem you choose to solve for your community – expressed in one clear sentence. Your mission must align with your profile. Consistency across your profile, posts, and interactions is what builds trust. Your profile is the storefront and your content is the products on the shelf – both must signal the same value proposition. Also bear in mind that very broad labels like "technology," "business," or "leadership" are too diluted. Narrowness creates memorability.

Your mission is not carved in stone. As you post, you can refine and tailor it. Reassess every few months – shifts in your field may open room to evolve without losing focus. Ask trusted peers, such as friends, family, or colleagues, to pressure-test and sharpen it.

Writing your first LinkedIn post

You have committed to LinkedIn. Your profile is set, your mission is clear, and a blank page is in front of you. This is where most people stall. Not because they cannot write, but because expectations feel heavy. They imagine colleagues judging, the feed ignoring, and the algorithm burying the post. So they wait. But *waiting* builds no reputation.

Don't bother with being a masterpiece. You only need a start.

Your first post is not about going viral. It is about momentum. When you press publish, you shift from consumer to contributor. That shift matters more than any single metric. Treat it like your first presentation at work. No one expects perfection. They remember that you showed up. On LinkedIn, showing up already sets you apart – most people never do.

How to write a post people will read

The structure of a strong LinkedIn post is simple. It includes four parts:

1. **The hook**: The first two lines decide whether people stop scrolling or keep moving. Start with a question, a bold statement, or a surprising fact, such as:
    - "Most AI pilots fail. Here's why"
    - "I almost quit consulting last year. Then this happened"
    - "99% of professionals waste this opportunity on LinkedIn"
2. **The story**: Once you've caught attention, give context. Share a short narrative, an observation, or a personal experience. Keep it human and relatable.
3. **The value**: Always deliver something useful. A lesson learned, a framework, a perspective. If readers walk away with a new way of thinking – or a tool they can use – you've won.
4. **The call to action**: End with a question or invitation to engage. Ask for perspectives, prompt reflection, or encourage readers to share their experience. Engagement drives reach, but more importantly, it turns your post into a conversation.

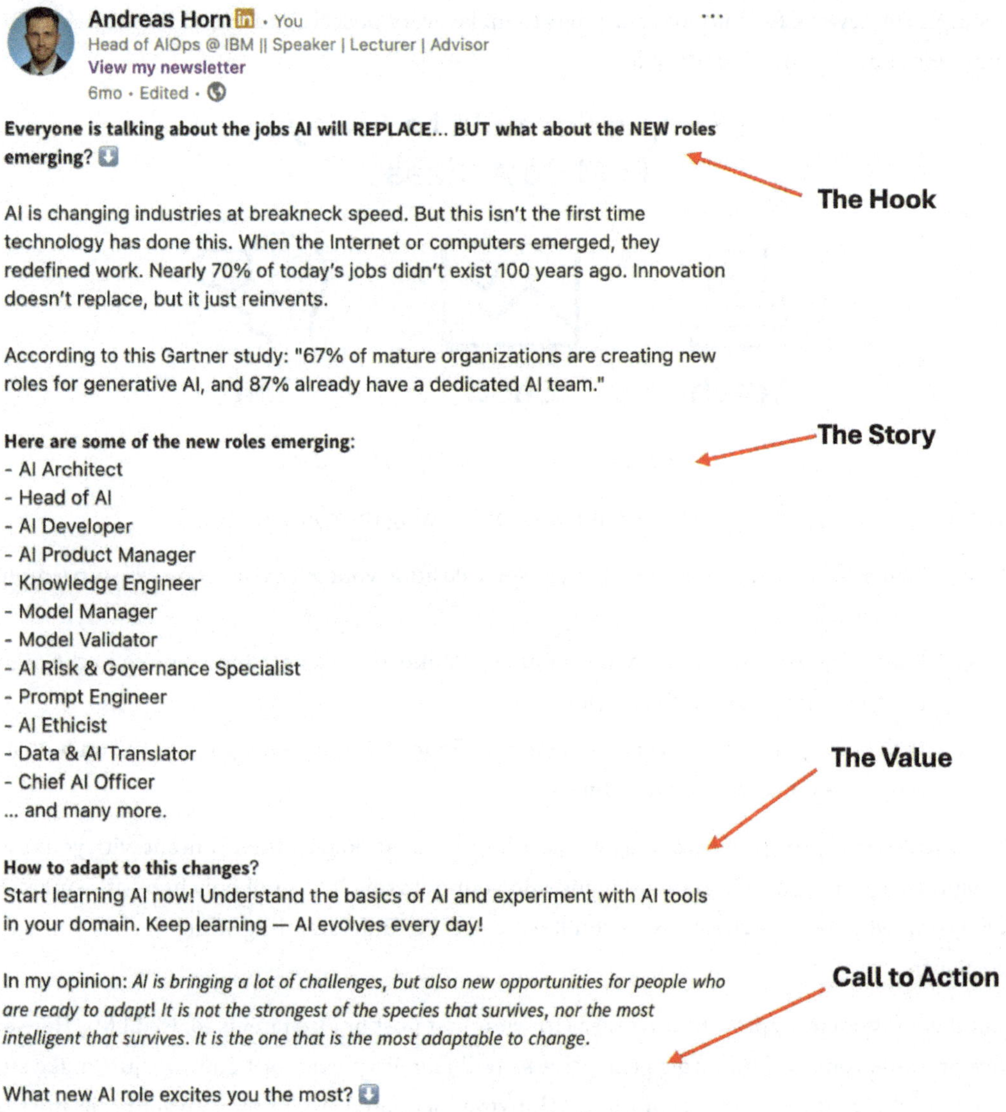

Figure 11.3: Anatomy of a LinkedIn post

A formula to always find post ideas

After your first post, an inevitable challenge shows up: how do you consistently generate strong ideas without burning out or lowering quality?

A simple framework for content creation is to make every post fit into one of three buckets. If a draft does not fit, refine it or drop it.

Figure 11.4: Framework for finding post ideas

There are three key actions to keep in mind when creating the content:

- **Teach**: Share insights, frameworks, lessons. Position yourself as someone who can simplify the complex.
- **Show**: Share real stories – wins, failures, behind-the-scenes. Show you're in the arena, not a commentator on the sidelines.
- **Tell**: Share perspective. This is where thought leadership lives – your "take" on industry trends, not just recycled headlines.

You can also study the profiles of bigger voices in your niche. Repost their content with your own perspective. As long as you give credit and add your own touch, it's not only fine – it's smart. By analyzing what resonates for them, you'll get closer to understanding which niches you want to play in.

Another very smart approach to get ideas for your first post or also later is to use LLMs. Here are five prompts you can feed into a generative AI tool (e.g. Perplexity or Gemini) – just make sure you have the internet search feature and "Thinking" activated. Adapt them to your role, mission, expertise, and interests:

- **Show expertise:** Give me 10 examples of LinkedIn posts I could write as a [JOB TITLE] to demonstrate credibility in [INDUSTRY].
- **Highlight passion:** Search examples of articles I can cover as a [JOB] to show I'm a good [JOB]. For example, I love [TOPIC].

- **Share a story**: Suggest LinkedIn post ideas where I tell a personal story from my work in [FIELD] and connect it to a lesson others can apply.
- **Teach something**: List simple tips or frameworks in [SPECIALIZATION] that I could turn into LinkedIn posts to help beginners.
- **Spark debate**: Generate post topics around the biggest myths or misconceptions in [INDUSTRY] that I can challenge with my perspective.

These prompts will help you overcome the blank page by framing ideas around what you already know. Run them through a tool, or just use them as thinking starters, and you'll have a useful starting backlog of ideas. You'll never face a blank page again. Together, these prompts can generate a useful starting backlog of ideas quickly, all of them tied neatly back to your buckets.

Another valuable approach is to stay deliberately informed about what is happening in your space. Track current industry trends in your sector. Pay attention to what universities are researching and publishing. Read what large companies are reporting in studies and trend reports. Observe what other credible thought leaders are discussing. Then do not just repeat it. Join the conversation by adding your own perspective, interpretation, or disagreement.

And always remember: the first post is not a one-time test. Your first post is the beginning of a long-term rhythm. You will get better with each iteration. Your voice will sharpen. Your confidence will grow. And don't worry if it doesn't land perfectly. A modest post can still create more learning and visibility than an idea that remains unpublished.

Using AI to draft your posts the right way

If you want to use ChatGPT or other AI tools to speed up your writing process, don't make the rookie mistake of typing "`Write a LinkedIn post about X.`" That will get you generic fluff.

Instead, give the AI a role, context, and framework so it writes like a specific persona, which will lead to better results. You can for example just say "write for a professional audience with practical expertise in the following industry" and then add context, or you can copy certain styles of people whose writing you like and infuse them with your approach. You can also feed it examples of writing styles you like and ask it to combine them with your own point of view. Even better, you can build a reusable writing guide based only on your own public writing samples, such as published posts, public articles, or newsletter issues you have the right to use. Do not use confidential employer materials, client documents, internal emails, or unpublished presentations. This gives the AI a clearer pattern for how you think, structure arguments, open posts, make transitions, and close with a point of view. The AI works best when briefed like a ghostwriter.

Here's a (generic) basic prompt structure you can steal and tweak:

```
Act as my LinkedIn writing partner.
Write a LinkedIn post for [audience] about [topic].
The goal is to [educate / challenge / inspire] them by making one clear
point: [main idea].
Use a sharp, practical, and confident tone. Avoid hype, generic
motivation, corporate jargon, vague claims, and AI slop. Do not use empty
phrases like "in today's fast-paced world," "game-changer," "unlock your
potential," or "the future is here."
Structure the post with:
A strong first line that creates tension or curiosity
A clear explanation of the problem or opportunity
One concrete example, insight, or implication
A final takeaway or question that invites discussion
Use short sentences and easy-to-scan paragraphs.
Write in a style inspired by [person you admire], but adapt it to my own
perspective and voice.
Maximum length: 250 words.
```

There are also writing assistants and custom GPT-style tools available in different marketplaces. Treat them as starting points, test outputs critically, and avoid uploading confidential or employer-owned material.

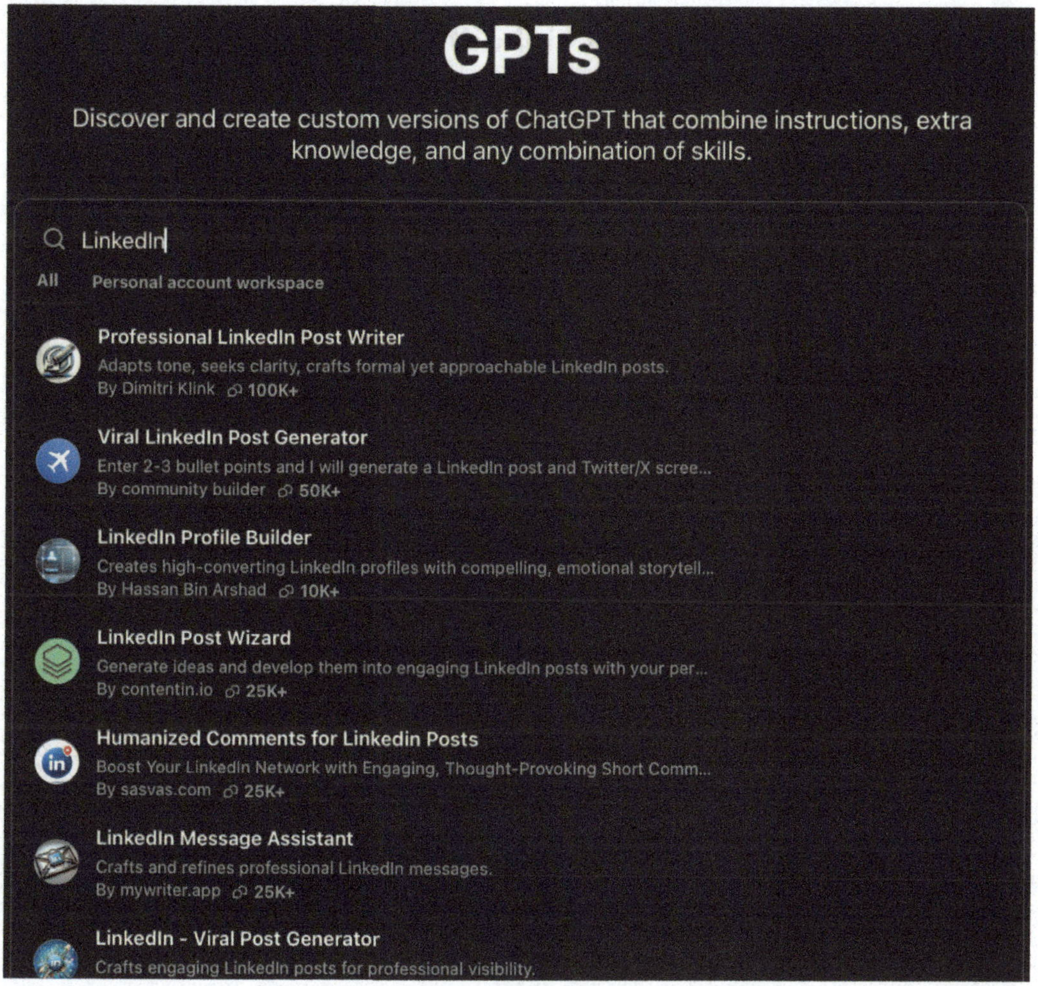

Figure 11.5: Overview of GPTs for LinkedIn posting

From blank page to LinkedIn post in 15 minutes

When you're writing with AI, always start with an outline. A simple structure – working title, 3–5 bullets, and key opening lines – gives direction and prevents the model from *guessing* your intent. Once you've set that frame, AI becomes far more effective: it can expand your points, polish the language, and generate drafts that actually sound like you. Think of the outline as scaffolding – you do the thinking, AI does the building.

How not to write your first LinkedIn post

Your first post won't be perfect. Getting started usually feels messy. But there are three common mistakes to avoid:

- Posting like a corporate press release – nobody cares
- Writing too long or too complex – LinkedIn is not an academic journal
- Ignoring comments – you miss opportunities to connect

Thoughtful personal reflections can sometimes build more trust than polished industry commentary, as long as they remain relevant and professional. Balanced vulnerability builds trust and credibility. But this isn't something you master on day one. It develops with experience, practice, and the confidence to show up as yourself. You should constantly evaluate what performs well and what doesn't. Pay attention to which posts spark engagement, comments, or shares – and which ones fall flat. This feedback loop is how you refine your voice, double down on what resonates, and drop what doesn't.

Creating a repeatable content strategy

After writing your first post you have already done most of the work and overcome it. Growth on professional platforms is rarely driven by one post. It usually comes from consistent, useful contributions over time. Consistency compounds. People need to see your face, your words, your ideas regularly before they trust you. Over time, this creates familiarity → trust → opportunities.

However, posting without a plan is like going to the gym without a workout routine. You'll move around, maybe lift a few weights, but you won't make progress. The same happens on LinkedIn: you post, but it doesn't add up to anything.

For professionals in enterprise environments, the system also needs boundaries. Your calendar should account for time availability, employer policies, confidentiality rules, and topics you should not comment on publicly.

With a **content calendar**:

- You stay consistent – your audience sees you show up week after week
- You save time – no more last-minute "what should I post today?" panic
- You build strategically – every post aligns with your bigger mission
- You avoid burnout – because you've already spread the load

Here's how to build a simple, effective content calendar plan:

- **Step 1: Decide your frequency**

  Pick a pace you can actually sustain. 3–4 posts per week works well if you want to grow faster. If it's mainly for your own presence, 2–3 posts per week is a solid sweet spot. Daily posting can work if you have the capacity, but remember: consistency beats intensity. For most people, posting every day quickly becomes hard to maintain.

- **Step 2: Choose your buckets (themes)**

  Buckets are the categories you rotate through so your content feels fresh but still connected. Pick 3–4 that tie directly to your mission. Example buckets:

  - Industry insights (commentary on trends, data, reports)
  - Personal stories (career lessons, failures, behind the scenes)
  - Tactical how-tos (frameworks, templates, step-by-steps)
  - Bold opinions (contrarian takes, myths busted, debates)

  These become your content DNA. When in doubt, go back to the buckets.

- **Step 3: Map out your month**

  Take a simple calendar – Google Sheets, Notion, or even a notebook – and assign content buckets to specific days. A content planning template can be found in the repository, ready to download and adapt. For example:

  - Monday → Industry insight
  - Wednesday → Story
  - Friday → How to

  This way, you create a predictable rhythm. And just as important: your audience learns what to expect. Before you start posting, outline at least three weeks of content in advance. This gives you momentum, removes the pressure of thinking on the spot, and helps you stay consistent. Keep in mind: it usually takes time until your posts gain traction—patience and persistence are key.

- **Step 4: Fill it with ideas**

  Block one recurring time slot each week to review ideas and prepare upcoming posts. Don't worry about polish. Just headlines or bullets.

- **Step 5: Review and adapt**

  After a month, look back: which posts got engagement? Which buckets felt natural? What fell flat? Double down on what works, cut what doesn't. A content calendar isn't fixed – it evolves with you. You don't need a fancy tool to start. A simple Excel sheet already works.

  If you prefer using a dedicated tool for your content calendar – and want something even easier to navigate – here are some solid options:

  - Notion – flexible, customizable, and integrates with your broader workflow
  - Trello – simple drag-and-drop boards that make scheduling visual
  - Airtable – spreadsheet power combined with calendar and kanban views

The tool doesn't matter as much as the habit. What really counts is having a system where you can see at a glance what's coming up next. Whether that's a simple Excel sheet or a dedicated tool (we'll go deeper into AI tools for writing in the next chapter) – both work.

The hidden hack – maintaining a backlog

If you want to stay consistent and make your life much easier, you should also start creating a content backlog. A backlog is a *living list* of draft ideas and potential posts. Some are just titles. Some are half-written. Some are 40% done. It doesn't matter. The point is: you're never starting from zero.

To build this, you don't need any tools. A pencil and notebook, a basic notes app, or even Microsoft Word are enough. The real value lies in capturing ideas consistently.

A backlog gives you big advantages:

- When work or life gets busy, you can pull from drafts instead of facing a blank page.
- Writing down ideas forces you to refine your thinking over time.
- The more you write, the more ideas come up. Writing regularly trains your brain to spot post material everywhere.

> Block time on the weekend to review and refine your backlog.
>
> - Carry a notebook or use your phone notes to capture ideas as they come.
> - Don't over-edit early. Keep adding. Keep building.

Over time, you'll notice a shift. When you write regularly, your brain adapts. You start spotting content ideas everywhere—in conversations, in work challenges, even while commuting.

That's the real power of a backlog: not just stored content, but an engine that trains you to think and communicate more sharply every day.

The hidden side of LinkedIn – networking and DMs

Most people treat LinkedIn like a broadcast platform. It's not. The real value lives in the backstage conversations. Every post is an excuse to connect, every comment a chance to build relationships. A practical networking approach is simple:

- Respond to every meaningful comment. Visibility is currency.
- Use DMs to build relationships, not sell. "Thanks for engaging on my post – curious to hear your perspective" goes much further than "Can I pitch you?"
- Keep track of people who consistently engage with your content over time, and reciprocate by genuinely engaging with theirs.
- Cold DMs trying to sell something are very common on the platform. Before you ask for something, think about what you can offer. Add value first. That's how relationships start.

That is how consistent contributors move from *posting into the void* to becoming part of a living, breathing professional network.

Using AI for personal branding

There are two camps: AI kills authenticity vs. AI writes for you. The truth sits in the middle.

If you hand everything to AI, your content turns generic. Worse, your voice starts to sound like everyone else's: same tone, same structure, same safe conclusions. If you ignore AI, you waste time. The winning approach is simple: use AI as an amplifier, not as a replacement.

Bring the substance yourself: lived experience, domain insight, project lessons, personal observations, messy notes, and real examples. Let AI help with structure, clarity, and speed. AI can improve the packaging. It should not invent the point.

These are the areas where it actually makes a meaningful difference:

- **Content creation support** – brainstorm ideas, generate hooks, and structure your thoughts.
- **Profile optimization** – analyze your LinkedIn profile for keywords, clarity, and positioning. Screenshot or copy your profile and ask AI to roast it.

- **Content strategy** – draft a cadence and topic map, pressure-test formats, and review engagement patterns.
- **Writing enhancement** – polish grammar and clarity while keeping your voice intact. This is especially helpful for non-native speakers.

But there's a hard stop to what AI can offer. AI cannot supply your lived perspective. Your stories, failures, and judgment are the differentiators. Authenticity cannot be automated. Use AI for ideation, structure, polish, and analytics, but keep the insights and narratives human – that is the edge.

You can use these prompts to anchor your voice:

- What problems do I solve that no tool can answer alone?
- Which experiences shaped my perspective?
- What outcomes do people get when they work with me?

These answers become brand pillars, giving you space to let AI do the heavy lifting around them—idea generation, structuring, formatting, and analytics. You provide the signal; AI scales it.

Audiences are already flooded with AI-generated noise. What cuts through is a professional voice that is genuine, useful, and consistent. AI is not here to replace your voice but to free time so you can use that voice more effectively.

AI tools for LinkedIn

A new industry has emerged around personal branding tools. Many of them are thin wrappers on top of LLMs – with solid prompting you can often get similar writing results directly. But the better platforms add real utility beyond drafting: integrated content calendars, scheduling, analytics, team workflows, asset libraries, and idea capture. Used well, they save time and reduce friction.

For your **first posts**, you don't need any of this. A simple outline and ChatGPT are enough. If you enjoy tooling – or plan to publish consistently – these platforms can help you get organized and scale.

Here's how you can evaluate tools:

- **Workflow fit** – do you get a calendar, backlog, and scheduling in one place, or just "write better" posts?
- **Control** – can you set your voice constraints, templates, and approval steps?

- **Feedback loop** – basic analytics at minimum, ideally post-level insights that inform your next iteration
- **Practicalities** – free tier to start, quick setup, and painless export of your drafts and data

Remember, however, that tools are accelerators, not prerequisites. Start with an outline and a clean prompt. Add a platform when the manual process becomes a bottleneck.

Tool	What it does
MagicPost	AI-powered LinkedIn post generator that drafts post variations and schedules posts
RedactAI	Generates clean, concise LinkedIn posts tailored by analyzing trending posts and tones
Taplio	AI-assisted post writing with engagement tracking, scheduling, content calendar
SocialPilot	Simple AI-generated LinkedIn drafts, scheduling and multi-platform management
EasyGen	Creates original LinkedIn thought-leadership posts from diverse content types (PDFs, images)
Hootsuite	AI post generator for social media managers, fast LinkedIn post templates
Draftly	Professional LinkedIn post writing, industry-specific templates, scheduling
Copy.ai	General AI writing tool with LinkedIn-specific templates and storytelling support
Writesonic	AI writer that crafts LinkedIn posts and long-form content, SEO-optimized
AuthoredUp	Focuses on LinkedIn content creation, drafts, hooks, post preview, scheduling, and analytics

Table 11.1: Overview of tools for LinkedIn

Tool features and availability change frequently — verify current details directly with the provider and avoid uploading confidential employer, client, or internal material.

Consistency – the real secret

Among everything covered in this chapter, one theme deserves to stand on its own:

Consistency.

Consistency might sound obvious – everyone says they know it matters. But knowing it and living it are two very different things.

Across professional content discussions, consistency often gets brushed aside – reduced to a throwaway line like "post regularly" before moving on to flashier tactics. Yet when people who have built sizable professional audiences are asked how they did it, the answer often comes down to this: consistency isn't an afterthought. It's the whole game.

A common question is: "What's the trick? How do people grow so fast?" The answer is simple: there is no trick. There is only the work. That's why most people fail. They put in two weeks of effort, don't see results, and quit. But audiences don't trust bursts. They trust patterns – and they trust the person who shows up again and again.

We live in an AI-powered world where anyone can generate polished content in seconds. But the rarest and most valuable signal is still human consistency. Consistency proves you're not just another automated account. It shows you'll be here tomorrow, not just today. You don't need to post every day. What you need is rhythm. Two or three strong posts a week, repeated over months, will outperform a flurry of daily activity followed by silence.

If there's one key takeaway from this chapter for you, it's this: **personal branding isn't about hacks or shortcuts. It's about showing up, again and again, long after others stop**.

Consistency compounds. It's not glamorous, and it's not easy. But it's the principle that separates those who talk about building a brand from those who actually build one.

Expanding beyond LinkedIn

So far, we've focused on LinkedIn – for good reason. It's the most direct and effective platform for career visibility, especially in corporate settings. But LinkedIn is not the only game in town. Depending on your goals, skills, and audience, other platforms can play a major role in building your personal brand.

The key is strategy over scatter: don't try to be everywhere at once. Pick one or two additional platforms that complement LinkedIn and strengthen your positioning. Think of them as amplifiers, each with its own "format" and community logic. Here are the most relevant options:

1. YouTube – build authority in motion

   If LinkedIn is your digital resume, YouTube is your digital stage.

   - Why it matters: YouTube is the second largest search engine in the world. People don't just scroll here – they search for answers. This makes it an ideal place to establish yourself as a teacher, explainer, or thought leader.
   - What works: Tutorials, explainers, trend breakdowns, case studies, or even documenting your learning journey. Videos have higher trust because they show your personality and expertise in action.
   - Pro tip: You don't need studio-quality production. Clear sound, decent lighting, and consistency beat fancy edits. Many careers have been built on simple "talking head + slides" formats.
   - How it connects to LinkedIn: Every video is repurposable into short clips, quotes, or posts. YouTube becomes the "content well" from which you draw daily material for LinkedIn.

2. GitHub – proof of work for tech roles

   Not a social network in the traditional sense, but for developers, engineers, and technical specialists, GitHub is a portfolio that speaks louder than words.

   - Why it matters: Recruiters and hiring managers for technical roles often check GitHub before LinkedIn. A strong contribution history signals hands-on capability. If you apply for tech roles, you should think about building a repo to showcase your skills.
   - What works: Hosting side projects, contributing to open-source repos, sharing code snippets or AI/ML notebooks. Even small contributions show initiative.
   - Pro tip: Don't worry if your repo isn't perfect – what matters is visible progress and clarity. Document what the project does and what you learned building it.
   - How it connects to LinkedIn: Write posts about the lessons you learned while working on your GitHub projects. "Behind the scenes" stories make technical work more relatable to non-technical audiences.

3. Medium (or blog platforms) – long-form thinking

   Some ideas need more space than a LinkedIn post allows. That's where blogs shine.

   - Why it matters: A blog is an evergreen asset. Well-written articles can rank on Google (SEO) and bring you inbound opportunities months or years later.
   - What works: Deep dives, how-to guides, personal reflections, or research-backed pieces. Medium, Substack, or your own WordPress site all work – the tool doesn't matter, the writing does.
   - Examples: Engineers explaining new architectures, consultants writing industry analyses, designers breaking down case studies.
   - Pro tip: Use your blog as a "home base" and distribute snippets to LinkedIn or X. Blogs compound authority over time.
   - How it connects to LinkedIn: Blog posts can be repurposed into carousels, summaries, or single sharp insights that drive traffic back to your long-form work.

4. X (formerly Twitter) – real-time conversation

   X is noisy, chaotic, and often politicized – but it still has pockets of high-value conversations, especially in tech and entrepreneurship.

   - Why it matters: Many investors, founders, and researchers share ideas on X first, before they hit mainstream channels. If you want to engage in real-time debates and spot early trends, it's useful.
   - What works: Short takes, threads, sharing resources, engaging in discussions. Virality is possible, but the shelf life of posts is short.
   - How it connects to LinkedIn: Use X for "in the moment" commentary, then bring the distilled, professional version of those insights back to LinkedIn. It's not as career-friendly as LinkedIn – recruiters rarely source there, and companies post less. For early-career professionals, it should not be the main platform.

5. Newsletters (Substack, beehiiv) – owning the relationship

   A newsletter is the ultimate long game. While social platforms control the algorithm, newsletters give you a direct line to your audience.

   - Why it matters: Email is still the most intimate digital channel. People who subscribe are choosing to hear from you regularly. That's a stronger bond than a "follow."

- What works: Curated updates, personal reflections, trend breakdowns, or practical guides. The format can be short or long, but consistency is key.
- Challenges: It's a heavy lift. Newsletters require discipline and long-term thinking. Don't start one until you've proven you can create consistently on LinkedIn or another platform first.
- How it connects to LinkedIn: LinkedIn becomes your "top of funnel" – drawing attention, growing reach. Your newsletter converts a slice of that audience into a loyal inner circle.

6. Pulling it together – an integrated approach

   It's not LinkedIn vs. YouTube vs. GitHub vs. blogs vs. newsletters. It's about stacking platforms in a way that fits your goals.

   - If you're in tech, LinkedIn + GitHub works well.
   - If you're in consulting or business, LinkedIn + blog/newsletter makes sense.
   - If you're aiming for thought leadership at scale, LinkedIn + YouTube is the strongest combo.

The mistake most people make is to chase everything at once. Start with LinkedIn: master consistency there, then add one complementary channel. Over time, you can build a content ecosystem where each platform feeds the other. The flywheel works like this: LinkedIn grows reach. YouTube or blogs build depth. GitHub or portfolio proves skills. Newsletter builds ownership.

Play the platforms like instruments in an orchestra. Alone they sound fine. Together, they make you unforgettable.

Why you should start now

AI and especially LLMs have changed how work is found, done, and recognized. Paths into roles are less linear, and proof of value happens in public. Your brand is the human signal in the algorithmic noise—the reason people remember and choose you.

We live in a culture of instant gratification. We check likes within minutes. We measure success in notifications. But personal branding doesn't work that way. It's a long game disguised as a series of small, unremarkable actions.

Post. Comment. Refine. Repeat.

And then, somewhere around month four or five – sometimes later – something shifts. The phone rings. The DM arrives. The opportunity appears. Not because you went viral, but because you were there, week after week, when everyone else had quit.

This chapter wasn't designed to make personal branding sound easy. It was designed to make it doable. Because the truth is, most people already possess everything they need: expertise from their work, stories from their failures, and perspectives shaped by experience. What they lack is a system to make that value visible—and the discipline to sustain it.

Let's revisit what that system looks like:

- **First, you position yourself by finding your mission**. Not as everything to everyone, but as the person who solves one specific problem better than most. Your mission isn't a corporate slogan. It's the answer to a simple question: if someone lands on your profile six months from now, what should they immediately understand about you? Clarity here is everything. Vagueness kills careers. Specificity opens doors.
- **Second, you build your online presence**. A profile that signals competence. A content rhythm that doesn't rely on inspiration. A backlog that ensures you're never starting from zero. These aren't glamorous tasks, but they're the difference between posting sporadically and building a presence. Think of them as the scaffolding – invisible once the building is up, but essential while you're constructing it.
- **Third, you build a repeatable system and use it consistently**. This doesn't mean spamming your network or chasing viral moments. It means showing up in the right rooms, engaging meaningfully, and letting your content do the heavy lifting. LinkedIn rewards consistency and conversation, not volume. Three strong posts per week, coupled with genuine engagement, will outperform a flood of mediocrity every time.

Throughout all of this, AI should serve one role: it is an amplifier. It will not write your story or manufacture your credibility, but it will help you draft faster, brainstorm smarter, and refine more clearly. The professionals who succeed will not be the ones who avoid AI or surrender to it; they will be the ones who use it to free time for the work only they can do: thinking, connecting, and showing up as themselves.

The professionals who thrive in the next decade will not necessarily have the most credentials. They will be the people others recognize, trust, and remember – the ones who show up, share what they learn, and turn expertise into a signal strong enough to cut through the noise.

The beauty of this moment is that you don't need to be a natural writer, have thousands of followers, or crave the spotlight. What you need is a decision: stop waiting for permission, stop doubting your value, and stop letting your best work disappear into the void.

Your first post will not be perfect, and your tenth probably will not be either. By your fiftieth, something will have changed – not only your content, but also your confidence, your network, and the opportunities in your inbox. The people who will shape your career are already out there; they are waiting to see if you will show up long enough to be noticed.

Personal branding is not a side project you pick up when work is slow or when you finally "have time." It is the work. It ensures that when opportunity knocks, you are not scrambling to prove yourself—you are already known.

The playbook is in your hands, the platforms are free, and the tools are accessible. The only question is whether you will commit to the one thing that separates people who talk about building a presence from those who actually build one: **Consistency**.

Not inspiration. Not talent. Not luck. Consistency – the quiet, unglamorous discipline of showing up again and again, long after the excitement fades and the novelty wears off. That is when the real work begins, and that is when the results follow.

Start today, not tomorrow, and not when your profile feels perfect. Write the outline, draft the hook, and hit publish. Then do it again next week and the week after that.

The future does not care about your doubts, but it rewards those who show up anyway. Your invisible parachute is waiting.

Time to build it!

Summary

In the age of AI, where content is easily automated and entry-level pathways are shifting, professional success relies on cultivating a deliberate personal brand – the human signal in a world of algorithmic noise. This chapter laid out a framework to build a durable AI identity, emphasizing that visibility must be treated as professional strategy, not vanity. The process rests on three pillars: first, defining a clear mission to anchor your focus and build trust; second, turning your LinkedIn profile into a platform that serves as your digital handshake and storefront; and third, implementing a repeatable system to keep content consistent and prevent burnout. AI is an amplifier, accelerating drafting, and idea generation, but your personal stories, judgment, and expertise are what differentiate you. The most important takeaway: success comes not from going viral, but from the quiet, strategic discipline of consistency – showing up, again, and again, long after others have quit, turning your expertise into lasting recognition.

In the next chapter, we will show you how to navigate the AI job market strategically, strengthen your professional presence, and excel in technical and behavioral interviews.

12

Conquering the AI Job Market – Strategic Search Techniques and Interview Excellence

> *"A strong resume helps you get through the first filter and earn an initial conversation with HR or a hiring manager. But a resume alone rarely closes the gap to an offer. In most hiring processes, there is a second screen that is less formal and often more decisive: your digital footprint."*
>
> *–Andreas Horn*

Generative AI is changing how labor markets match talent to jobs. Job seekers use AI to apply at scale. Employers use AI to filter at scale. The result is a new hiring reality: algorithms increasingly decide who gets seen, and humans decide who gets hired.

To navigate this landscape, you need two things at the same time. First is technical optimization to pass the algorithmic gatekeepers (**Applicant Tracking Systems** (**ATS**), keyword filters, automated screens). And second are human trust signals that make a hiring manager want to work with you. This chapter is about building both.

The important part is this: algorithms can make you visible. Trust is still earned human to human. People hire people. Your network is still the single highest-impact channel, especially in AI-adjacent roles where trust, learning speed, and ambiguity tolerance matter. In an AI-filtered job market, the smartest move is often to avoid the hiring funnel entirely. Many roles are filled through internal mobility, referrals, and networks before they ever hit a public job board. A warm introduction does not guarantee an offer, but it materially increases the chance that a human reads your profile and considers your context. Most larger companies and many startups have referral systems that route applications directly to **human resources** (**HR**) and often accelerate screening. Do not ask people who barely know you to refer you. It puts them in an awkward position and can feel unethical. The best referrals come from people who have worked with you, seen your work, or can credibly vouch for your skills, judgment, or character.

This is why you should build your network consistently. Stay in touch and help others when they are in job search mode. A network functions as a professional bridge and a parachute. You do not build it when you need it. You build it long before, through small, consistent signals of trust and usefulness. With a strong network, asking for referrals feels natural, and your odds go up fast.

But network is not enough. You still need clarity on the role you want, the company environments where you can win, a resume that survives screening, and interview stories that hold up under pressure. This chapter walks you through the pre-work that takes you from outreach to offer in today's job market.

In this chapter, we will:

- Understand how AI is reshaping hiring and the AI job market
- Define your career objectives, target role, skill shape, and company list
- Build a resume that passes automated screening and earns human trust
- Use AI tools to improve your resume, cover letter, and job search process safely
- Create a portfolio and digital footprint that show real proof of work
- Prepare for interviews with reusable stories, project deep dives, and AI-assisted rehearsal

How AI is changing the job market

The job market is going through a structural reset. Entry roles are fewer, expectations are higher, and traditional career ladders are less reliable than they were a decade ago. Getting a foothold appears to be harder in many AI-exposed entry-level roles, as confirmed through a recent large-scale study conducted by Stanford University (`https://digitaleconomy.stanford.edu/wp-content/uploads/2025/08/Canaries_BrynjolfssonChandarChen.pdf`). Data confirms that companies are hiring fewer workers aged 22–25 in AI-vulnerable jobs, such as software engineering, customer service, and marketing. A decrease in entry-level positions matters because it reshapes the early-career on-ramp. There are fewer structured programs, fewer "learn on the job" roles, and less tolerance for slow ramp-up. That means early-career professionals need to build proof earlier: projects, portfolios, internships, certifications, open-source contributions, or concrete examples that show they can learn fast and apply skills in practice. AI is not the only driver. These changes are happening on top of a broader market correction. The post-COVID cycle matters: overhiring, cheap money, and then a fast correction as interest rates rose and budgets tightened.

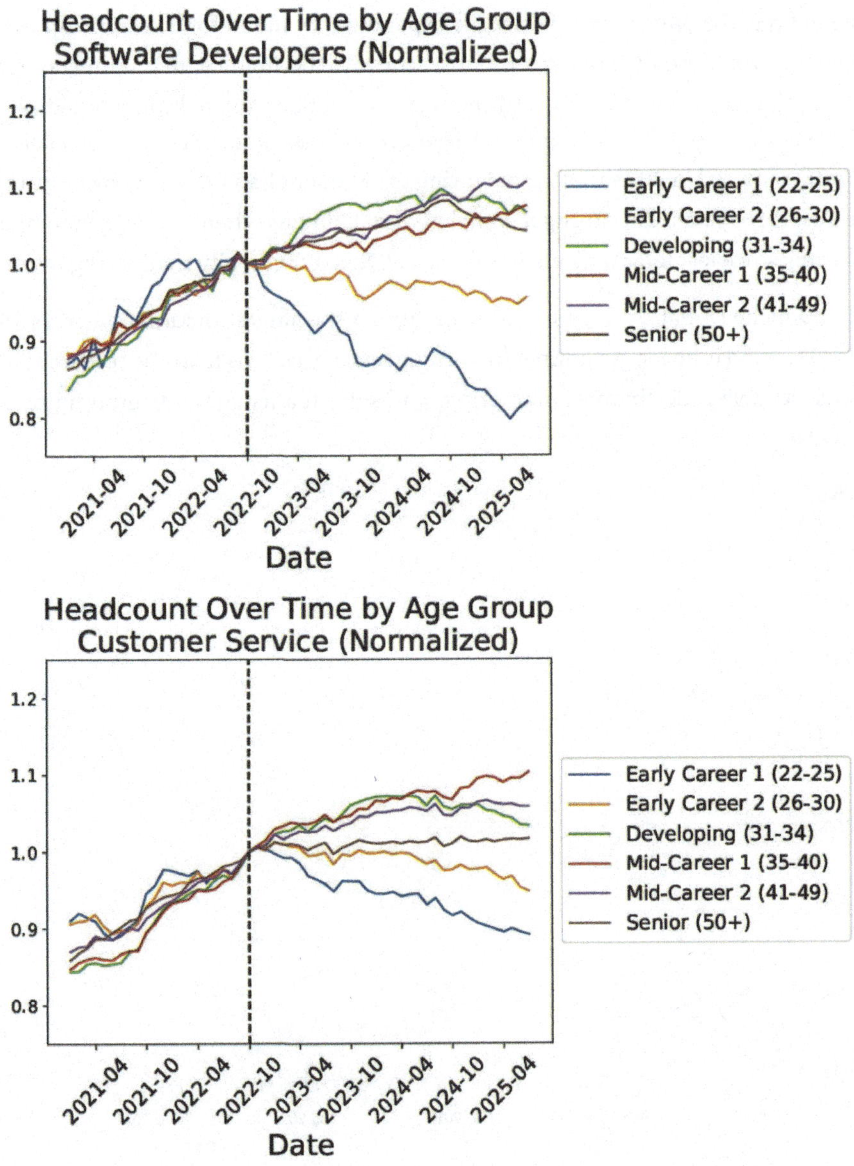

Figure 12.1: Employment changes for software developers and customer service agents by age (Stanford University 2025)

However, AI changes something much deeper than just headcount. It changes the mechanics of hiring. The pipeline is increasingly mediated by software: ATS filters, keyword screens, automated assessments, and ranking systems. In many processes, the first selection is made by algorithms and only later handed to humans.

At the same time, the opportunity surface is expanding. Demand for AI capability is spreading beyond engineering into product, operations, strategy, HR, finance, marketing, and sales. You can see it in the language of hiring and the pace of AI talent acquisition. LinkedIn (`https://economicgraph.linkedin.com/content/dam/me/economicgraph/en-us/PDF/Work-Change-Report.pdf`) reported in 2025 that global hiring for AI talent had increased by more than 300% over the past three years. The stronger signal is what happens when AI hiring is compared with overall hiring: since last fall, AI hiring has grown 30% faster globally than hiring overall.

This is not a niche signal. It shows AI moving from a specialist function to a cross-functional capability. Demand is no longer limited to AI engineers or machine learning researchers. Product, operations, strategy, HR, finance, marketing, and sales teams are all beginning to absorb AI-related skills.

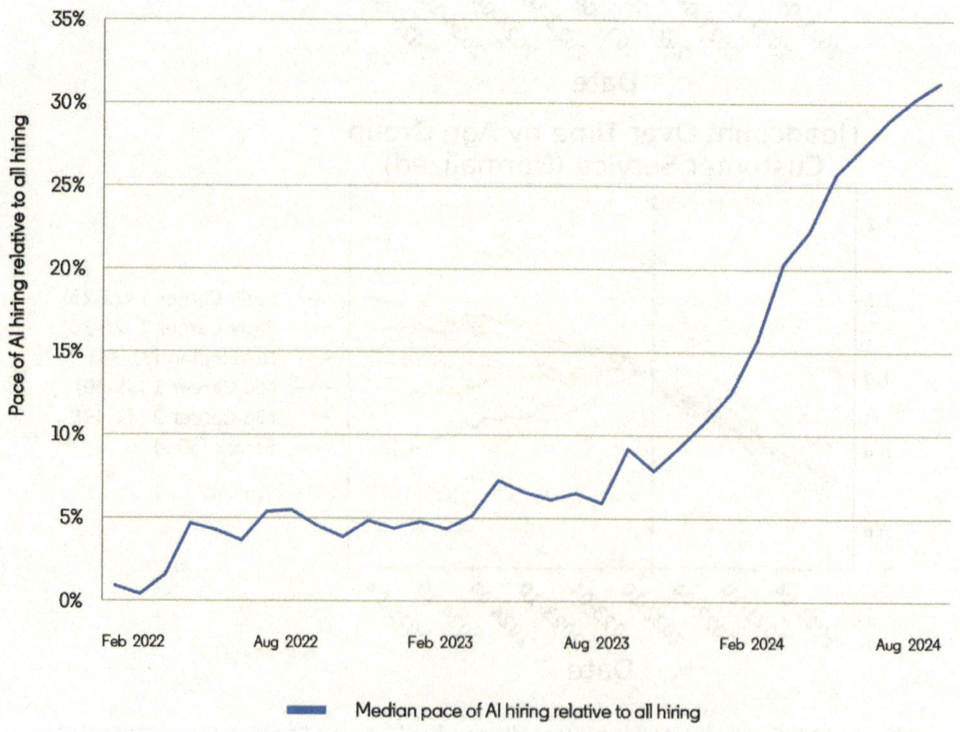

Figure 12.2: Change in global AI hiring relative to all hiring (LinkedIn, 2025)

So yes, AI removes tasks. But it also creates roles, reshapes functions, and upgrades expectations across many jobs that are not "deeply technical." The winning profile in this market is not just someone who can use AI tools. It is someone who can apply them to real workflows, produce outcomes, and do it responsibly.

That is the career shift: from AI usage to AI impact.

Before you optimize your resume or start applying, you need direction. The next section helps you define your target role, understand the company environments where you can win, and position yourself strategically in the AI job market.

Laying the groundwork – defining your career objectives and identifying target companies

Before you use AI tools to "optimize" your job search, you need a target. Otherwise, you will produce a highly polished version of the wrong application.

Start with a simple self-assessment. Define the role family you are aiming for. A role family is the broad category of work you want to be hired into, such as AI engineering, product management, data strategy, solutions architecture, operations, or change management. Then clarify the industry context you want to operate in and the skills you want to be hired for in the next six to twelve months. This is not a philosophical exercise. It is a filter that determines which opportunities you pursue—whether through applications, referrals, direct outreach, or internal conversations—how you present your experience, and what proof you need to build.

If you are reading this and have worked through the previous chapters, you should now have an understanding of what is possible with AI – and a clear view of your own strengths, as well as the areas you want to develop further. The most reliable way to make this visible is to write it down and shape it intentionally as a **T-shaped** profile. A T-shaped profile means depth in one core area, combined with working literacy across adjacent domains (see *Figure 12.3*). This concept is especially relevant in AI-driven work because most AI roles cut across functions. You need depth to be credible and breadth to connect your work to product, data, engineering, risk, operations, and business outcomes.

The vertical bar of the "T" represents deep expertise – the skill that makes you clearly hirable. The horizontal bar represents breadth – enough understanding to collaborate, scale impact, and connect dots across disciplines.

In practice, that means going deep in one stack. For example, AI Engineering can be your vertical spike. On top of that, you layer horizontal literacy in areas like product, data risk, or thought leadership and communication. Not to compete with specialists in those fields, but to operate effectively across them. That combination is what stands out in 2026 applications.

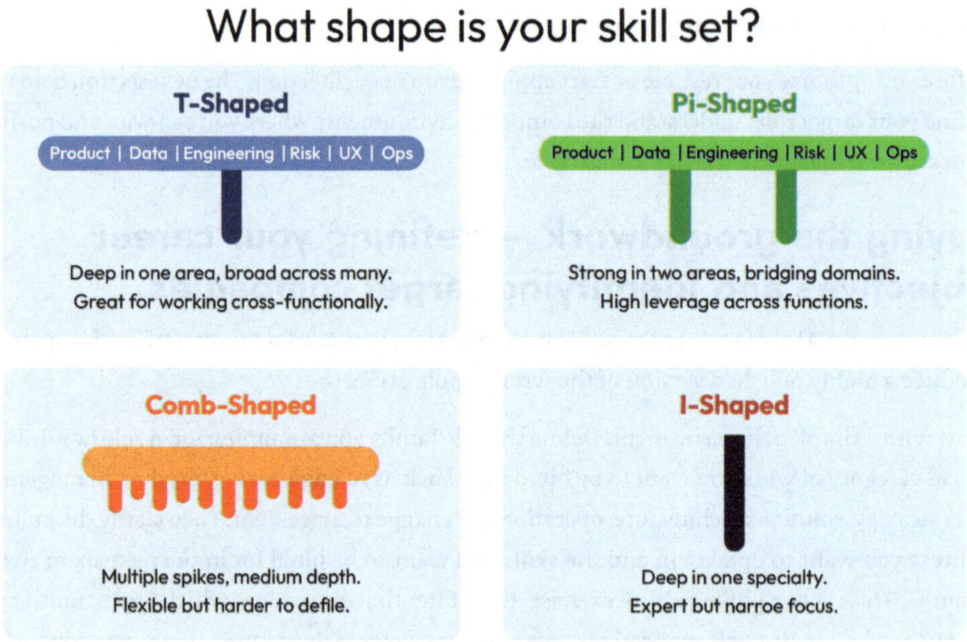

Figure 12.3: How to think about your career as a skill shape

As your career evolves, you will encounter other skill profiles and shapes. A **Pi-shaped** profile means depth in two domains, for example, product and data, or security and AI. This pays off once you operate at the intersection of teams and can bridge competing priorities. A **comb-shaped** profile shows multiple medium-depth spikes across areas. It offers flexibility, but it is harder to position unless you can clearly articulate where you create value. An **I-shaped** profile represents deep specialization in a single domain. This can work in narrow expert roles, but it limits your ability to influence end-to-end outcomes. The T-shaped model remains a reliable foundation for building credibility, adaptability, and long-term career durability in an AI-driven market. This model is widely used in consulting, technology, and cross-functional business environments.

If you are early in your career or transitioning into AI, focusing on a T-shaped profile first is a strong starting point. One clear depth makes you hirable, and broad literacy makes you effective. The other shapes become more interesting later, once you have earned trust, built proof, and can afford to combine strengths deliberately.

The four roles that actually exist in the AI job market

In the AI job market, most roles fall into four archetypes. Use them as a compass for your T-shaped profile: decide where you go deep, where you stay broad, and which skills you need to demonstrate for the roles you are targeting. Your goal is to shape your profile to match one archetype deliberately:

- Builders create models, agents, and data foundations – roles like ML Engineer, LLM Engineer, AI Engineer, and Data Engineer
- Integrators connect AI capabilities to real products and platforms – including AI Product Manager, Solutions Architect, and Platform Engineer
- Operators run AI systems in production and tie them to reliability, security, and scale – such as AI operations specialists, MLOps engineers, reliability engineers, and security analysts applying AI in detection and response
- Enablers drive adoption and sustainability – covering AI Educators, Change Leads, Responsible AI specialists, and analysts using LLMs to redesign workflows

Do not choose the archetype that sounds exciting. Choose the one where you can produce credible proof: relevant experience, transferable skills, shipped work, measurable outcomes, or artifacts that show you can actually do the work. The highest demand sits where value can be measured and defended. If you cannot translate your work into outcomes, you will struggle in interviews even if your resume looks perfect.

From random applications to a focused target list

Most job seekers have no strategy and just blindly apply to every role or filter roles by title, salary, and brand. In the current job market, that is a weak strategy. What determines whether a role becomes a career accelerator or a frustrating detour is company maturity.

GenAI work is not only about models. It is about whether an organization can deploy, evaluate, govern, and scale AI without struggling to operationalize. Two companies can advertise the same job title. In one, you will ship in weeks. In the other, you will spend more time on internal coordination than on delivery. That is why company maturity matters. It determines whether your work turns into shipped outcomes or gets slowed by internal complexity. Your job search should understand the difference and make a deliberate choice based on what you need at this stage of your career.

A practical target is to build a list of twenty to forty companies. Cluster them into tiers: first-choice targets and second-tier options. This may feel like extra work upfront, but it saves time later because you stop pursuing opportunities randomly. You can tailor faster, prioritize outreach, and tell a more coherent story in interviews because your narrative is built around a clear set of environments, not a scattered set of applications.

A practical framework to define your personal skill shape, target market map, and opportunity thesis

There are 6 key questions you should ask yourself:

- "What role do I want to be hired for in the next 6 to 12 months, and what would success look like in that role?"
- "Which type of work do I want to do most days – building, integrating, operating, or enabling AI in an organization?"
- "What proof do I already have that I can deliver outcomes in that archetype – metrics, artifacts, shipped work, stakeholder wins?"
- "In which workflows do I understand the pain deeply enough to be credible – support, IT ops, finance, developer productivity, risk and compliance, or something else?"
- "Which company environments will accelerate me rather than slow my growth – maturity, data reality, governance, leadership appetite?"
- "Act as my career strategist. Help me define a T-shaped job profile that fits my target role and seniority level without overshooting."

`Target role [YOUR INPUT]:`

Target level: [New grad/Mid-level/Senior/Executive]

`Target time horizon: [6-12 months]`

Archetype (choose one): [Builder/Integrator/Operator/Enabler]

Domain workflow credibility (where I know the pain): [Support / IT Ops / Finance / Dev Productivity / Risk and Compliance / Other]

`Proof I already have (metrics, artifacts, shipped work, wins): [YOUR INPUT]`

Company environment that fits me (maturity, data reality, governance, leadership appetite): [YOUR INPUT]

Once you know your target role, archetype, and company list, the next step is to turn that strategy into a clear application narrative. Your resume is where this starts. It should translate your positioning into evidence: the skills, outcomes, and proof points that make your fit easy to understand.

Start building your resume

After you know your target role, T-shaped profile, and opportunity thesis, the next step is to translate that strategy into a sharp resume. A well-written resume can make a significant difference in getting the interview.

However, before an application reaches a human recruiter, many companies first process it through automated screening systems known as **Applicant Tracking Systems (ATS)**. In 2026, these systems have evolved from simple keyword counters to sophisticated semantic analysis engines. Many modern recruiting platforms have moved beyond simple Boolean keyword searches (where recruiters combine exact terms using operators like AND, OR, and NOT) and increasingly use semantic matching or AI-assisted ranking— analyzing meaning and identifying relevant matches even when the exact words do not appear. For example, a recruiter can search for "candidates with 7+ years in high-growth startups," and the AI will identify profiles that reflect that specific context, even if those exact words are not present. Jobscan reported in 2025 (`https://www.jobscan.co/state-of-the-job-search`) that the vast majority of Fortune 500 companies use ATS platforms. Because most applications are submitted online, you should assume your resume is parsed by software before a human ever reads it.

This new reality around AI-driven automated screening systems is turning hiring into a more algorithmic process. Matching engines increasingly rank candidates based on skills, preferences, and inferred fit, and they surface roles that might never show up in a manual search. The implication is simple: you must optimize for two audiences at the same time. First, the systems that decide whether you get seen. Second, the humans who decide whether they trust you.

That is the AI-to-AI reality: your resume may first be written, tailored, or checked with AI, and then read, parsed, or ranked by another AI system before a human ever sees it. The goal is not to game the machine. The goal is to make your real experience clear enough for both systems and people to understand. However, optimizing for the machine does not mean writing for a machine. It means making your real experience easy to parse, easy to verify, and hard to ignore. Before you optimize anything, make your skills visible.

How to write an AI-resilient resume

An AI-friendly resume is machine-readable. It parses cleanly, gets indexed correctly, and matches the keywords and structures these systems search for. Let's have a look at how to survive the first wave and build an AI-resilient resume.

Step 1: Get the format right (so you do not fail on a technicality)

Many ATS-related issues have less to do with experience and more to do with formatting and parsing.

Use a simple, single-column layout. Avoid tables, text boxes, images, icons, and multi-column designs. Keep section titles obvious: Experience, Education, Skills, Certifications, Projects. Write dates consistently (MM/YYYY or YYYY). Keep your contact details as plain text. An ATS-friendly resume file is available in the repository for download and adaptation.

Choose a file format that matches the employer workflow. If a posting requests a specific format, follow it. If it does not, submit either a .docx file or a text-based PDF and avoid scanned PDFs. Many systems parse text-based PDFs well and recommend PDF unless the employer requests .docx. The practical rule is simple: whatever you submit, test it by copying a full section from the file and pasting it into a plain text editor.

Step 2: Write for search and for trust

Think of your resume as a searchable database entry and a credibility document at the same time.

To make it searchable, you need the right terms in the right places. Recruiters often search an ATS database using keywords from the job description, especially skills, tools, and certifications. That means your job title and summary cannot be poetic—they must be aligned.

To make it credible, your bullets need to show outcomes, not activity. A strong bullet has five parts: action, scope, mechanism, outcome, metric. Not all five need to be long, but all five need to be there.

Example shift in tone: "Worked on GenAI initiatives" is not evidence. Better: "Cut quarterly report generation time by 40% by automating the data pipeline with Python and dbt." Strong resume bullets do not just describe what you touched; they show what changed because of your work.

Step 3: Keywords without keyword stuffing

The fastest way to get filtered out is to look generic. The second fastest way is to keyword-stuff your skills section like a shopping list.

Do it cleanly instead:

- Extract 10–20 keywords from the job description that represent skills, tools, responsibilities, and outcomes.
- Mirror the exact phrasing for the ones that matter (for example, if they say "MLOps" do not rename it "model operations").
- Do not duplicate keywords just to satisfy a system. Use the skills section for clear scanning, and use experience bullets to prove the most important skills through real work, outcomes, and evidence.

Step 4: Make your resume AI-resilient by adding proof that systems cannot fake

AI has made it easier to produce polished resumes, which means polish is now cheap. Add proof signals that are hard to generate without real experience:

- Numbers tied to a mechanism (what changed, how it changed, and by how much)
- Constraints you worked under (latency, compliance, stakeholder complexity, scale)
- Artifacts you can reference (portfolio link, case study PDF, GitHub, slides, talks)

This is where most candidates lose. They describe what they worked on, but they do not show what changed because of their work.

Step 5: Keep LinkedIn and your resume consistent

Recruiters will cross-check. If titles, dates, scope, and claims do not match, you create doubt. Your goal is not perfection, but it is consistency.

Make sure your LinkedIn and any other platforms you use to demonstrate skills reinforce the same role thesis as your resume. Use the Featured section to highlight work samples, project links, case studies, talks, or posts that a one-page resume cannot fully capture.

Step 6: Use AI tools, but do not outsource your truth

AI can accelerate tailoring, rewriting, and keyword alignment. It can also quietly destroy your credibility if it invents details or smooths your voice into something generic.

Use AI for structure and clarity, not for fabrication. If you cannot defend a claim in an interview, it does not belong on the page.

A practical workflow for resume alignment and ATS readiness

Once you've worked through the steps above, here are five key instructions for your LLM to sharpen your resume and align it with your target roles.

Instruction 1 – Keyword extraction and mapping

Extract the 10–15 most important keywords and requirements from this job description. Group them into skills, tools, responsibilities, and outcomes. Then map each one to a specific line in my resume where it should appear, but only if I can truthfully support it. Job description: [paste]. My resume: [paste]

Instruction 2 – Bullet rewrite into proof format

Rewrite my experience bullets using action, scope, mechanism, outcome, and metric. Preserve truth; do not add new facts. If a metric is missing, suggest 2–3 defensible proxy metrics I could use instead. Bullets: [paste]

Instruction 3 – Consistency check against LinkedIn

Compare my resume and my LinkedIn for consistency. Flag any mismatches in titles, dates, scope, or claims. Then propose a revised LinkedIn headline and 4-line About section that matches my resume and includes the most relevant keywords for this target role: [role]. Resume: [paste]. LinkedIn text: [paste].

Instruction 4 – Minimal tailoring for a specific job (fast and safe)

Using the job description and my master resume, produce a tailored resume version by editing only: (1) the professional summary, (2) the top 2 most relevant roles, and (3) the skills section. Keep formatting ATS-safe. Do not invent facts. Integrate the highest-priority keywords naturally where I can truthfully support them. Output the revised sections only and list the exact keywords you added and where. Job description: [paste]. Master resume: [paste].

Instruction 5 – ATS audit

Act as an expert resume writer and ATS specialist. I will paste my resume below. Score it from 1–100 for ATS compatibility. List issues in three buckets: formatting (parsing blockers), structure/sections (missing or unclear), and content and keywords (weak proof, vague bullets, missing terms). Then give the 10 highest-impact fixes that improve ATS parsing and recruiter readability. Resume: [PASTE RESUME]

Keep in mind that you should tailor your resume slightly for each role. Not a full rewrite every time, but targeted edits where it matters: summary, top experience bullets, and skills.

Create one master resume that contains your full inventory of projects, responsibilities, outcomes, metrics, and proof points. From there, create a role-specific version tailored to one archetype and one target role. The master resume is your working inventory. The tailored resume is the focused version you submit.

Using AI tools for resume creation and ATS optimization

There is a growing market around AI tools for ATS optimization and resume creation. While a standard LLM is sufficient, specific tools offer better user experience and accelerate the creation of ATS-friendly resumes.

Tool	What it does
Teal	Job search workspace with ATS resume checker, match scores, keyword insights, and job-tracking board.
Jobscan	Deep ATS resume scanner that compares resume vs JD, keyword density, and delivers a match-rate score.
Resume Worded	AI resume and LinkedIn analyzer giving scores, line-by-line suggestions, and ATS-readiness feedback.
Rezi	AI resume and cover letter builder using ATS-friendly templates and keyword optimization.
Resume.io	Template-based resume and cover letter generator with simple ATS-friendly designs and export options.
Zety	Online resume and cover letter builder with guided suggestions and ATS-compatible formats.
Enhancv	Visual but ATS-aware resume builder with AI suggestions and role-specific tailoring.

Table 12.1: Overview of AI tools for resume creation and ATS optimization

Using AI for cover letter writing

With the surge of AI, cover letters have become less important. Fewer companies require them. So, we will not spend too much time here.

When a cover letter is requested, take it very seriously, because it shows whether you can connect your experience to the role with clarity. LLMs can help by generating a first draft and accelerating tailoring, but only if you treat the output as raw material. Recruiters can quickly spot generic AI text. If a cover letter is explicitly requested, put extra attention into it, because it will play a significant role. If your letter reads like it could be sent to any company, it does not help you – it hurts you. Use AI for structure and speed. You supply the specificity and proof.

A practical workflow for cover letter writing

A practical workflow for your LLM to help with cover letter writing is simple: extract the job's vocabulary, map it to your resume, then write a short letter that proves fit with two or three concrete examples. Keep it tight. In most cases, one page is already too long.

Instruction 1 – Extract role requirements and keywords

Act as a recruiter. Analyze the job description and extract the top 8 must-have skills, the top 5 nice-to-have skills, the tools and technologies mentioned, and the keywords that are repeated or emphasized and likely matter for screening. Output everything as a prioritized list. Job description: [PASTE JD].

Instruction 2 – Map requirements to your experience

Using my resume, map each must-have requirement to one or two concrete proof points from my experience. If a requirement is missing, either suggest a truthful way to address it or clearly flag it as a gap. Resume: [PASTE RESUME].

Instruction 3 – Draft the cover letter (human tone, proof-first)

Write a cover letter for [company] and [role]. Constraints: 200–300 words, no clichés, no generic admiration, no invented facts. Use only the mapped proof points above. Structure it as follows: a short opening that signals role fit, two body paragraphs each anchored in one concrete example with outcomes, and a single-sentence close. Job description: [PASTE JD]; Proof points: [PASTE MAPPING]

Final rule: never paste the AI draft as-is. Consider it to be at 70–80%. Edit for voice, remove filler, and make sure every claim connects to something you can defend in an interview. It's also very helpful to send it to colleagues or friends to reflect and add some human touch.

A resume is not enough – the portfolio as evidence

A strong resume helps you get through the first filter and earn an initial conversation with HR or a hiring manager. But a resume alone rarely closes the gap to an offer. In most hiring processes, there is a second screen that is less formal and often more decisive: your digital footprint.

This gains high relevance in companies with multi-round interview processes. In large AI organizations, it is normal to speak with 8 to 15 people across multiple rounds. The more interviewers you meet, the higher the probability that someone will look you up. They will not do it because they are skeptical. They do it because it is the easiest way to validate your skills: what you built, how you think, and whether your work holds up beyond a polished resume.

In AI and machine learning, a static resume is often insufficient. The field moves too fast, and credentials alone do not prove competence. What separates candidates is evidence of execution: projects that show you can go from idea to running system, not just from idea to notebook. Recruiters look for end-to-end implementation and production awareness: latency, scalability, monitoring, evaluation, failure modes, and responsible handling of data.

In an era where AI can generate a perfect cover letter in seconds, your portfolio is one of your strongest proof points. It is your proof layer. A well-maintained GitHub is the simplest version of that proof layer. Not because everyone will read your code line by line, but because it demonstrates three things quickly: you can ship, you can document, and you can sustain a project over time.

Here are five portfolio projects that signal real technical AI maturity:

1. **RAG system with evaluation and monitoring:** Build a retrieval-augmented generation system on a real dataset. Add offline evaluation (retrieval quality, answer quality) and online monitoring (latency, error rates, user feedback). Include a clear "how to run" guide and a short report of what improved results.
2. **Agentic workflow with guardrails:** Implement an agent that completes a bounded business workflow, for example: support ticket triage, incident summarization, or invoice extraction. Add guardrails: tool permissioning, deterministic fallbacks, and a human-in-the-loop checkpoint. Show failure cases and how your system handles them.
3. **Model serving with performance constraints:** Deploy an LLM or smaller model behind an API with caching, rate limiting, and basic observability. Track latency percentiles, throughput, and cost per request. Show how you optimized the system and what trade-offs you made.

4. **Automated evaluation harness for prompts or models:** Create a small eval framework that runs a test suite of prompts against different models, compares outputs, scores them, and produces a report. This signals maturity because most AI projects fail due to lack of evaluation discipline.
5. **Data pipeline plus feature store mindset:** Build a mini pipeline that ingests data, cleans it, versions it, and makes it queryable. Even if you are not training a model, show that you understand data lineage, quality checks, and reproducibility. This is the foundation most AI teams struggle with.

In AI portfolios, a deployment link is increasingly a strong signal because it removes ambiguity. Anyone can claim they built some projects. A working demo lets a recruiter or hiring manager test in 30 seconds whether the claim is true or not.

Platforms such as Hugging Face Spaces, Streamlit Community Cloud, or similar hosting tools can help demonstrate working AI prototypes. You can ship a small AI app using Gradio or Streamlit and make your work interactive, not theoretical. That is a strong signal, especially for AI engineering, applied ML, and product-adjacent roles, because it shows you can move from notebook to usable interface. If you want to stand out, build one demo that shows a real workflow, include clear instructions, and link it directly from your resume and LinkedIn.

One final point: your portfolio does not have to be huge. It must be coherent. Two or three strong projects with clear documentation and measurable outcomes beat ten unfinished repos every time.

AI-assisted job search

After you've done the groundwork, built your resume and profile, you start applying for your job.

If you want the most up-to-date view of open roles, start with the company website itself. Begin with the 20–40 target companies you identified earlier, go to each company's careers page, and search there first. Job boards often lag. Company career pages are the most authoritative source for current openings and are typically far more reliable. Then layer in job boards to widen coverage and catch roles you might miss. Use LinkedIn Jobs or Indeed. LinkedIn can be particularly useful because it often connects job postings with people, teams, and company context.

Also, use your existing network deliberately. Start by looking at where your peers, former colleagues, classmates, and friends work. That is your highest-probability entry point. Warm context wins. Cold outreach to random strangers has a low hit rate and often wastes time. Focus on bridges where there is already a reason to help.

Build an active pipeline of targeted applications at the beginning. Response rates can be low, so one or two applications are rarely enough. The goal is controlled volume: apply to enough roles to create momentum, but keep the search focused enough that you can tailor your resume, prioritize outreach, and learn from each response. It is good training and helps you build rhythm and experience early on. It also creates optionality. Having multiple applications in progress makes you calmer and more objective, and it puts you in a stronger position when it comes to negotiation.

As discussed earlier in this chapter, the job market is tough right now. Do not get discouraged if you do not receive interview invitations immediately. This can be normal. Keep going, iterate, and treat early rejections as part of the process rather than a signal to stop.

Once your resume, profile, and portfolio are ready, the work shifts from preparation to execution. The next step is to navigate the actual job market: finding the right roles, using outreach intelligently, and building enough targeted application activity to create momentum.

After you have done the groundwork, built your resume, and sharpened your profile, you can start moving into the market with more focus.

Tips for job interview preparation

Once you start applying, the first interview invitation is a milestone – but it is also where the real work begins. This is not the moment to relax. You want to walk into interviews extremely well prepared. Many candidates make the mistake of easing off too early. They treat interviews as conversations they can "wing," and then wonder why they do not progress.

In the first 10 to 15 minutes, the interviewer forms a view on three questions: can you do the work, do you understand the problem, and will you be easy to work with?

So do not prepare to "answer questions." Prepare to reduce uncertainty. The interview job is simple: make the decision easy.

Your preparation should produce a small set of assets you can reuse across interviews:

- A clear 30-second intro (elevator pitch)
- A 2-minute "why this role, why this company" answer
- A story bank of 8 to 12 proof stories
- 2 to 3 deep dives you can discuss end-to-end
- A question set that reveals maturity and competence

If you have these, most interviews become repetition with minor customization. Let's have a look at how to get well prepared.

Step 1: Understand the company and role, or do not show up

Read the job description like a contract. What are they paying for? What are the responsibilities that will determine success? What are the implied constraints: scale, compliance, speed, cross-functional dependencies?

Then research the company in a targeted way. You are not writing a history essay. You are looking for three things: what they sell, what they are building now, and what they are likely struggling with. Read their website and product pages, skim recent announcements, and check the team's hiring patterns. If it is a technical company, look at public engineering blogs or GitHub activity. If it is not, look at customer stories, product updates, or press coverage. If you know people at this company or have connections on LinkedIn, reach out and request a short call—fifteen minutes is enough. Prepare a few questions beforehand to get insights into the team, department, and culture you would be joining.

Step 2: Build a story bank that you can deploy under pressure

Many candidates fail behavioral questions for one reason: they ramble. They start with context, lose the thread, and never land the proof. The fix is structure.

A simple structure that works across roles is STAR. It stands for Situation, Task, Action, Result. It is a way to tell a work story that is easy to follow and easy to evaluate. But most people misuse it by spending too much time on the setup.

Use STAR but run it like a performance review. Situation and Task should be 20% of your answer. Action and Result should be 80%. End with what you learned or what you would do differently next time. That last sentence is what makes you sound senior. Most behavioral answers are too long on context and too light on proof. Use this single-entry template for every story:

- **Situation (1–2 lines):** What was happening and why it mattered
- **Task (1 line)**: What you owned, including the constraint and the KPI
- **Action (3–5 lines):** What you did that was uniquely yours: decisions, tools, collaborators, trade-offs
- **Result (2–3 lines):** Outcome with numbers, time window, what you learned, and one artifact you could show if asked

Example entry – STAR framework (copy the structure, swap the content)

Note: this is an illustrative example for interview preparation, not a specific case study. The numbers and timeline are indicative only—adapt the structure to your own experience.

Situation:

Imagine a procurement team buried in vendor contract reviews—dozens of agreements every quarter, each requiring the same clause checks. The team wants to test an LLM-based assistant to extract and flag key clauses, but trust is low because earlier rule-based attempts had missed edge cases and created false positives

Task:

The goal is to reduce average review time per contract within a few weeks, while staying within the company's data-handling requirements. The team also needs a simple way to prove quality, not just claim that the model is working

Action:

A useful first step is mapping the review workflow and identifying the most common clause types. From there, a gated extraction flow can be built so the assistant proposes clause matches that a reviewer confirms or overrides. Sensitive fields are masked, the model is connected only to approved templates and policy documents, and a fixed evaluation set of past contracts is reviewed regularly. Confidence thresholds, an escalation path for ambiguous clauses, and a rollback plan give the team a safety net

Result:

Within roughly 6–8 weeks, review time per contract can drop by around 20–30% without an increase in missed clauses on the evaluation set, and the majority of incoming contracts end up routed through the new flow. The biggest lesson is that trust does not come from using a bigger model. It comes from guardrails, measurement, and giving people a clear way to intervene

Now build your story bank. Create 8 to 12 stories that cover the patterns hiring managers screen for:

- Delivering impact under constraints
- Influencing without authority
- Handling ambiguity and missing data

- Failure and recovery
- Stakeholder conflict and alignment
- Learning fast and shipping anyway
- Making a risk or ethics call
- Improving a process, not just shipping a feature

Step 3: Prepare your deep dives, because that is where offers are decided

Most interviews eventually reach the same moment: *Tell me about a project you're proud of.* This is not small talk. This is the main evaluation.

Pick two to three projects you can walk through end to end:

- What problem you solved and why it mattered
- What you shipped, not what you explored
- What trade-offs did you make and why
- What broke and how you handled it
- What changed in the business afterward

For AI roles, expect extra scrutiny around reliability and governance. Be prepared to explain how you handled evaluation, hallucinations, guardrails, privacy, and monitoring. AI is moving fast and demonstrating that you are at the cutting edge – with hands-on experience using the most in-demand tools – can give you an additional edge. Many AI roles today focus on LLMs and agentic AI, where real-world experience is still limited. Even large companies are largely in an experimental phase.

Step 4: Technical preparation, but targeted

If the role is technical, prepare in the direction of the job, not in the direction of ego. Look for the core stack and workflows the role touches. If you can infer tooling from job requirements or team profiles, align your preparation: APIs, data pipelines, deployment, MLOps, security, observability, product analytics, or whatever is relevant.

If you expect coding interviews, practice. But practice intelligently: focus on the patterns the role uses, not random puzzles.

If you expect system design, do not overcomplicate it. Practice the basics: requirements, constraints, architecture, trade-offs, bottlenecks, and back-of-envelope reasoning. Many candidates lose here because they either dive into details too quickly or never show quantitative thinking at all.

Step 5: Prepare your questions, because they reveal your level

Always bring questions. Not because it is polite, but because your questions signal judgment.

Your questions should do two things: clarify success metrics and reveal maturity. In AI roles, ask about data access, evaluation, deployment, and ownership of risk. If they cannot answer, you are likely walking into a role where outcomes are not defined and accountability is unclear.

Avoid questions you could have answered with a five-minute website scan. That signals laziness.

Step 6: Use AI for rehearsal, not for performance

AI is great for mock interviews because it can simulate pressure without costing you social capital.

Use it to:

- Practice your 30-second intro until it is tight
- Stress-test your stories with follow-up questions
- Rehearse objections and weak points in your resume
- Run a case prompt and get feedback on structure

But do not let AI write your answers in a way that removes your voice. Interviewers can hear it when you sound like a template.

Tools for interview preparation

There is now a fast-growing set of tools built specifically for interview simulations for technical roles, drilling coding, system design, data/ML cases, and debugging. LeetCode and HackerRank lead for coding practice, Pramp for mock interviews, and Interviewing.io for anonymous practice with engineers. AI-native platforms provide interviewer-style simulations with feedback loops, though scoring should be treated as directional.

In parallel, use *question intel* sources to reduce surprise. Sites like Glassdoor often contain reported interview questions, and role-specific communities on Reddit, Blind, or dedicated forums sometimes share the patterns companies use. Do not assume every question is accurate or current but look for repetition across multiple posts. The goal is not to memorize answers. The goal is to recognize the question types the company tends to screen for, then rehearse your own proof-based responses.

A step-by-step guide to create your mock interview preparation guide with NotebookLM

This is a simple NotebookLM playbook you can copy. If you want a concrete workflow, use NotebookLM. It is built for grounded preparation because it works from sources you provide.

- Go to NotebookLM and create a New Notebook.
- Click Discover sources and use this prompt: "I need sources to prepare for my [JOB TITLE] interview at [COMPANY NAME]. Focus on the business model, the relevant product area, recent announcements, and any public AI initiatives."
- Add the job description as a source manually as well. This is your ground truth.
- Add your own materials as sources: your resume, portfolio, case studies, and any project notes you can share.
- Add 2 to 5 high-signal company sources: relevant product pages, a recent blog post, a press release, a talk, or a podcast episode transcript if you can find one.

Keep it disciplined. Ten strong sources beat fifty random links.

Now go to settings and choose a Custom style. Set NotebookLM to behave like a strict interview coach. A useful custom instruction is:

You are a strict hiring manager. Ask questions that test depth, trade-offs, and impact. Be concise. Challenge vague answers. Do not flatter. Push for metrics and evidence. If an answer is generic, force me to make it specific.

Turn sources into a role-specific question bank

Most people ask an AI model for interview questions without giving it the right inputs. Then they get generic output. With NotebookLM, you already fixed that. Now use it properly.

Prompt:

Based on the sources in this notebook and this job description, generate 15 high-probability interview questions for this role. Group them into role and domain, execution and delivery, cross-functional influence, AI reliability and risk, and metrics and ROI. For each question, add what a strong answer must include and what common weak answers sound like.

This produces a checklist you can prepare for. It also creates a standard you can use to judge your own answers.

Simulate a real interview, not a study guide

This is where NotebookLM becomes a weapon. You can rehearse under pressure, with follow-ups, in the exact style that typically breaks candidates.

Prompt:

Run a mock interview for [JOB TITLE] at [COMPANY NAME]. Ask one question at a time. After my answer, ask one follow-up that tests depth and evidence. Interrupt if I ramble. If I make a claim, ask for a metric or artifact. After 10 questions, grade me on clarity, credibility, structure, and role fit. Then tell me the 5 weakest points to fix and how to fix them.

If you do this twice, you will immediately notice patterns: where you go vague, where you over-explain, where you lack proof.

Add interviewer-specific questions using public information

Many interviews are shaped by who is in the room. If you have the interviewer's name or LinkedIn profile, you can tailor preparation without guessing.

You do not need private data. Public information is enough: their function, past roles, what they post about, and the projects they are associated with. Copy the public profile text into your notebook as a source.

Prompt:

Here is the LinkedIn profile text of my interviewer: [paste]. Here is the job description: [paste]. Based on this, generate 8 likely questions this person might ask, with emphasis on their background and priorities. Then generate 6 questions I should ask them to build rapport and test maturity.

This makes the interview feel less random because you are preparing for a real human, not a generic process.

Use AI to draft, then rewrite in your voice

AI can draft your *why this role* answer and your story bank quickly. You still need to own it.

Prompt:

Create a 3-sentence *"why this company, why this role"* answer using only the job description and the sources. Then create a story bank of 10 STAR stories based on my resume. Do not invent facts. Highlight where I need stronger metrics or proof.

Then rewrite the answers in your own language, with your own examples. If you do not, you will sound like a template. Interviewers hear that instantly.

You do not just prepare. You rehearse until your answers are clear, defensible, and fast.

Interview performance – the dos and don'ts that decide outcomes

Interviews are not a vibe check. They are a signal test. This checklist keeps you out of unforced errors and helps you show up like a professional.

Category	Recommended (DOs)	Avoid (DON'Ts)
Before the interview	• Print extra resumes • Research the company • Plan outfit a day early • Sleep well the night before • Practice common questions • Prepare your own questions • Check the location	• Skip company research • Arrive without questions • Forget to check your tech • Ignore the job description • Wing it without preparation • Choose flashy, loud clothing • Stay up late
During the interview	• Show enthusiasm • Use the STAR method • Give a firm handshake • Ask thoughtful questions • Listen carefully • Smile and make eye contact	• Be late (ever!) • Check your phone • Lie about experience • Interrupt the interviewer • Use slang or curse words • Ask about salary right away • Badmouth former employers
Body language	• Sit up straight • Smile naturally • Keep hands visible • Lean slightly forward • Mirror interviewer's energy • Maintain eye contact • Nod to show you're listening	• Fidget or tap • Check the time • Cross your arms • Avoid eye contact • Slouch in your chair • Play with hair/face • Use closed body language

Category	Recommended (DOs)	Avoid (DON'Ts)
After the interview	• Send a thank-you within 2 hours • Connect on LinkedIn • Mention specific topics • Express continued interest • Follow up once after a week • Reflect on your performance	• Call repeatedly • Stop your job search • Skip the thank-you note • Forget to request feedback • Feel discouraged if rejected • Pester with daily follow-ups • Post about it on social media
Tough questions	• Use the STAR method • Take a pause if needed • Turn negatives into positives • Be honest about weaknesses • Focus on growth and learning	• Lie or exaggerate • Use fake weaknesses • Ramble without a point • Give memorized answers • Criticize previous employers
Virtual interviews	• Find a quiet location • Use a neutral background • Test technology early • Dress professionally (all over) • Look at the camera, not the screen	• Have poor lighting • Let pets/family interrupt • Forget to mute when needed • Have distracting backgrounds • Use an unprofessional username

Table 12.2: Interview performance do's and don'ts

Summary

In this chapter, we covered how to compete in the AI job market in 2026. Hiring is now partly automated, so you must optimize for screening systems and still win human trust. The goal is simple: prove value, show evidence, and communicate clearly under pressure.

Start with targeting. Define your role family, archetype, and the company environments where you can ship and learn, then build a shortlist before you apply. Translate that focus into a resume that is ATS-friendly and AI-resilient: easy to parse, consistent with your LinkedIn profile, and anchored in measurable outcomes. Treat your portfolio and digital footprint as proof, because recruiters and interviewers will validate what you claim.

Then prepare like it matters. Use AI tools for mock interviews and question banks, but do not outsource your thinking. For behavioral interviews, use STAR (Situation, Task, Action, Result) with evidence: short context, clear actions, measurable results, and one artifact you can point to. For technical interviews, think aloud, state assumptions, and show how you reason.

Finally, do not forget to use your personal network along the way. Ask for referrals and use conversations with people already in the roles you want to sanity-check requirements, team reality, and what success looks like. This often beats the traditional hiring funnel and improves your odds before you even apply.

The next chapter focuses on sustaining growth once you land the role: some expert insights, community, and the operating habits that compound.

13

Expert Insights and Sustaining Growth – Building a Career That Compounds

> *"Protect your capacity to last. Burnout is not a badge of honor. The people who build decade-long careers are not the ones who work the most hours. They are the ones who stay curious and healthy long enough to let their skills compound."*
>
> *–Andreas Horn*

Landing your first AI role is a milestone. Building a career that stays relevant, grows into leadership, and compounds over decades is a different challenge entirely.

That is what this chapter is about.

The earlier chapters helped you understand the AI job market, position yourself, build proof, and prepare for interviews. This chapter focuses on what comes after the offer: how to accelerate in your first 90 days, build credibility inside and outside your organization, keep learning as the field changes, navigate career transitions, and avoid burning out in a market that rewards constant motion.

This has always mattered in technology careers. The difference now is speed. AI is moving fast, roles are changing quickly, and the skills that feel valuable today can become baseline sooner than expected.

What separates professionals who build long careers from those who plateau early is not only technical depth. It is judgment, continuous learning, strategic positioning, and the habit of contributing back to the ecosystem that helps you grow.

The New York Times reported recently that 60% of jobs today did not exist in 1940 (`https://www.nytimes.com/2023/07/10/opinion/ai-economy-productivity-jobs-workers.html`). The pattern is now compressing even further. Many roles that dominate AI hiring today, such as AI Engineer, Prompt Engineer, AI Strategy, AI Safety, barely existed a decade ago. The jobs you will hold in ten years may not have names yet.

The way people move through careers is shifting too. Average tenure at a single company has dropped significantly over the past two decades. The share of people who have stayed with a single employer for 10+ years is at record lows across most age groups (`https://www.bloomberg.com/opinion/articles/2024-10-17/haven-t-worked-at-the-same-place-for-10-years-join-the-club`). You cannot expect an employer to develop you over a fifteen-year arc the way previous generations could. The responsibility for growth has shifted to you. That means you cannot coast after landing a role.

As a reader of this book, you already understand AI's potential. You are not here because you need convincing. You are here because you understand the reality: baseline AI fluency is now a minimum requirement. By itself, it does not create career advantage. What compounds is *deep knowledge* and *judgment*.

Deep knowledge means understanding what sits underneath the interface: how models work, how they behave, where they fail, and what it takes to make them reliable inside real systems. It is knowing the difference between a good answer and a dependable outcome. It is understanding context limits, retrieval quality, tool reliability, and data lineage. It is recognizing how small changes in prompts, inputs, or system design can shift results. It is being able to reason about latency, cost, privacy, security, and failure modes—not after something breaks, but before you deploy it.

Judgment is the operating system on top. Knowing when to trust a model's output, when to override it, when a workflow needs a human checkpoint, and when an AI-native approach changes the economics of a problem entirely. It is recognizing when uncertainty is too high, when the data is too sensitive, when the stakes are too real, and when "good enough" is not good enough. That judgment does not come from reading. It sharpens through repetition, critical evaluation, and exposure to increasingly complex use cases – shipping, observing, measuring, and iterating. Over time, you stop asking "Can AI do this?" and start asking the only important question: "Can we make this accurate, safe, and scalable enough to matter?"

This chapter is about turning that mindset into a career strategy you can run for years. You will learn from practitioners who have lived through multiple cycles of AI evolution, the pitfalls that derail otherwise strong careers, and the habits that create compounding returns over time.

This chapter covers the following topics:

- How to tackle the first 90 days of a new role for maximum acceleration
- How to develop thought leadership and visibility
- Mentorship, community, and lifelong learning as force multipliers
- Practical career advice from AI leaders on the frontier

Insider advice for the first 90 days

Landing your first AI role is worth celebrating. But the real work starts on day one. The first 90 days decide your reputation—not your long-term potential, but your reputation. In AI roles, that reputation is built on two things:

- Can you ship something real?
- Can you do it without creating risk?

This is where judgment – the skill that compounds – starts to show. Anyone can propose ideas. The professionals who build lasting careers are the ones who deliver outcomes early, build trust fast, and create the conditions for bigger bets later.

For now, let's start by looking at the first 30 days.

Days 1 to 30: Map reality and ship a quick win

Your first job is to understand how work actually flows. Map three things:

- **Systems** – the tools, data sources, and handoffs that touch the workflow you are entering
- **People** – those who own decisions, approvals, budgets, and risk
- **Metrics** – what the business cares about, and what the team is already measured on

Do not assume the org chart reflects how work gets done. It rarely does.

Then ship one quick win with visible impact. It could have a small scope as long as it has a real workflow and a measurable outcome. A quick win is not a demo. It is something real users touch. Even if it is basic: a triage template, a retrieval-backed FAQ, or a workflow automation that removes a repetitive step. Your goal is momentum and trust. You are not trying to impress anyone with complexity. You are proving you can close the gap between idea and production.

Output by day 30: one working improvement in production or controlled use, plus a baseline metric and a before-after story you can explain in two minutes.

Days 31 to 60: Run a small pilot with structured evaluation

Now you move from quick win to pilot. Keep it small, but real. Define the workflow, the users, and the success metric before you build anything else. Then install an evaluation loop from day one: a fixed test set, a review cadence, and clear thresholds for what counts as acceptable.

If you cannot evaluate, you cannot improve. If you cannot improve, you cannot scale. This is where most AI work quietly fails – not because the model was bad, but because nobody defined what "good" looked like. In parallel, publish a one-page operating guide. This is underrated. It forces clarity. It tells the organization what this is and what it is not, who owns it, how it is used, what data it touches, how it is measured, and when to escalate to a human. That single page will save you dozens of Slack threads and months of misaligned expectations.

Output by day 60: A pilot running with real users, a simple evaluation dashboard or scorecard, and a one-page operating guide that reduces confusion.

Days 61 to 90: Harden, expand, and make outcomes visible

If the pilot works, expand carefully. Increase coverage, harden guardrails, and improve reliability. Add monitoring. Add rollback paths. Make failures safe. This is where most AI initiatives die: scaling a prototype without building the operating model to support it. You do not want to be the person who shipped something impressive that broke in production and eroded trust for the next team. Then share outcomes org-wide. Not as hype but with a clean brief: baseline, intervention, measured change, trade-offs, risks, and next steps. Your job is to turn "interesting" into "credible."

Executives do not need to understand how your system works. They need to understand what changed, what it costs, what it risks, and whether it is worth continuing. Finally, propose a roadmap tied to business goals. Rather than a list of features, present a sequence of workflow upgrades with owners, dependencies, and success metrics. The roadmap should make it obvious how the organization moves from pilot to measurable value, and what needs to be true for each step to succeed.

Output by day 90: An expanded pilot with guardrails and monitoring, a short outcome brief shared with leadership, and a roadmap that links future work to business metrics.

If you want a structured playbook for this phase, a useful reference is *The First 90 Days* by Michael D. Watkins. It's a practical framework for onboarding and role transitions: how to diagnose the situation, align expectations, secure early wins, and build momentum.

The first 90 days help you earn internal trust. You prove that you can understand the environment, ship responsibly, measure outcomes, and communicate impact. But a career that compounds cannot depend only on internal reputation. The next step is to build external credibility by making your expertise visible beyond your current team and employer.

Developing thought leadership and visibility

The first 90 days build your reputation inside the company. That matters, but it has limits. If you leave, get laid off, or want to negotiate from strength, internal reputation does not transfer. What transfers is external credibility: proof that people outside your organization already know your work, trust your judgment, and can point to your output.

That is what thought leadership actually is. Self-promotion and LinkedIn platitudes only go so far. Real thought leadership involves making your expertise visible to people who have never worked with you. Done well, it builds career equity that compounds independently, regardless of titles, team changes, or the employer.

There are multiple paths to do that: you can write a book, start a newsletter, post on LinkedIn or other social platforms, launch a podcast, speak at conferences, or contribute to open source. Each has different effort-to-impact ratios, and which one fits depends on your strengths, your audience, and how much time you can invest. The key is to pick one and start. Most people overthink the channel and never begin. Let's look at three of the most impactful of these methods.

Writing

Among the options above, writing tends to deliver the strongest return on time invested. A post you publish today can generate opportunities three years from now. Writing scales in a way that conversations do not. And it forces you to clarify your thinking – you cannot hide behind vague claims when the words are on the page. The lowest barrier to entry is LinkedIn. You already have a profile and a network. You do not need to build an audience from zero. One post per week, consistently, compounds faster than most people expect. *Chapter 11, Crafting Your AI Identity: Personal Branding for Impact,* covers the full breakdown on LinkedIn strategy – how to structure posts, what performs, and how to build visibility without becoming a content machine. There are other ways to publish your writing. You can publish on a personal blog, a newsletter (Substack or beehiiv), or platforms like Medium. The format matters less than consistency and substance.

Speaking

Speaking builds trust faster but scales slower. On stage, you cannot hide behind slides. People evaluate your judgment, clarity, and composure.

Start small: internal lunch-and-learns, local meetups, and virtual events. Once you have a few talks, propose sessions to larger conferences. If you get rejected, do not take it personally – but do not ignore the signal either. Use it to sharpen your title, abstract, audience promise, and proof that your session will create value.

Acceptance puts you in front of people who now associate your name with specific expertise.

Contributing to open source

Contributing to open source builds a different kind of credibility. It signals you can ship code others depend on. You do not need to maintain a popular repo. Bug fixes, documentation improvements, example implementations – maintainers notice contributors who make their lives easier. Your GitHub profile becomes a portfolio. Make it easy for hiring managers to see you build real things. Strong GitHub portfolios consistently help candidates get interviews, land jobs, and stand out in hiring loops.

Open source helps people see what you can build. Mentorship helps you see where to grow next. A career compounds faster when visible work is paired with people who challenge your thinking, expand your perspective, and open doors you would not find alone.

Mentorship: seek it early, provide it often

Building a network and seeking mentorship are essential for career growth in any industry. In AI, where the pace of change makes formal training outdated quickly, mentorship becomes even more valuable. Connecting with experienced professionals provides insights into job opportunities, emerging trends, and nuanced career advice that you will not find in documentation or courses.

There are many ways to find mentors, including within your company: ask for introductions, use the intranet to see who works on topics you care about, attend internal or external events, go to conferences, join online communities (e.g. Discord), or join meetups.

Remember, effective mentorship is not transactional. It develops over time through consistent engagement, mutual respect, and reciprocity. The best mentorships start with small, specific asks – a 15-minute chat about a decision, feedback on a project, or advice on navigating a career transition. Over time, they can grow into long-term relationships where both people benefit.

Once you have gained some experience, consider mentoring others. This is not just altruism. Teaching forces you to articulate what you know, identify gaps in your own understanding, and develop communication skills that matter in senior roles. Mentoring junior teammates often improves technical clarity and leadership capability more than most formal training programs.

Community engagement – join, contribute, lead

The AI community extends far beyond your immediate team or company. Engaging with this broader ecosystem accelerates learning, expands your network, and creates visibility that opens doors. The most effective engagement follows a progression: join communities, contribute actively, and eventually take leadership roles.

A practical caveat: Community engagement is high-leverage but also time-intensive. For mid-career and senior professionals balancing full-time roles, family responsibilities, and existing commitments, start with a single channel—one community, one cadence—rather than trying to do everything at once. Even one focused conversation per week compounds over a year. The goal is consistency at a sustainable level, not maximum coverage.

Start by joining online groups and forums where practitioners discuss technical challenges, share resources, and debate best practices. Platforms like Reddit, Hacker News, and specialized Discord servers host active discussions where you can ask questions and learn from experienced professionals. In big cities, there are also plenty of in-person meetups – hosted by companies or by people interested in a specific field. In San Francisco, for example, you can find dozens every week. But even in smaller tech hubs, you'd be surprised how much is happening once you start looking around. Join, then participate actively: ask thoughtful questions, help organizers, support sponsor outreach, share what you have learned from real projects, and help others. If you do it right, you will learn faster, build relationships, and actually have a lot of fun.

Attending industry events and meetups provides similar value in a more structured format. Virtual and in-person AI conferences, webinars, and local meetups offer opportunities to hear about new research, learn practical techniques, and connect with potential collaborators or employers. In-person events provide context that online content cannot. You see how other people and teams think, how they solve similar problems, and how they make trade-offs in real time. You also build relationships that often evolve into collaborations and job opportunities. Meeting people in person helps build relationships that last. Many professionals lost that muscle during COVID, and rebuilding it is one of the most underrated ways to grow a career.

Contributing to open-source AI projects is not only a strong way to build thought leadership, but also one of the strongest forms of community engagement. Platforms like GitHub and Hugging Face host thousands of projects where you can contribute code, documentation, or examples. You will also find many calls for support on X, Discord servers, and Slack communities. Choose a tool ecosystem you want to get hands-on with, join the most active communities around it, and watch what the maintainers and power users are doing. Follow the threads where real work happens: bug reports, feature requests, benchmarks, and implementation discussions. That is where the best contribution opportunities show up first.

Community contribution is not only a way to be seen. It is also one of the fastest ways to learn, because it exposes you to real problems, real users, and real standards. The next discipline follows naturally: treating learning as an ongoing operating system for your career.

Lifelong learning – the only sustainable strategy

The AI field evolves faster than any formal education system can track. Models improve, frameworks change, and best practices get rewritten constantly. Professionals who maintain relevance are those who adopt a lifelong learning mindset: treating continuous skill development as infrastructure, not as a project with an end date.

Online courses and certifications provide structured paths for building foundational knowledge. Platforms like LinkedIn Learning, DataCamp, Coursera or Udemy offer structured programs on AI, machine learning, and data science, many aimed at beginners. Certifications can demonstrate commitment to employers, especially when combined with hands-on projects. However, courses alone are not sufficient. They teach concepts but do not build the judgment that comes from applying those concepts under real constraints. Keep in mind that AI is moving so fast that many courses become outdated quickly.

Staying updated requires active engagement with the field's information streams. That means reading selected research papers, following researchers and practitioners, subscribing to a few high-signal industry blogs, and attending webinars where new techniques and tools are discussed. The goal is not to read everything. It is to build filters: a way to decide what matters for your work, what is interesting but irrelevant, and what is mostly noise.

On top of that, building personal projects remains the most effective learning strategy. Working on your own AI projects, building models from scratch, and trying out new tools for creating applications that use AI components forces you to confront real implementation challenges: dealing with messy data, debugging model behavior, optimizing performance, and shipping something that works. Platforms like Kaggle provide datasets for experimentation, and tools like Hugging Face Spaces make it easy to deploy small applications. These projects create portfolio artifacts that prove capability in ways that certificates cannot.

Within organizations, fostering a culture of experimentation and communal learning is vital for building effective AI capabilities. Companies that encourage skilled users to share knowledge, run internal workshops, and document lessons learned create environments where learning compounds. If your organization lacks this culture, you can help build it: start a Friday technical deep dive group, share interesting papers in team channels, or volunteer to present on new tools and techniques you are exploring.

Learning keeps you relevant, but career growth also requires knowing when to move, how to reposition yourself, and how to turn accumulated skills into the next opportunity.

Navigating career transitions in AI

AI careers rarely follow linear paths. Professionals move between roles, companies, and even industries as opportunities emerge and priorities shift. Navigating these transitions effectively requires understanding when to move, how to position yourself for new roles, and how to minimize risk during periods of change.

The decision to change roles should be driven by growth. If your current position no longer challenges you, if you have stopped learning, or if the company's direction diverges from your values, those are legitimate reasons to explore options. However, moving too frequently without building depth in any one domain creates a resume that signals inconsistency rather than adaptability. A useful heuristic is to stay in a role long enough to ship something meaningful, see it operate in production, and learn from its successes and failures.

When transitioning between companies, treat it as an opportunity to upgrade your role, not just replicate your current one. Use the move to shift into higher-impact work, broader scope, or environments with stronger AI maturity. This requires positioning yourself deliberately: highlight the outcomes you delivered in your previous role, demonstrate that you understand the new company's challenges, and articulate how your experience translates to their context.

For professionals considering shifts between different AI archetypes – from Builder to Integrator, or from Operator to Enabler (*Chapter 12, Conquering the AI Job Market – Strategic Search Techniques and Interview Excellence* covers this in detail) – the transition requires building bridge skills that connect your current expertise to the target role. If you are moving from engineering into product management, develop skills in user research, roadmap planning, and stakeholder communication. If you are moving from research into operations, gain experience with production systems, monitoring, and incident response. These bridge skills make the transition credible rather than aspirational.

Career transitions are one part of long-term growth. But growth is not only about moving faster, taking bigger roles, or expanding your scope. Before turning to advice from leaders in the field, one part of career building deserves attention: sustainability.

Balancing ambition and sustainability

The AI field rewards ambition, but unconstrained ambition leads to burnout. Sustainable careers require boundaries that protect your capacity for long-term contribution. This is not about working less. It is about working strategically and protecting the conditions that enable sustained performance. This is important even though it is often glossed over in career advice. Many people implicitly celebrate extreme hours and constant output without discussing the cost. In reality, your career is not a sprint. It is a multi-decade compounding game. If you burn out early, you lose the very thing that makes you valuable: consistency, judgment, and the ability to keep learning.

> Learn to recognize the early signs of burnout before they become severe: persistent fatigue, cynicism about work, declining quality of output, and withdrawal from colleagues. These signals often appear gradually, which makes them easy to rationalize. Address them early by adjusting workload, taking time off, or asking for support from a manager or mentor. Ignoring them can turn a manageable problem into a recovery process that takes months.

Clear boundaries between work and personal life become harder when you are genuinely excited about the field. The temptation to read papers, build side projects, and track every release can quietly consume evenings and weekends. Some of that is valuable. Unchecked, it erodes the recovery time you need to perform at a high level.

Protect time for activities unrelated to AI: physical exercise, creative hobbies, relationships, and simple rest. These are not distractions from career development. They are prerequisites for it. Family and health are not "nice to have" categories you revisit when work calms down. They are the foundation that makes sustained performance possible.

Finally, cultivate relationships outside the tech industry. Friends and family who do not work in AI provide perspective and help you avoid echo chambers where everything feels urgent and every trend feels revolutionary. That perspective is grounding. It keeps your identity bigger than your job, and it reminds you that AI is a tool for improving lives, not an end in itself.

Thirteen chapters of frameworks, tools, skills, and strategies—from AI fundamentals to agentic systems, and from landing your first role to building use cases that actually ship. Before this chapter closes, some of the brightest minds in this field weigh in.

Enterprise AI leaders on building a lasting career

The following section gathers perspectives from enterprise AI leaders across the industry: Chief AI Officers, AI Fellows, VPs of AI Strategy, Heads of AI at leading companies, engineers shipping production systems at scale, and founders who built AI businesses from zero. Some have been in the field for decades. Others built their careers in the recent wave. All of them – across industries and continents – have navigated the hype, made hard calls, and learned what actually lasts. They were asked two questions:

1. What skills, mindsets, and experiences will matter most over the next few years for building a serious AI career – not chasing trends, but building something real?
2. What would you tell young professionals or career switchers who want to break into the field?

Read closely – there's sharp, hard-earned advice in here.

"Being a good AI researcher will mean being able to innovate in AI beyond incrementally improving current LLM-based techniques. This requires knowledge of all available AI techniques, including those that do not learn from data, which may be useful to mitigate and overcome some of the limitations and risks of machine learning systems.

More generally, people in many sectors will also need to know how to collaborate with AI, since this can greatly increase their productivity and accelerate the achievement of their goals. This means being aware of the opportunities and challenges of collaborating with an AI co-worker, compared to a human co-worker, including the risks of over-trust and under-trust, exhaustion, impacts on human cognitive abilities, and learning how to direct, verify, and govern the work done by AI rather than doing it from scratch. This will require some level of multidisciplinary training to understand not just the technology but also its social and cognitive impact on people.

I would recommend that you learn the basics of AI, including its current capabilities, limitations, and risks, as well as how such risks can be identified in use cases and appropriately mitigated through governance and tools. This is important to be able to trust AI at the correct level, avoiding over-trust, which may bring excessive risks to companies, as well as under-trust, which may cause you to miss useful productivity opportunities. AI adoption will increasingly be based on trust and governance, beyond technical capabilities. This is even more so in agentic AI, where task delegation to autonomous agents should be done with care to avoid negative impacts on people, communities, and companies."

Francesca Rossi

IBM Global Leader for Responsible AI and AI Governance; IBM Fellow

"The only thing that is certain today and in the future is change. The way to succeed in any field, especially in a fast-paced, deep-tech world, is to cultivate curiosity and embrace lifelong learning. Curiosity will help you discover new fields, and upskilling and reskilling will help you build on your existing knowledge, not only to stay relevant but to succeed. Curiosity, learning, and a pinch of serendipity have enabled me to pursue multiple careers as a chemical engineer, consultant, deep-tech advisor, and lecturer.

Do not be afraid of radically reinventing yourself every few years. Believe me, great things happen when you choose courage over comfort. This is why I have moved from Canada to Germany and to India throughout my career. If you are in AI, why not expand into quantum technologies? If you are already in quantum, why not space tech, and so on? This applies to technical skills as well as management and leadership skills.

As you progress in your career, unlearning becomes equally important. Be ready to unlearn practices, attitudes, and beliefs that served you well in the past but, over time, become a hindrance to reaching your full potential as an individual and a leader. Also, be ready to give back. If you have built a successful, satisfying professional and personal life, give back and help the next generation of professionals succeed."

Dr. Renata Jovanovic

Chief Scientific Officer, Deloitte; Head of Frontier Labs and Quantum Ambassador

"For young professionals or career switchers, my best recommendation is to move beyond the 'art of prompting' and master agentic literacy: understanding how autonomous systems can and should orchestrate complex, multi-step work. Don't learn the tech in a vacuum. Anchor your skills in a high-stakes domain like healthcare, energy, or law. The most valuable people will be those who can bridge deep industry problems with AI's evolving capabilities.

Finally, focus on system-level thinking and ethics. As models become commodities, the real career moat will be your ability to govern, integrate, and operate them in the real, messy world responsibly. The future belongs to those who treat AI not as a replacement, but as a catalyst – a tool that helps us make better decisions and act with greater responsibility."

Robert Engels

Head of Global AI Futures Lab at Capgemini

"If you want to position yourself in the AI space, you should learn early to think about technology, business, and responsibility as one. Technical excellence is a necessary foundation, but it is not sufficient. What matters is the ability to apply AI in a way that creates real impact – simplifying processes, improving decisions, and delivering measurable value.

At the same time, people skills and conscious leadership matter just as much as technical capability. In an era where AI technologies will outperform many cognitive tasks, we need to focus on what makes us human: empathy, judgment, a strong sense of responsibility, and the ability to build trust.

For roles like Chief AI Officer, systems thinking is essential, as is the ability to align diverse interests and establish governance structures that hold. AI does not create value in isolation – it only delivers results through the interplay of organization, law, culture, and technology.

Looking back, the most valuable decisions I made were the ones where I did not chase the next hype cycle, but instead invested in scalable platforms, durable capabilities, and a shared technological foundation. Anyone who wants to shape technological change must take central responsibility while enabling decentralized execution.

In the end, a career is not built through titles, but through the willingness to solve complex problems and take responsibility when it matters."

Dr. Michael Drass

Chief AI Officer at Deutsche Bahn
(Germany's National Railway Operator)

"Over the next 2–3 years, AI tools will keep lowering the barrier from idea to working prototype – not just for computer scientists, but for anyone willing to learn the workflow. The advantage won't be knowing the latest model; it will be engineering discipline: clear success criteria, rigorous evaluation of quality and failure modes, and fast iteration when reality disagrees. Because AI makes creation cheap, the world will be flooded with AI-assisted output, so the bar will rise – work must be more refined, reliable, and measurably valuable than ever before. Build a few end-to-end projects where you own the full loop: data → model/tooling → integration → evaluation → monitoring. Learn to create with modern AI coding tools (and their successors), but don't confuse tool familiarity with capability – tools change fast; fundamentals and judgment don't. Document what broke, how you measured it, and what you changed; that portfolio signal beats certificates. Most importantly, focus on the value of the idea and the persistence to carry it through obstacles – in a world where everyone can generate something, follow-through and refinement are what stand out."

Shaun Tyler

Vice President Global Software Engineering and AI Strategy at Körber Pharma

"To experience the full potential of AI, you need to try new ideas and new ways of doing things and let go of old habits. At the same time, the difference between brilliant AI output and utter rubbish is often subtle, and spotting it requires a sharp eye. Real AI success comes from alternating between two opposing mindsets: childlike enthusiasm and cynical discernment.

AI is eating everything: whatever job you want, soon it's going to be an AI job. That's why AI skills are valuable regardless of the career path you choose. Specific technical skills go out of date quickly – this has been true for decades. So, if you want a technical AI role, the most important prerequisite is being genuinely comfortable learning new things."

Richard Cotton

Senior Data Evangelist at DataCamp

"Be hands-on. Find a deeply technical niche and build real expertise there. The field is too broad to master everything, so pick an area where you can develop depth: inference optimization, training infrastructure, reinforcement learning, data pipelines, evaluation – whatever pulls you in.

From experience, open-source contributions are one of the most effective ways to build credentials that actually matter. Contributing to widely used repositories shows you can work on production-grade code, collaborate with others, and solve problems end users care about. Delivering real value through contributions is an unfair advantage. When you have a track record of merged pull requests, well-documented projects, or tools that people actually use, you're no longer competing on credentials alone. People can see your work and hire you based on it – instead of relying on proxy metrics.

And one more thing: distinguishing short-term hype from true innovation requires depth. You need enough context to evaluate claims critically and spot when a 'new' technique is a genuine advance versus a repackaging of old ideas. That only comes from sustained work and strong fundamentals."

Maxime Labonne

Head of Post-Training at Liquid AI;
Author of ***LLM Engineer's Handbook***

"We cannot look into the future, but it's safe to say that more people will work with more AI. AI will enable employees to perform tasks that were previously out of reach without it. As a result, many roles will broaden.

Focus will become the most important skill, as it's a prerequisite for effective work with AI and GenAI. GenAI produces answers, but are they answers to the question you actually meant? Are they missing context? In the future workforce, focus will help people navigate a wider scope of responsibilities without getting pulled into noise or false confidence.

As technology becomes more democratized, domain expertise will matter more, not less. And because work will broaden, many employees will need fluency across multiple domains."

Ben Torben-Nielsen, PhD, MBA

Executive Strategy and Portfolio Leader at Roche

"Whatever you want to call it: Artificial Intelligence, Machine Learning or Deep Learning. It's a field packed with opportunities to improve business, operations, and everyday life. But if you're new, it can feel daunting to break in. There's competition. There's noise. There's a lot to learn. And you won't get there in a day. Anyone telling you otherwise is lying. You CAN get there with consistent, persistent effort.

When I need to lock in, this is my daily formula (yes, every day—even weekends):

1. Make a cup of coffee and sit down at your computer.
2. Write one line of code. PyTorch, LangGraph, or SymPy are great places to start.
3. Practice one math technique. Differentiation and probability are high-leverage fundamentals.
4. Show your work. Publish it: GitHub, LinkedIn, YouTube - whatever fits. Let people see what you can do."

Nicholas Renotte

Chief AI Engineer and Head of AI Developer Advocacy at IBM

"To control an AI agent and ensure it has properly understood your request, you need strong computer science skills. When building software, there is rarely a single best solution. Instead, it's about carefully weighing consequences, benefits, and drawbacks across different options, and choosing the one that best fits the roadmap. Even if AI becomes capable of doing all our programming, someone will still need to guide it in the right direction – even in 2–3 years' time. Building a serious career in AI starts with a solid computer science foundation. Learn everything from microchips to large-scale infrastructure and understand how computers and cloud environments work from the ground up. The more you know, the more effective you will be at guiding AI agents to build meaningful systems."

Johan Sanneblad

Founder and CEO at TokenTek

"Over the next few years, the most valuable skill in AI will be a command of the full stack. Understanding how models interact with data pipelines, infrastructure, governance, people, and business processes matters far more than knowing the latest architecture by name. Intellectual humility is equally important. The field moves quickly, but not always in straight lines, and those who are comfortable saying 'I don't know yet' and doing the work to find out will outperform those who over-index on confidence or buzzwords. Communication is also underrated. Being able to clearly explain what a system does, what it does not do, and what it will cost in plain language is becoming a key career differentiator. For people looking to build a career in AI, I would not start with the goal of 'working in AI' itself. Start with a domain you care about – finance, healthcare, climate, logistics, sports – and learn how AI is actually applied there. Domain fluency combined with AI literacy is far more powerful than generic technical knowledge. Build things that run. Side projects, open-source contributions, internal tools – anything that forces you to deal with data quality, deployment, and edge cases. And focus on fundamentals: statistics, software engineering, and distributed systems. These foundations age well, even when toolchains do not."

James Corcoran

Head of AI, STAC (Strategic Technology Analysis Center)

"Deep foundational knowledge – mathematics, statistics, machine learning, and software fundamentals – will matter far more than surface-level familiarity with the latest tools. The field evolves every few months, so the ability to learn quickly is essential. Focus on identifying real problems worth solving and learning directly from users. Build things and share them publicly for visibility and credibility. If you already have technical skills, develop the mindset to turn them into products that solve actual problems. Someone who understands production guardrails and can drive a prototype to production will shine. Don't overlook human skills: persuasion, communication, empathy, and the ability to translate vague customer needs into meaningful solutions. These remain irreplaceable. Finally, weave ethics and safety considerations into everything you do – they're not optional. Pick one domain and dive deep. Experiment extensively with AI tools to gain hands-on experience, then build a small portfolio of practical projects. Get excellent at using modern AI tools while keeping ethics and safety front of mind. Focus on fundamentals – anyone can write code with AI today, but you'll stand out if you can guide tools to produce clean, robust, maintainable code that handles edge cases. Stay informed about developments in AI but filter out the noise and focus on what's truly useful. Don't wait for the perfect plan. Start, fail, learn, and improve. Network with people in your chosen domain, contribute to open-source projects, and share your work. There's no perfect day to begin – the best time is now."

Prashant Rathi

Principal AI Architect at McKinsey & Company

"AI is reshaping the world in a fundamental way: many skills that once differentiated individuals are increasingly becoming commoditized, as they can be outsourced to AI models. In this environment, the advantage shifts to those who know how to work with these systems rather than compete with them at the task level. My advice to people positioning themselves in AI is to focus less on mastering specific tools and more on understanding how intelligent systems actually work in real environments. The technologies will change quickly, but the ability to reason about problems, design systems, and adapt to the unknown will remain enduring. The skills that truly matter go beyond short-term hype and include systems thinking, strong fundamentals in data and computation, and the ability to translate technical capabilities into real human or organizational impact. To take full advantage of AI as a multiplier, people need to stay current with emerging tools and workflows and use them deliberately to increase their own productivity. Rather than writing every line of code yourself, leverage code productivity tools to move faster, write an order of magnitude more software, and focus your energy on system-level and application-level design. Looking back, the most valuable decisions in my career were choosing roles at the intersection of research, engineering, and real-world application, which provided the adaptability needed to navigate repeated waves of technological change."

Merve Unuvar

Director, Agentic Middleware and Applications at IBM Research

"Learn to speak two languages fluently: what AI can do, and what your business actually needs. I've seen product managers, strategists, and operators become far more valuable than ML experts by asking the right questions: How will we measure if this works? What happens when it fails? Who owns fixing it? The gap between an 'impressive demo' and 'this creates value' is massive. Position yourself in that gap. Whether you're in strategy, operations, product, or engineering, develop a nose for the unsexy work that makes AI reliable. That's where careers get built.

Three things transcend job titles. First, defining success before building: most AI initiatives fail because of fuzzy goals, not bad technology. Can you articulate what 'good enough' looks like? Second, systems thinking: AI doesn't work in isolation. Understanding how it fits into workflows, breaks down, and affects people matters more than understanding transformers. Third, healthy skepticism: the courage to slow down when everyone wants to move fast, and to ask, 'should we?' alongside 'can we?'

The people who treat AI as a powerful tool that requires thoughtful integration will outlast those who treat it like magic. Experience with messy, real-world constraints beats theoretical knowledge every time."

Sandipan Bhaumik

Data and AI Technical Lead at Databricks

"The ability to connect deep domain knowledge with a solid understanding of the full technology stack – from hardware and systems to software and AI models – will be crucial. An open, curious mindset, comfort with rapid change, and hands-on experience building and integrating AI (especially agentic and open-source systems) will matter more than chasing any single framework. AI will be a team sport, so collaboration, systems thinking, and the ability to translate research into real-world impact will define long-term success. Build a strong foundation in computer science and systems first, then layer AI and domain expertise on top. Actively experiment, contribute to open source, and learn how AI is deployed in real products, not just demos. Most importantly, stay curious, think across disciplines, and learn to work in teams that bridge research, engineering, and business."

Jens Stapelfeldt

Global AI Lead for AUP (AMD University Program) at AMD

"Sustaining a career in AI over the next few years won't be about chasing the next hot tool. It will be about cultivating agency: the ability to identify real-world problems, assemble systems, and take ownership of outcomes. And ownership requires depth. As AI shifts from horizontal demos to vertical impact, domain expertise becomes the anchor that keeps your work grounded in reality rather than hype. But depth alone isn't enough. You also need breadth. Systems thinking is the missing superpower: those who can connect models, data, interfaces, and feedback loops into coherent architectures will lead. So, my advice to young professionals is this: stop trying to become 'AI people.' Become useful people who happen to wield AI in domains that actually matter. The most valuable work now lives at the intersections, and you can't get there with a single skill."

Rakesh Gohel

Founder and Chief AI Strategist, JUTEQ Inc.

"Dare to look under the hood. Build a deep understanding of AI, especially (but not only) transformers, at a detailed level. Most people have only surface-level knowledge; this is a clear way to differentiate yourself. Alongside theory, do not neglect practice: build your own use cases. If you have the opportunity (for example, in a large enterprise), focus on scaling: how do we turn 'nice ideas' into hardened, SoC-compliant, scalable production solutions? Also, AI, especially agentic AI, is closely tied to automation, so it helps to build strong fundamentals in automation more broadly (e.g., BPMN models, orchestrators, and related concepts). Maintain openness to technology, a willingness to change, and patience over the long term. We are in another hype cycle right now, and it will cool down again, just as it did after previous AI winters, so stay the course, because the potential is real. At the same time, develop a strong instinct for choosing the right tool for the right problem: AI can be an extremely powerful heavyweight tool, but not every problem is a nail. Where it truly is the right tool, act decisively and execute. Finally, stay young in mindset (even as you get older) and stay alert. Recognize opportunities, don't chase every opportunity, but when you decide to pursue one, do it with full commitment, ambition, and engagement. And it should be fun, too – without that, it rarely works out in the long run."

Andreas Exner

Head of AIOps at Deutsche Telekom

"Over the next few years, the skills in demand will be the open-mindedness to understand customer challenges, plus the ability to build solutions they cannot clearly articulate yet. As coding becomes more and more of a commodity, the value will be with people who can truly understand customer needs and match those needs with solutions. It will be more about listening and observing, and then being smart about taking various technical solutions and using them as building blocks for crafting solutions for customers... but you have to be quick and adaptable, because the pace of change is accelerating."

Indrek Vainu

Head of Conversational AI at Zurich Insurance Company Ltd

If all of this advice feels like a lot, start simple. These AI leaders came from different industries, different continents, different career paths. But their message converged on the same truths:

Depth beats breadth. Pick a domain, go deep, and build things that work in the real world.

Fundamentals outlast frameworks. The tools will change. Your ability to think clearly about systems, and understand the basics of AI and algebra, can never be taken away.

Start before you're ready. The gap between "interested in AI" and "working in AI" is closed by action, not preparation.

Stay human. Communication, empathy, trust-building – these are not soft skills. They are the skills that determine whether your technical work ever reaches production.

Summary

The first 90 days in your new role shape your reputation – ship something real, build trust fast, and create the conditions for bigger bets later. But what you do after those 90 days shapes your career and career growth. That means doing the work. Showing up. Being the colleague people want on their team – reliable, honest, someone who makes others better. Loyalty and integrity are not outdated concepts. They are how trust compounds over years.

Beyond the day job: writing, speaking, mentoring, contributing to open source. Building side activities with reach that no single employer can take away. Find mentors early. Then become one. The best learning happens in relationship, not isolation. Join communities – online and in person. The people you meet at a random Tuesday meetup might become collaborators, co-founders, or the person who refers you to your next role.

Protect your capacity to last. Burnout is not a badge of honor. The people who build decade-long careers are not the ones who work the most hours. They are the ones who stay curious and healthy long enough to let their skills compound.

Although this is the final chapter of this book, it is only the beginning. The real work starts now.

The tools you master today may become outdated. The models, platforms, and job titles will change. What will not become obsolete is your ability to learn, adapt, and build with whatever comes next.

That's how careers compound.

Now go build something!

14

Unlock Your Exclusive Benefits

Your copy of this book includes the following exclusive benefits:

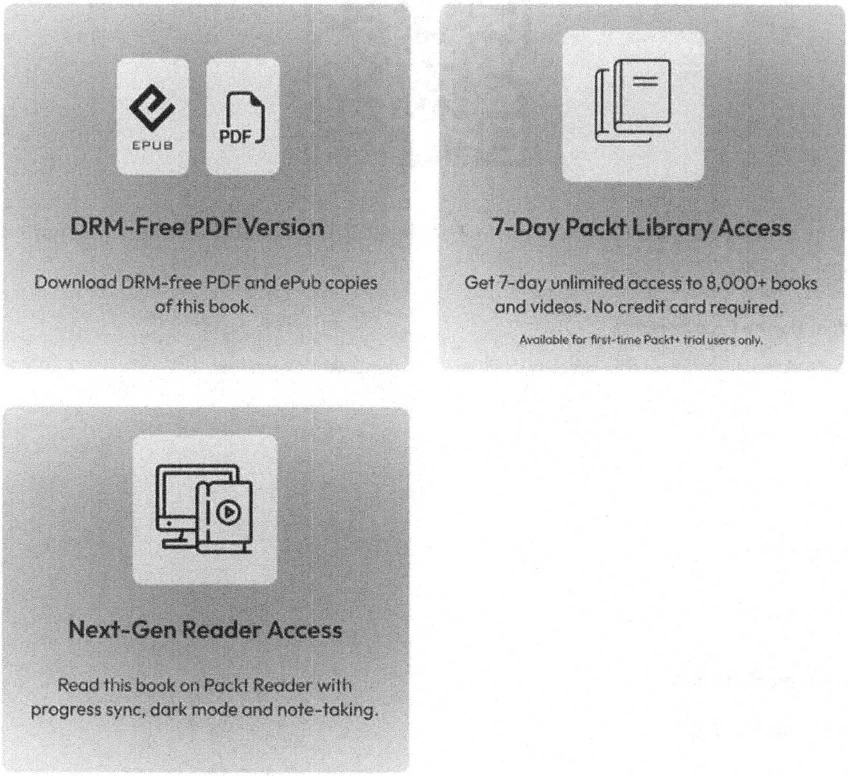

Follow the guide below to unlock them. The process takes only a few minutes and needs to be completed once.

Unlock this book's free benefits in 3 easy steps

Step 1

Keep your purchase invoice ready for *Step 3*. If you have a physical copy, scan it using your phone and save it as a PDF, JPG, or PNG.

For more help on finding your invoice, visit `https://www.packtpub.com/en-us/unlock?step=1`.

If you bought this book directly from Packt, no invoice is required. After *Step 2*, you can access your exclusive content right away.

Step 2

Scan the QR code or go to `packtpub.com/unlock`.

On the page that opens (similar to *Figure 14.1* on desktop), search for this book by name and select the correct edition.

Figure 14.1: Packt unlock landing page on desktop

Step 3

After selecting your book, sign in to your Packt account or create one for free. Then upload your invoice (PDF, PNG, or JPG, up to 10 MB). Follow the on-screen instructions to finish the process.

Need help

If you get stuck and need help, visit `https://www.packtpub.com/unlock-benefits/help` for a detailed FAQ on how to find your invoices and more. This QR code will take you to the help page.

If you are still facing issues, reach out to `customercare@packt.com`.

Other Books You May Enjoy

If you enjoyed this book, you may be interested in these other books by Packt:

Generative AI at AWS

Nestor Gandara, Eduardo Ordax, Srikanth Daggumalli, Ashutosh Dubey

ISBN: 9781806104444

- Understand how generative AI creates business value
- Compare models, prompts, fine-tuning, and RAG
- Navigate the AWS generative AI stack with confidence
- Prepare data and select models for real use cases
- Build MVPs and production-ready AI applications
- Apply governance, ethics, and responsible AI controls
- Evaluate agentic AI patterns and emerging trends
- Measure impact across enterprise AI initiatives

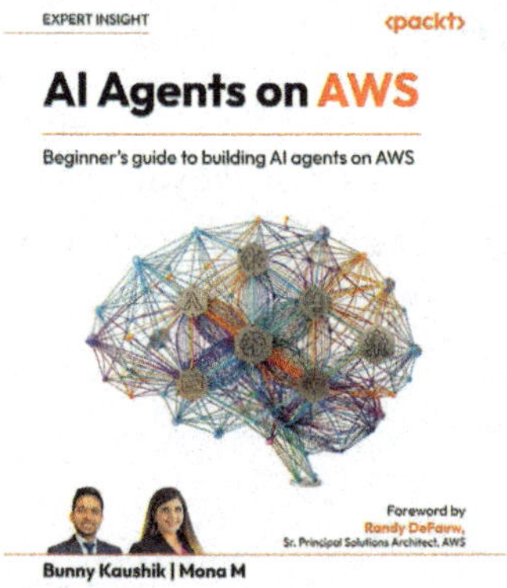

AI agents on AWS

Bunny Kaushik, Mona M

ISBN: 9781806387212

- Understand how AI agents think, act, and collaborate
- Design single-agent systems with tools and reasoning
- Build agents on AWS using Bedrock and SageMaker AI
- Add memory for context-aware and adaptive behavior
- Create multi-agent systems and orchestrated workflows
- Use MCP and A2A for agent communication and tools
- Deploy and scale agents for production environments
- Monitor, evaluate, and govern agent performance

Packt is searching for authors like you

If you're interested in becoming an author for Packt, please visit `authors.packt.com` and apply today. We have worked with thousands of developers and tech professionals, just like you, to help them share their insight with the global tech community. You can make a general application, apply for a specific hot topic that we are recruiting an author for, or submit your own idea.

Share your thoughts

Now you've finished *The Generative AI Career Masterplan*, we'd love to hear your thoughts! Scan the QR code below to go straight to the Amazon review page for this book and share your feedback or leave a review on the site that you purchased it from.

`https://packt.link/r/1806691450`

Your review is important to us and the tech community and will help us make sure we're delivering excellent quality content.

Index

A

O

P

Q

R

S

T

U

V

W

X

Z

Made in United States
Orlando, FL
04 November 2026

90201338R00188